AF567056

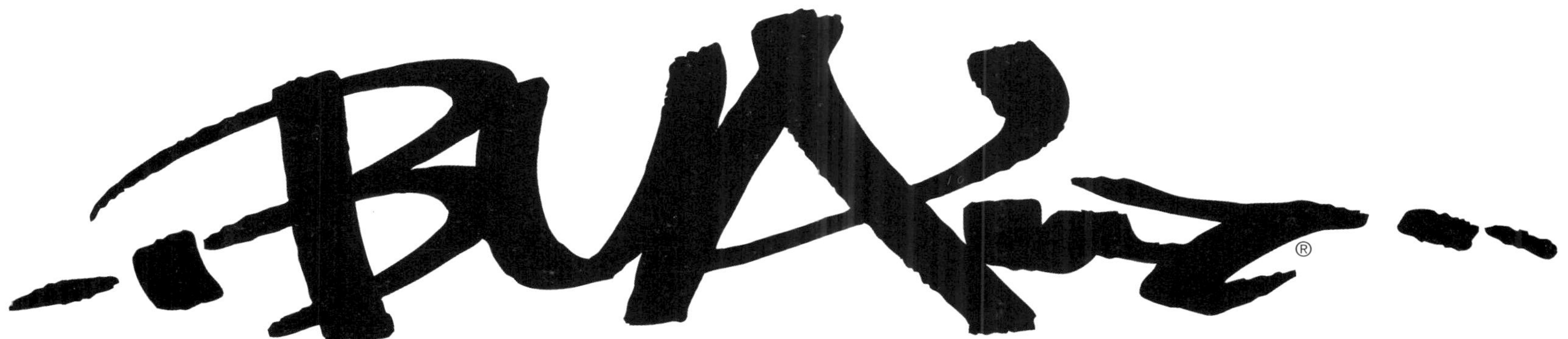

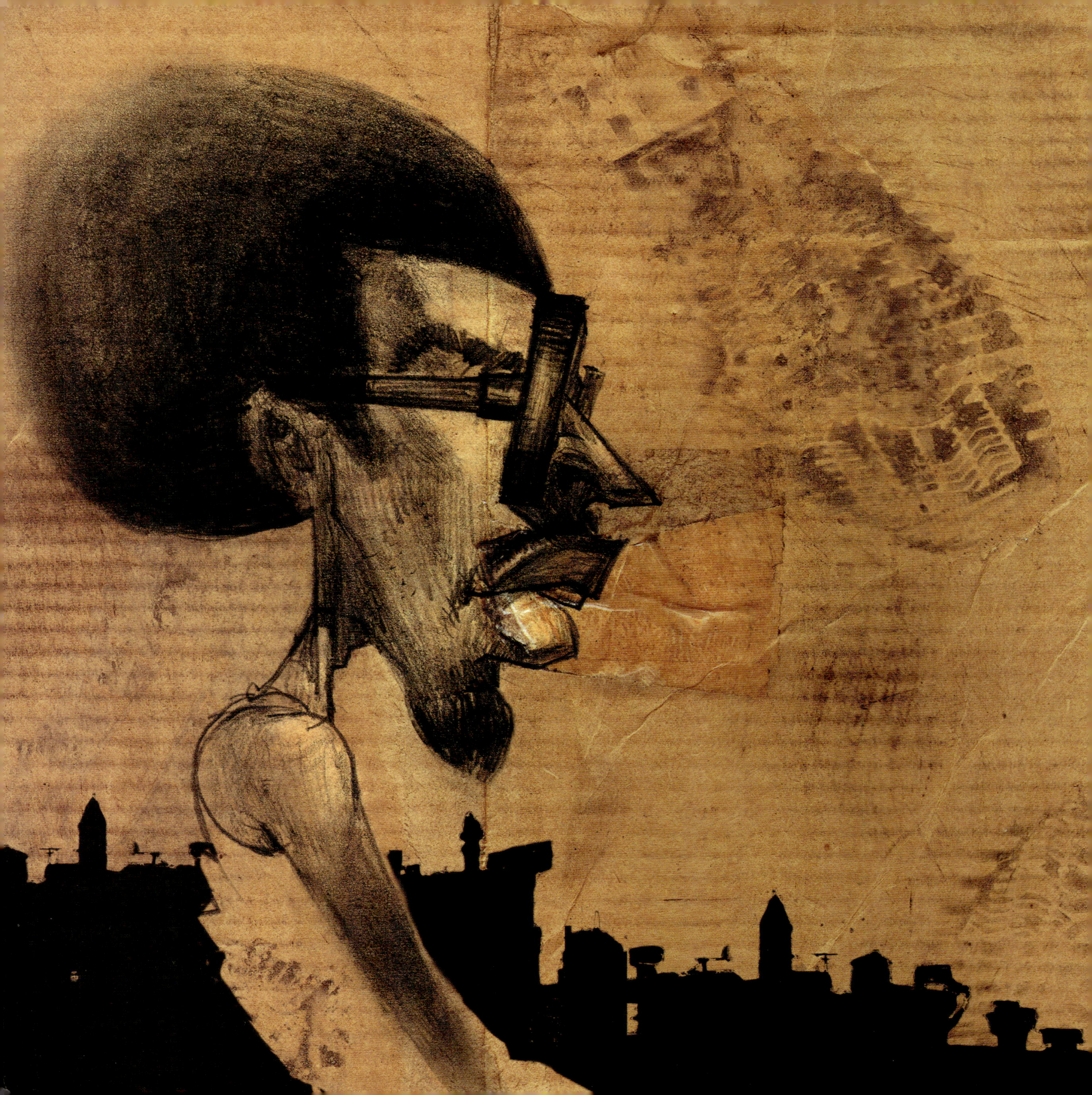

THE BEAT OF URBAN ART

The Art of Justin BUA

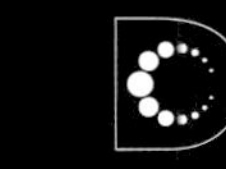

COLLINS DESIGN
An Imprint of HarperCollinsPublishers

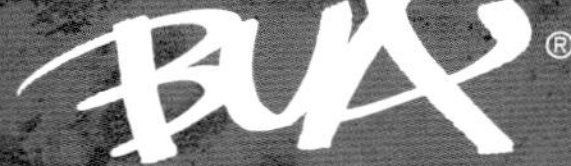

HarperCollins books may be purchased for educational, business, or sales promotional use. For information, please write: Special Markets Department, HarperCollins*Publishers*, 10 East 53rd Street, New York, NY 10022.

First edition published in 2007

First paperback edition published in 2009 by
Collins Design
An Imprint of HarperCollins*Publishers*
10 East 53rd Street
New York, NY 10022
Tel: (212) 207-7000
Fax: (212) 207-7654
collinsdesign@harpercollins.com
www.harpercollins.com

Distributed throughout the world by
HarperCollins*Publishers*
10 East 53rd Street
New York, NY 10022
Fax: (212) 207-7654

Designed by BUA Studios
Los Angeles, California, USA

Library of Congress Cataloging-in-Publication Data has been applied for.

ISBN 978-0-06-173499-1

Printed in China
First Paperback Printing, 2009

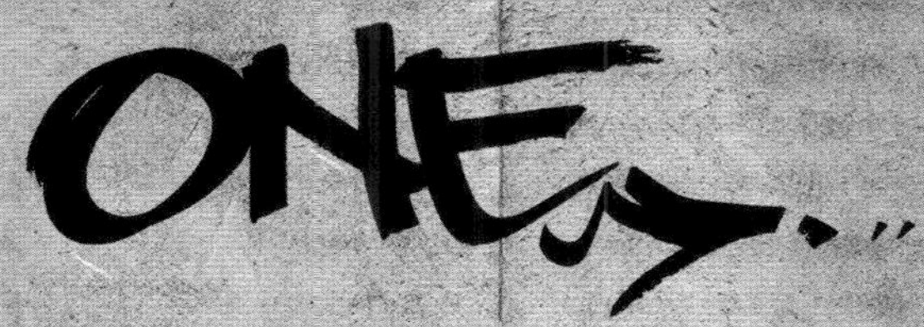

The characters I draw and paint represent who I am and what I value. They are from different backgrounds that together form one urban culture. People ask me what I am. Puerto Rican? Italian? Jewish? African-American? Like my characters, I can't define myself by any one race. I have so many different bloodlines flowing through my veins and grew up in such a uniquely integrated culture, that I am just me. I am part of an urban race united by the city. As kids, we weren't separated by the color of our skin. We judged each other by the content of our character. This is where the slang word "ONE" comes from. We are ONE. Urban life challenges us to thrive among diversity and vibe off one another in a positive way.

This is the gift of a city.

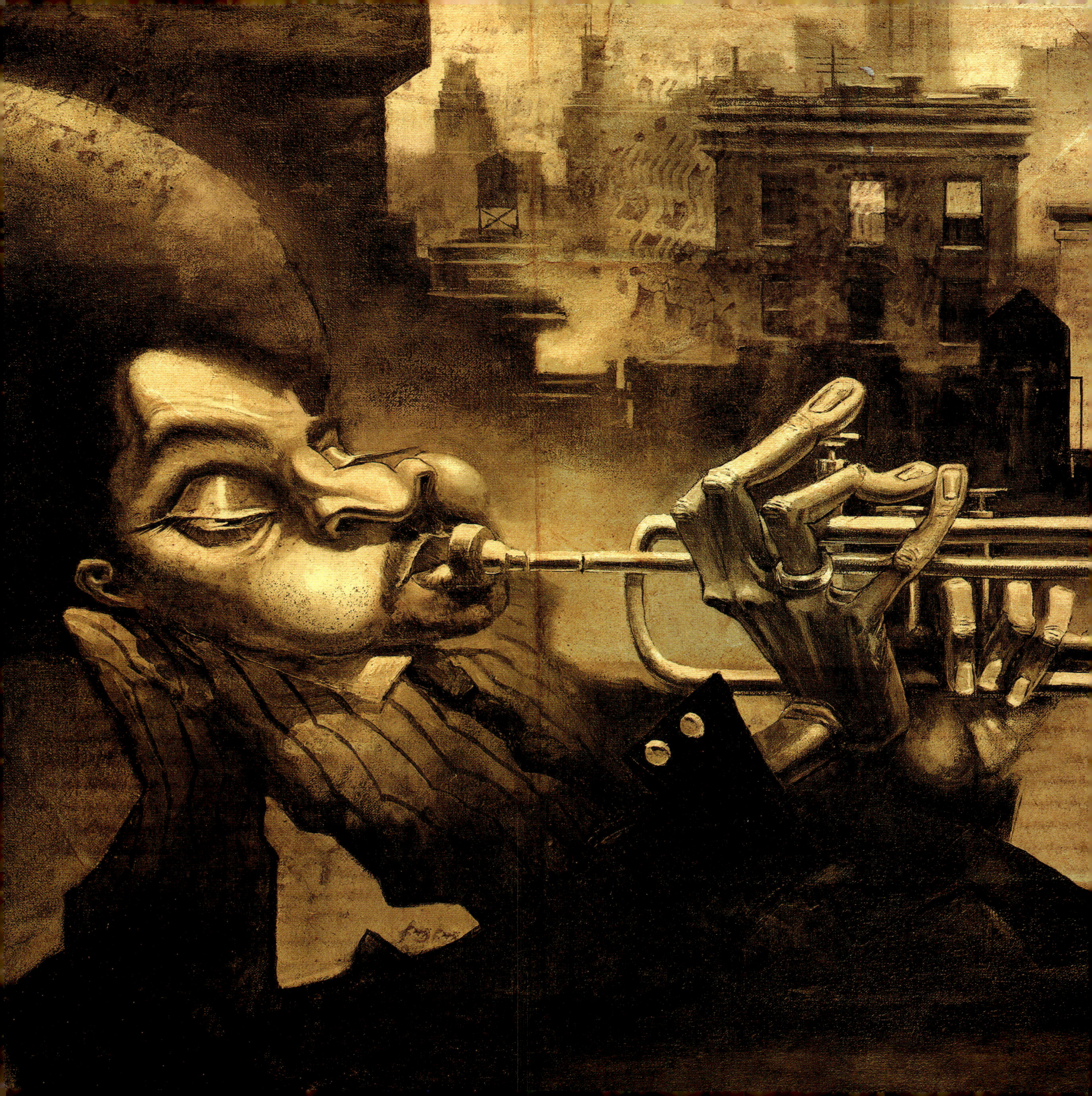

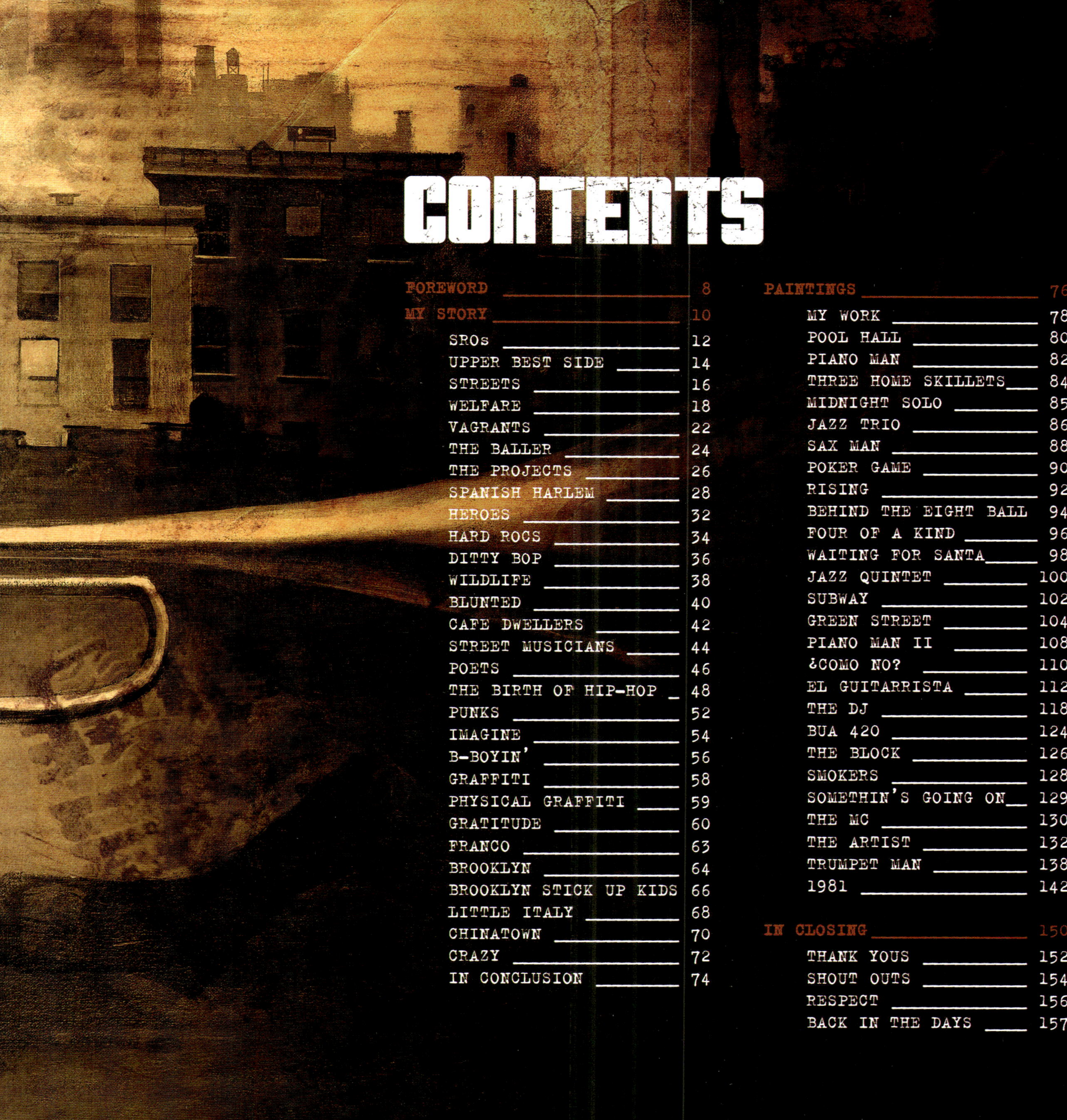

CONTENTS

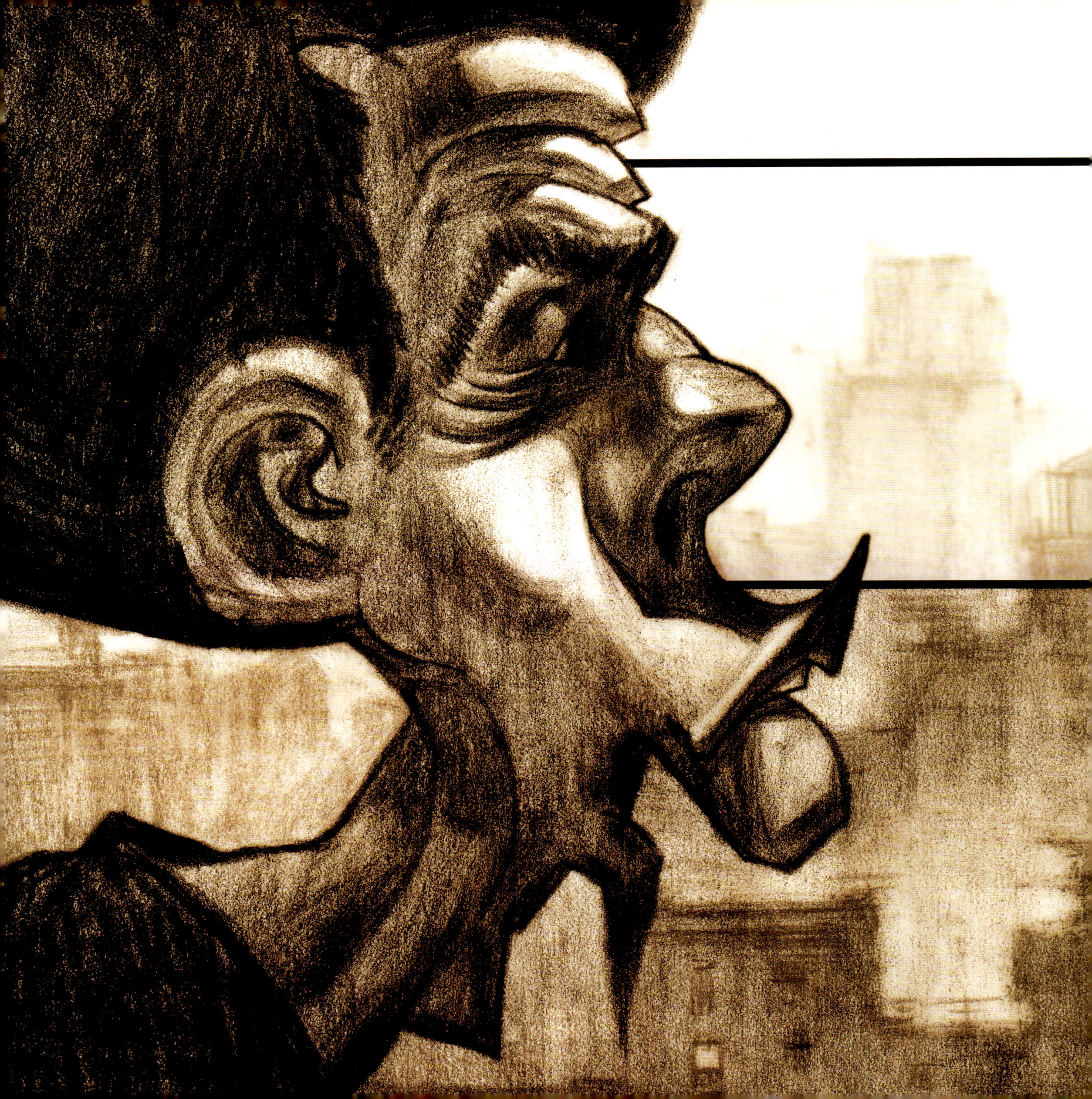

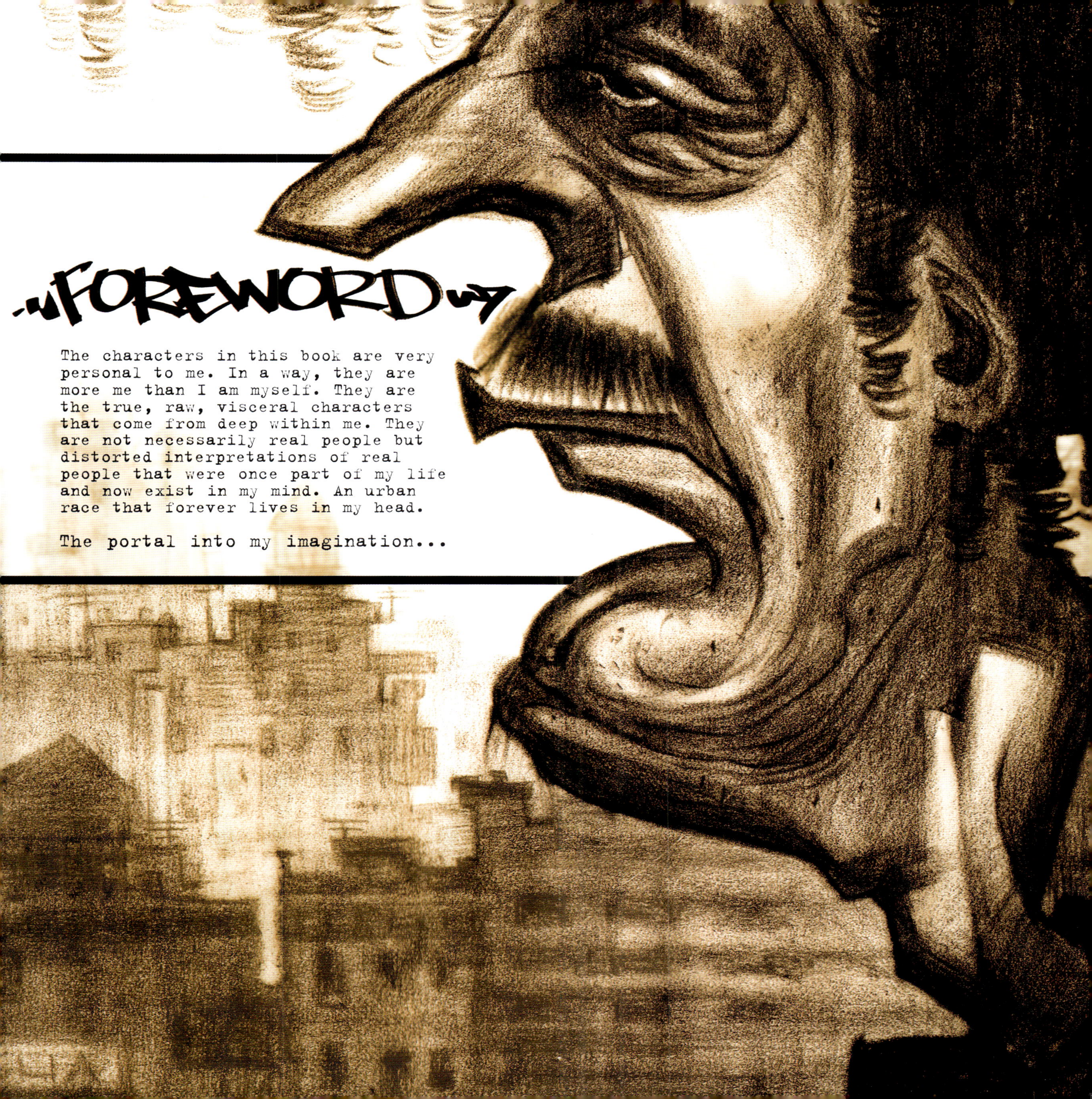

FOREWORD

The characters in this book are very personal to me. In a way, they are more me than I am myself. They are the true, raw, visceral characters that come from deep within me. They are not necessarily real people but distorted interpretations of real people that were once part of my life and now exist in my mind. An urban race that forever lives in my head.

The portal into my imagination...

MY STORY

I am originally from New York City's Upper West Side. I grew up next to an SRO (Single Room Occupancy) hotel that was home to many hard working, low income people—some of whom illegally crammed their children in with them. In the early 1970s, local and federal funding was cut and New York was forced to close many mental institutions. Instead of providing community-based housing with the enormous amount of money that was saved from closing facilities like Willowbrook and Creedmore, the government dumped the mentally ill onto the streets and into SRO hotels. Suddenly, people and families living in the SROs were side by side with the mentally insane.

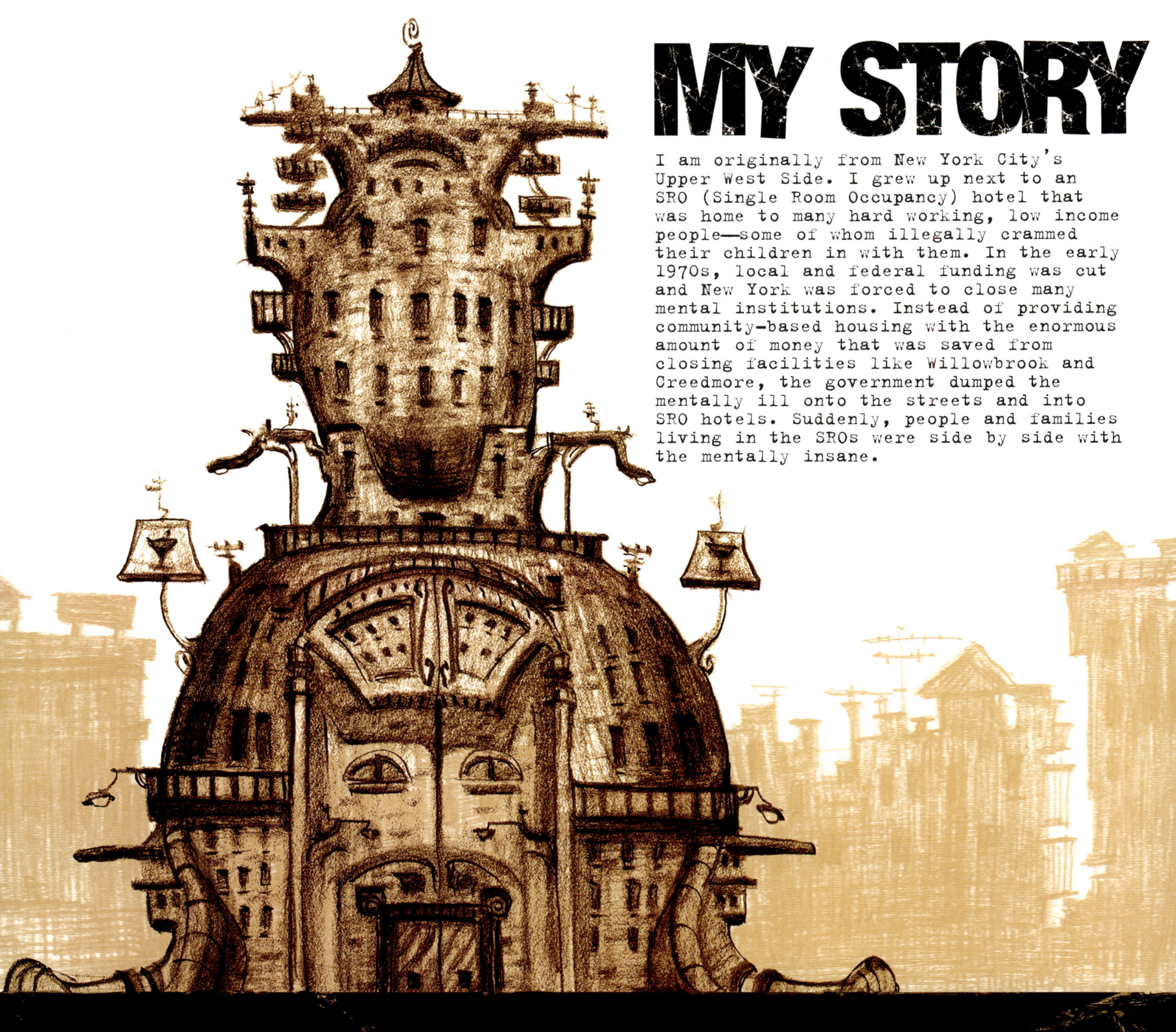

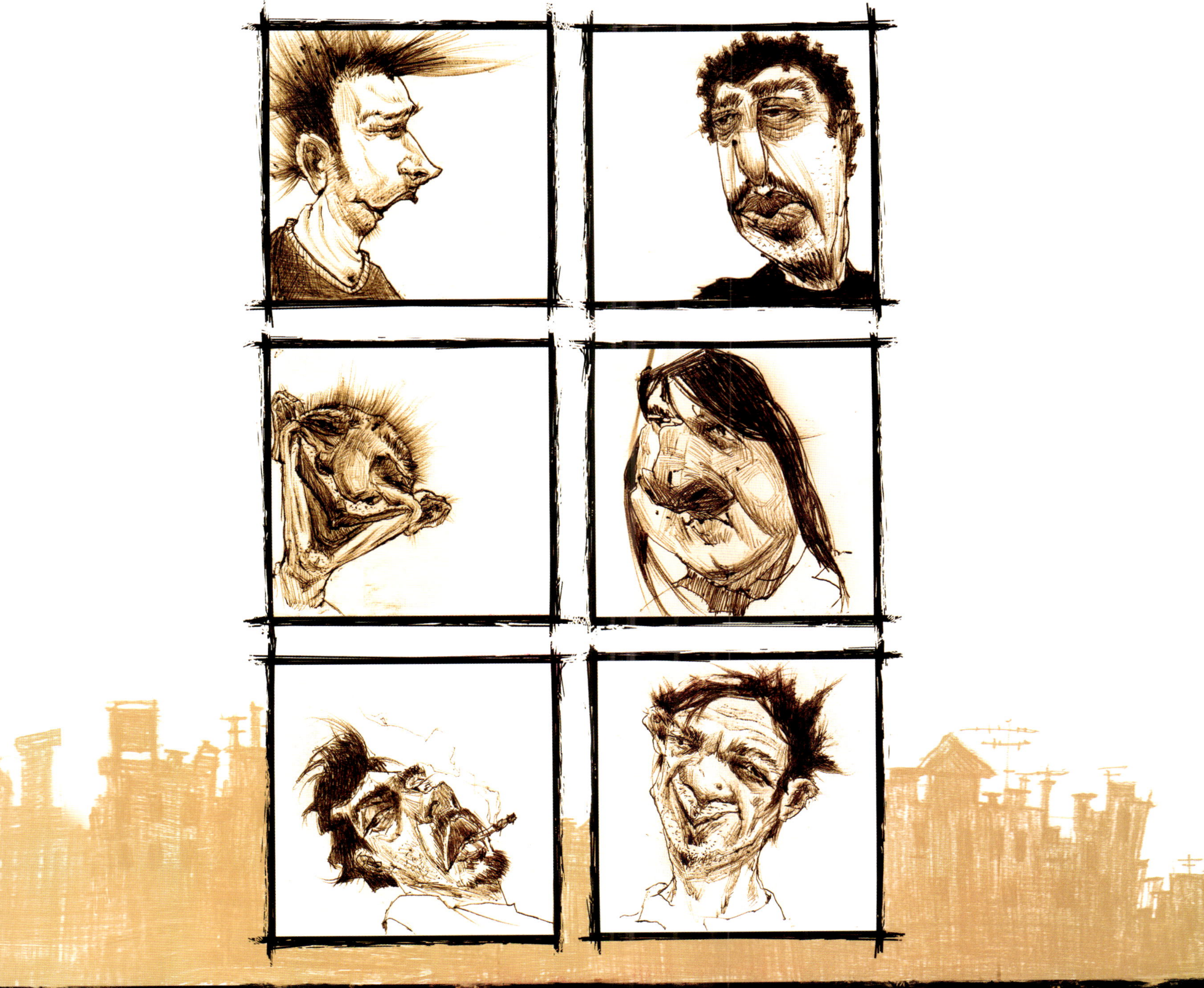

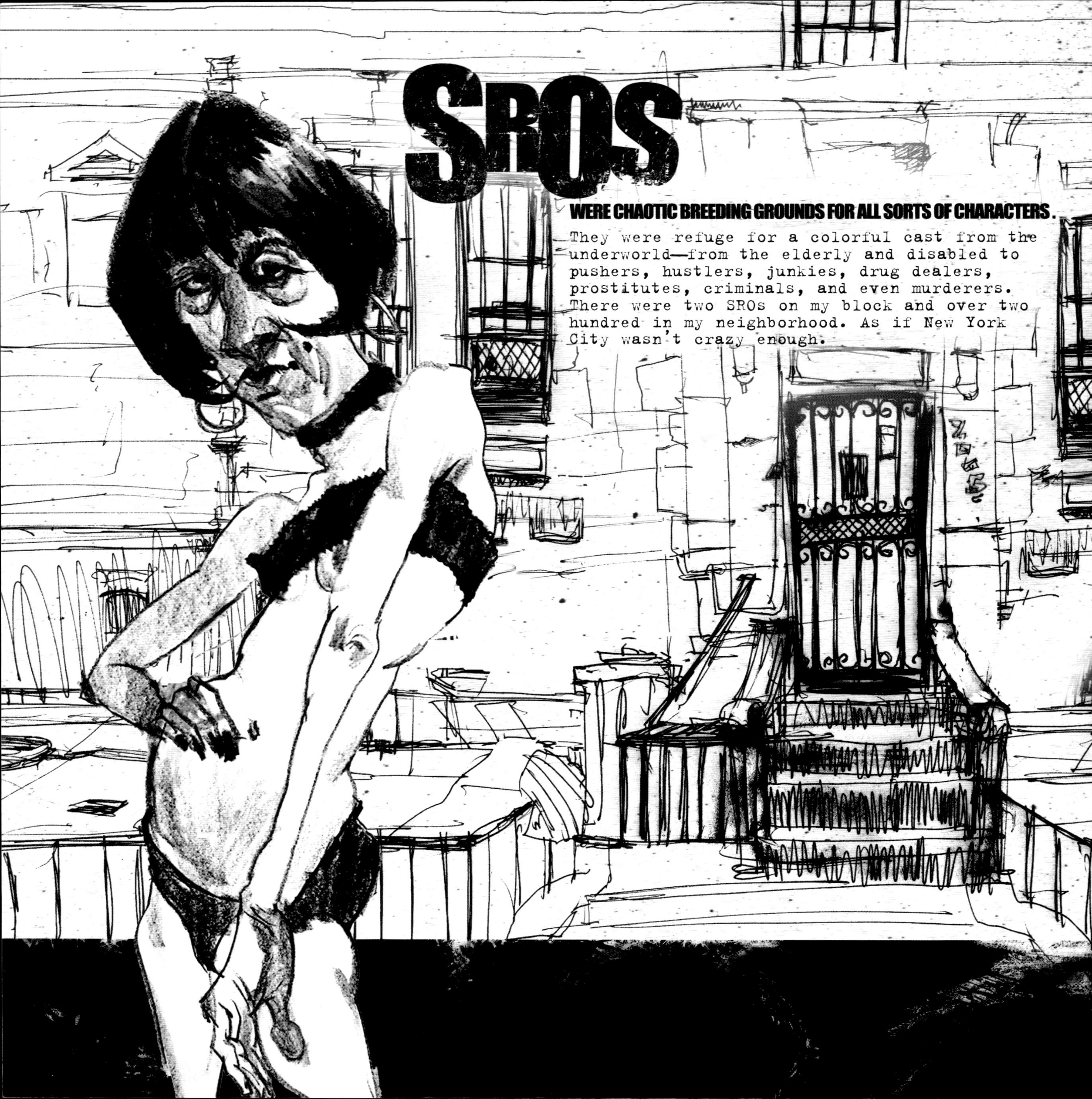
SROs
WERE CHAOTIC BREEDING GROUNDS FOR ALL SORTS OF CHARACTERS.
They were refuge for a colorful cast from the underworld—from the elderly and disabled to pushers, hustlers, junkies, drug dealers, prostitutes, criminals, and even murderers. There were two SROs on my block and over two hundred in my neighborhood. As if New York City wasn't crazy enough.

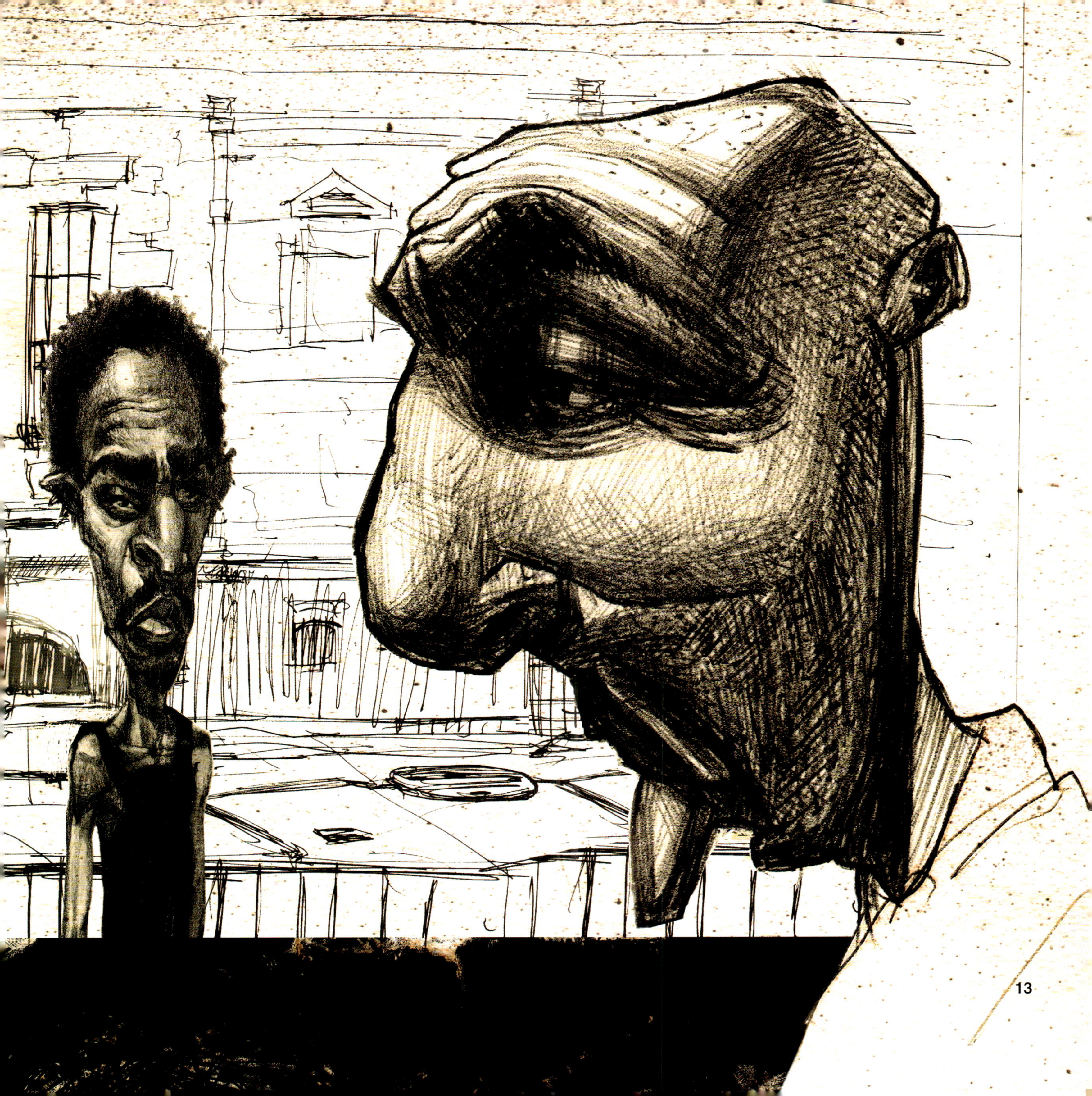

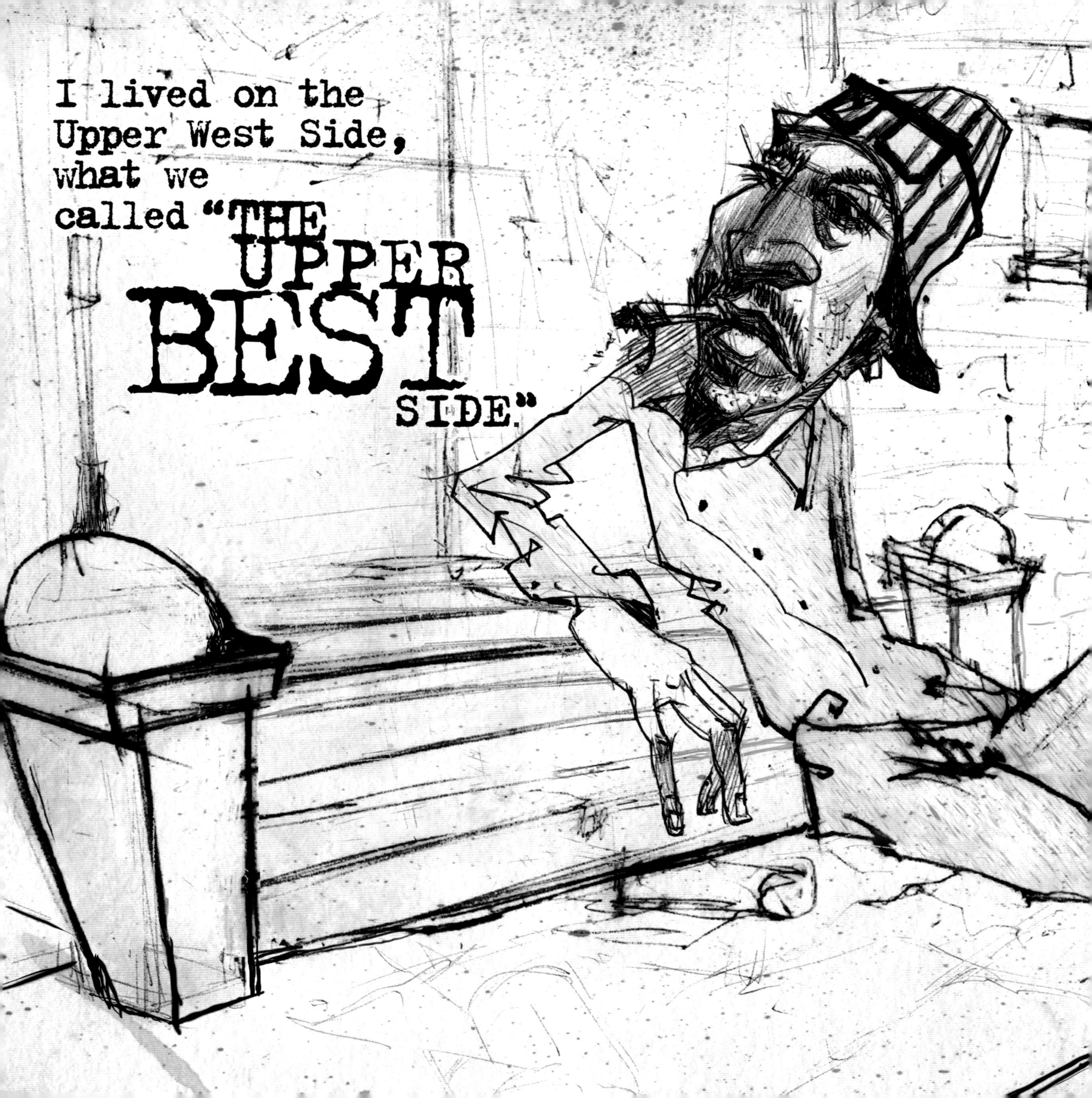
I lived on the
Upper West Side,
what we
called "THE
UPPER
BEST
SIDE."

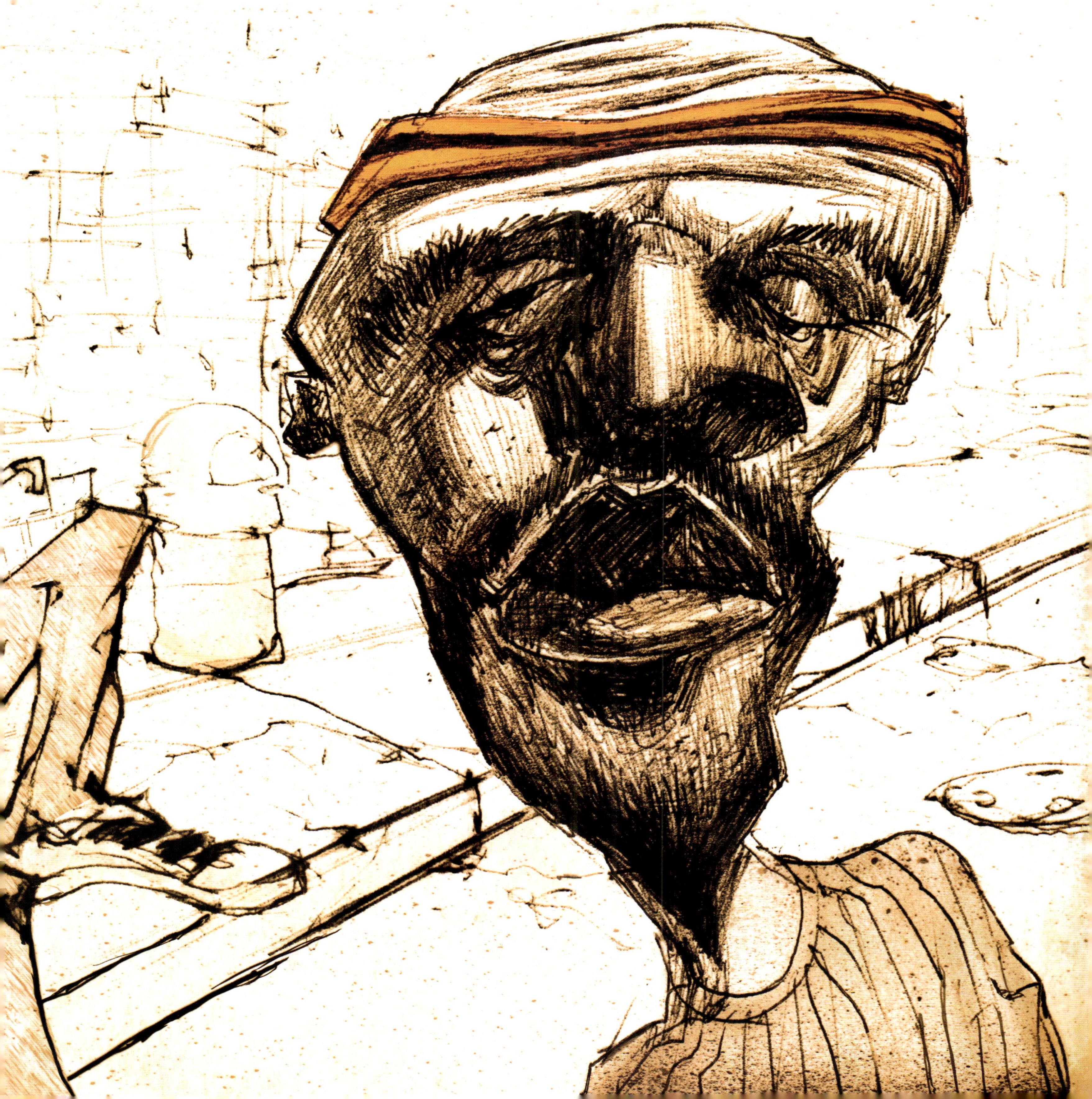

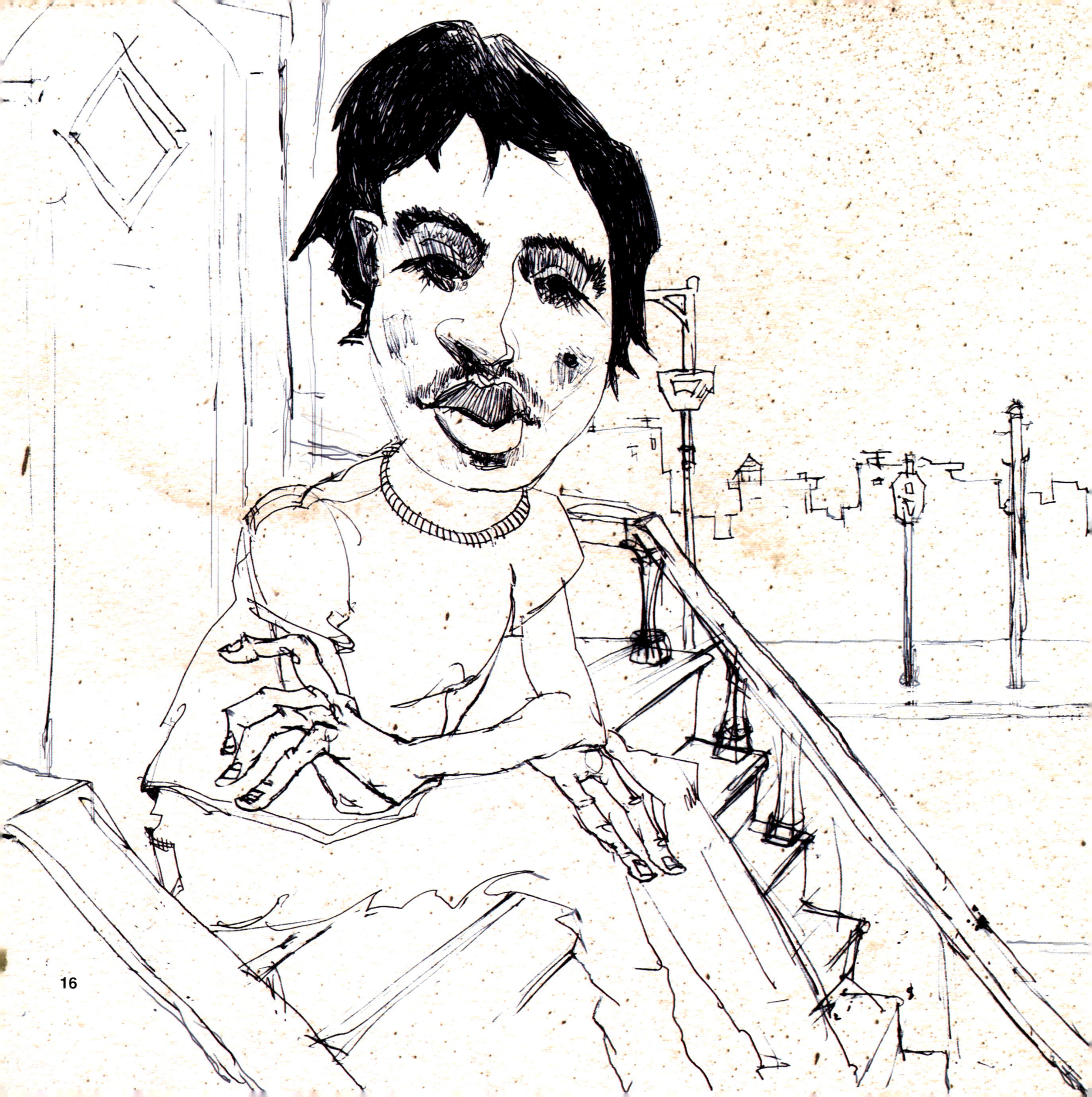

BEING A LATCHKEY KID I SPENT MOST OF MY TIME HANGIN OUT IN THE STREETS.

I was proud to be from uptown, but I was in an environment that was decaying rapidly. On our block, people weren't even hiding their guns anymore.

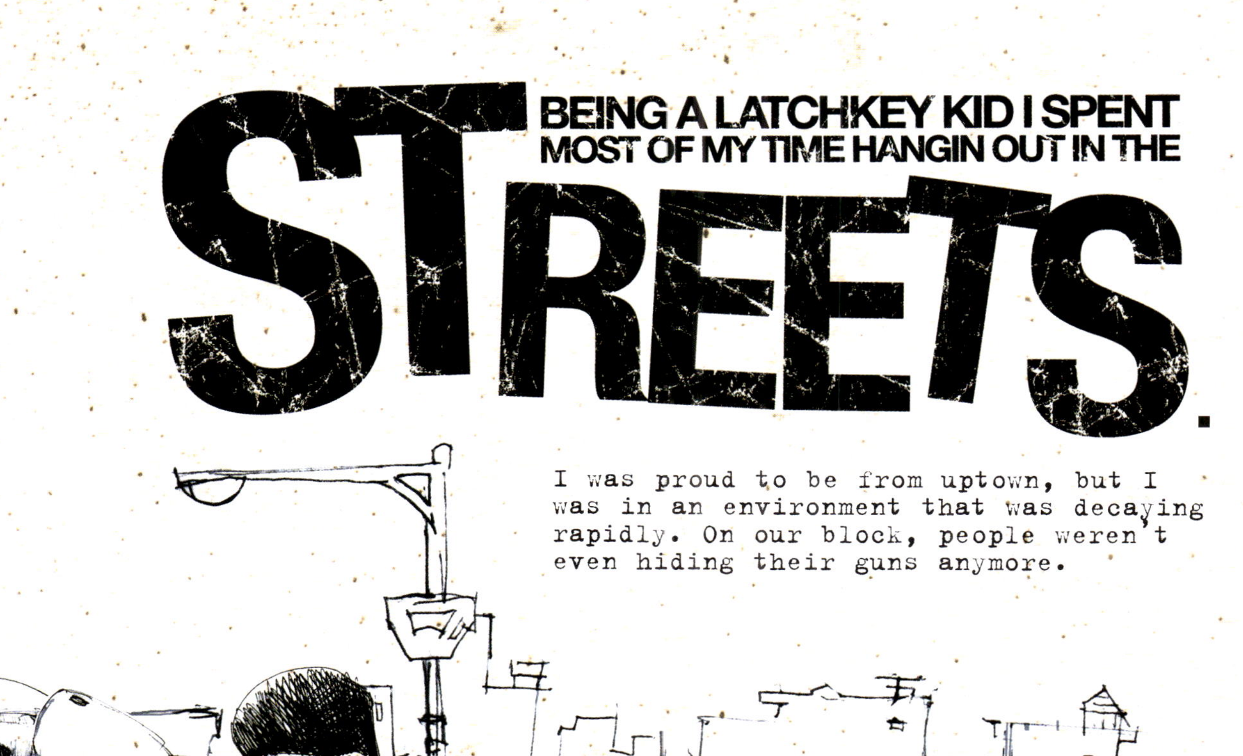

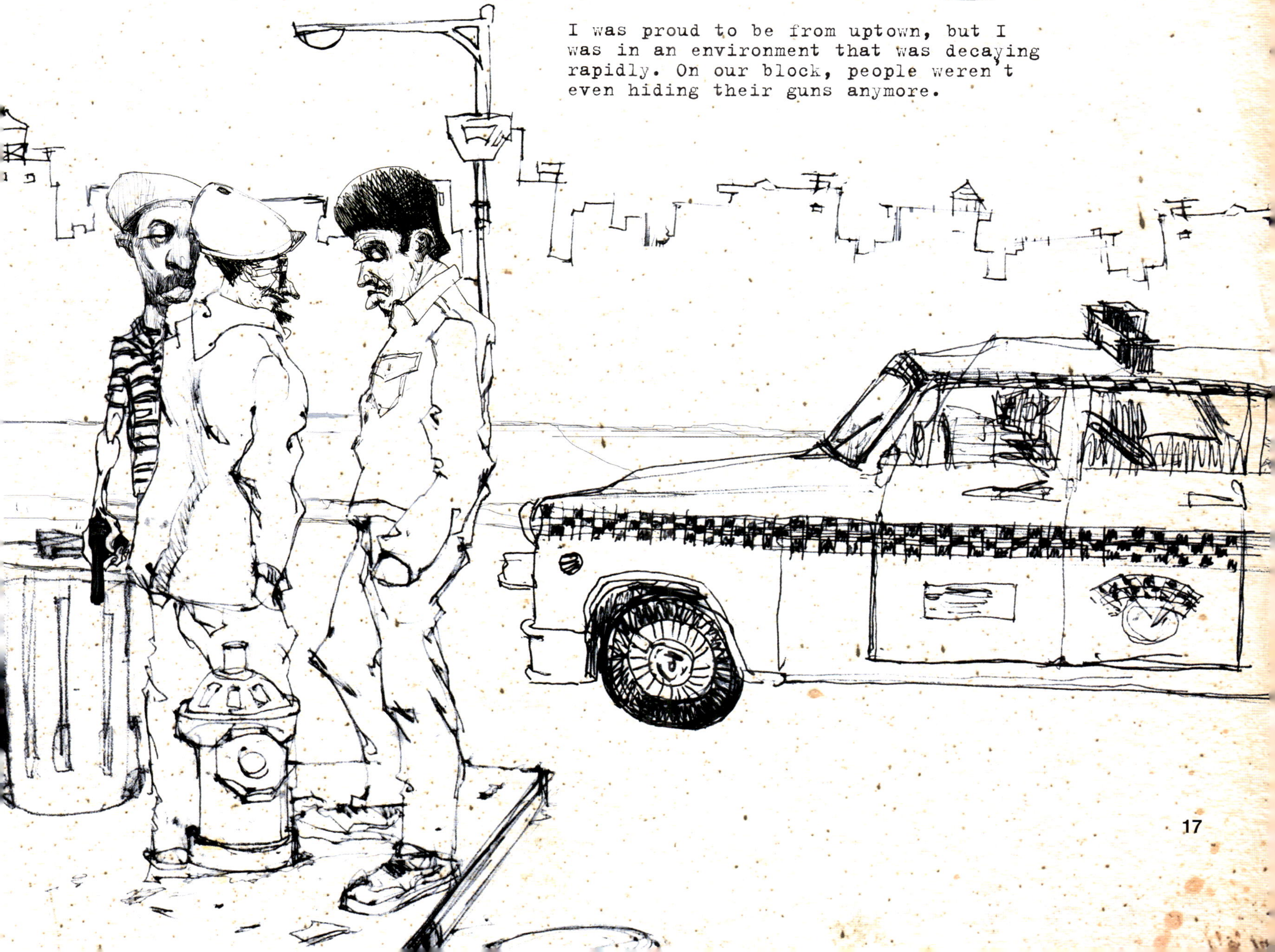

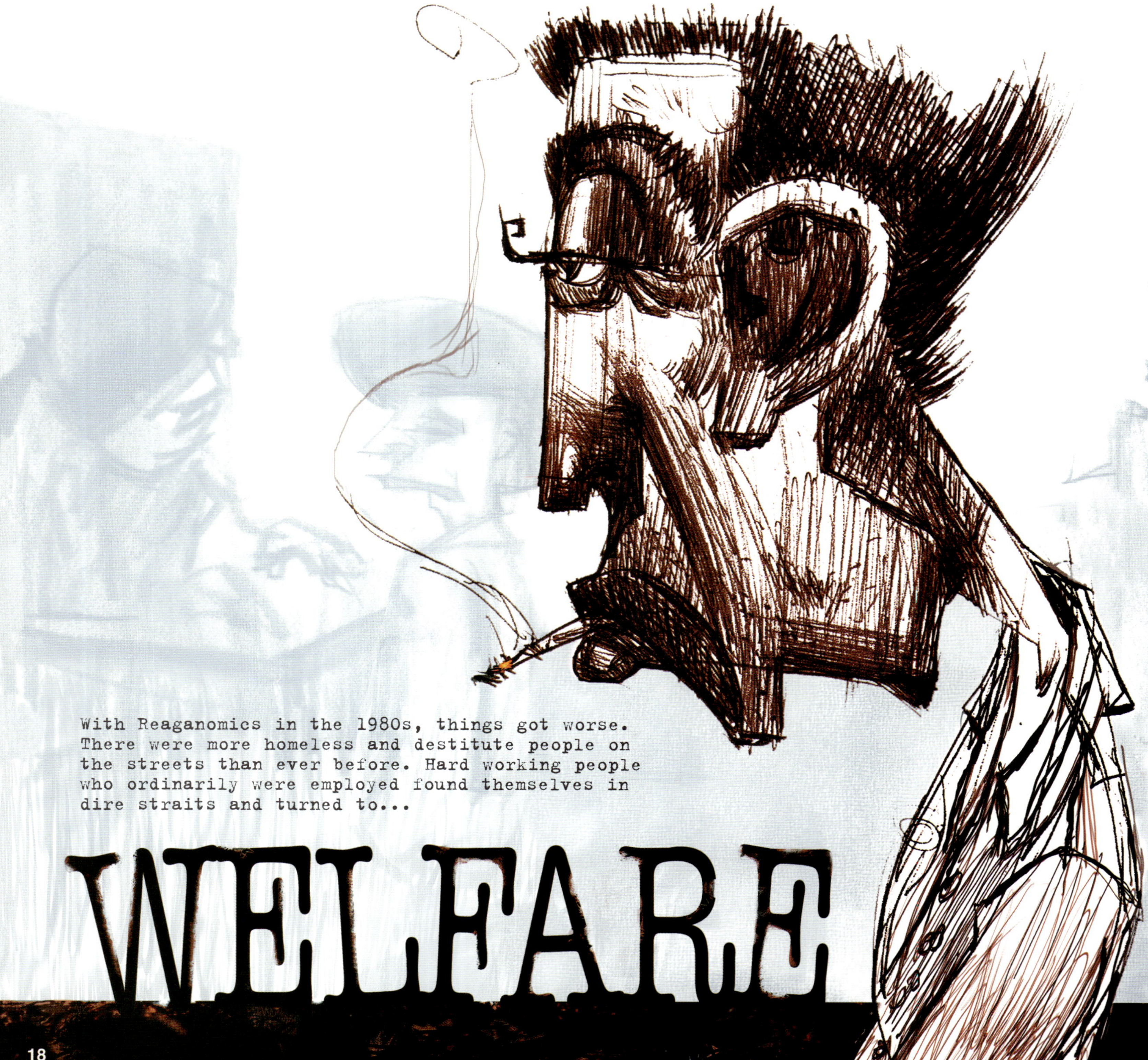

With Reaganomics in the 1980s, things got worse. There were more homeless and destitute people on the streets than ever before. Hard working people who ordinarily were employed found themselves in dire straits and turned to...

WELFARE

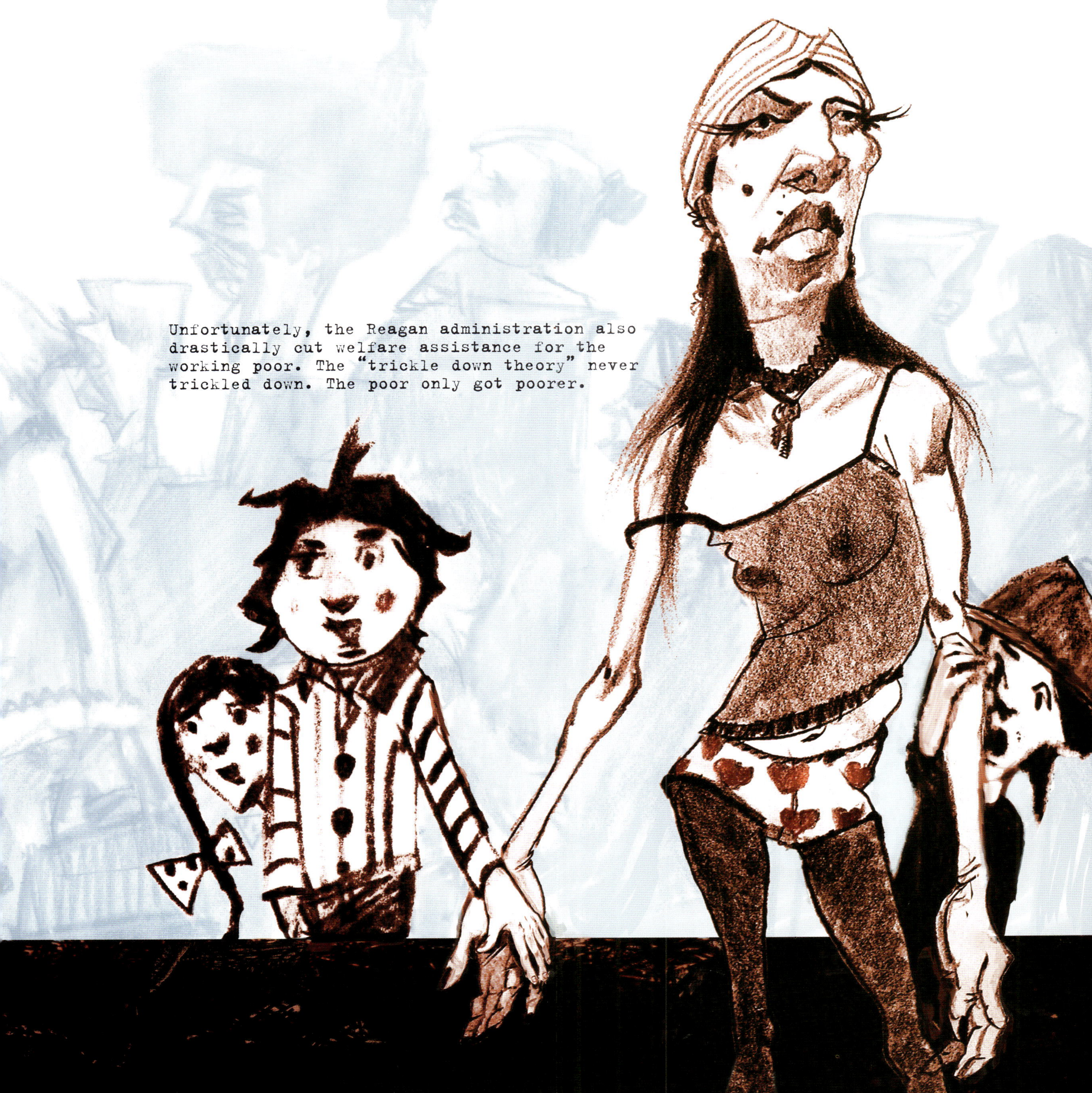
Unfortunately, the Reagan administration also drastically cut welfare assistance for the working poor. The "trickle down theory" never trickled down. The poor only got poorer.

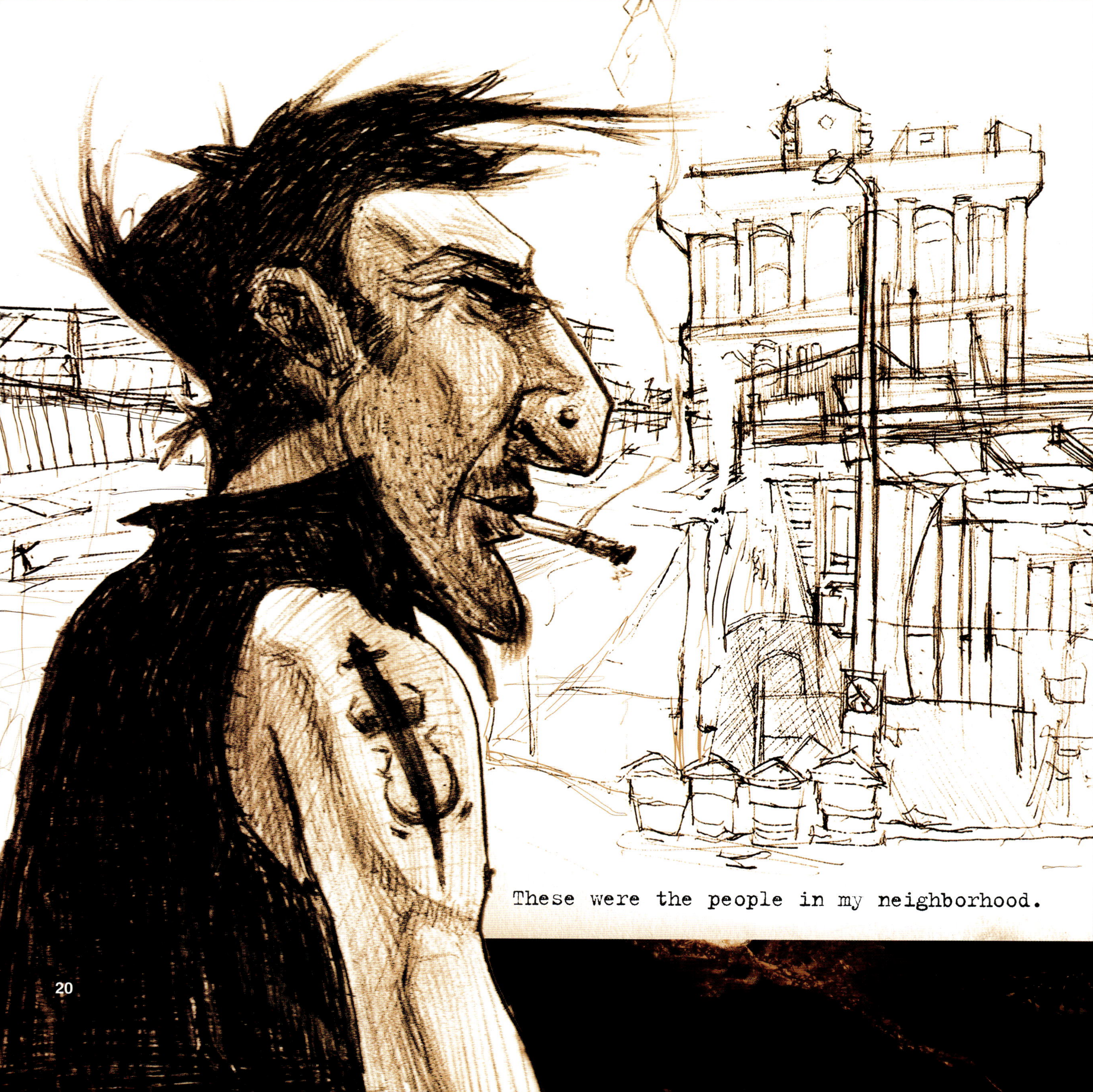
These were the people in my neighborhood.

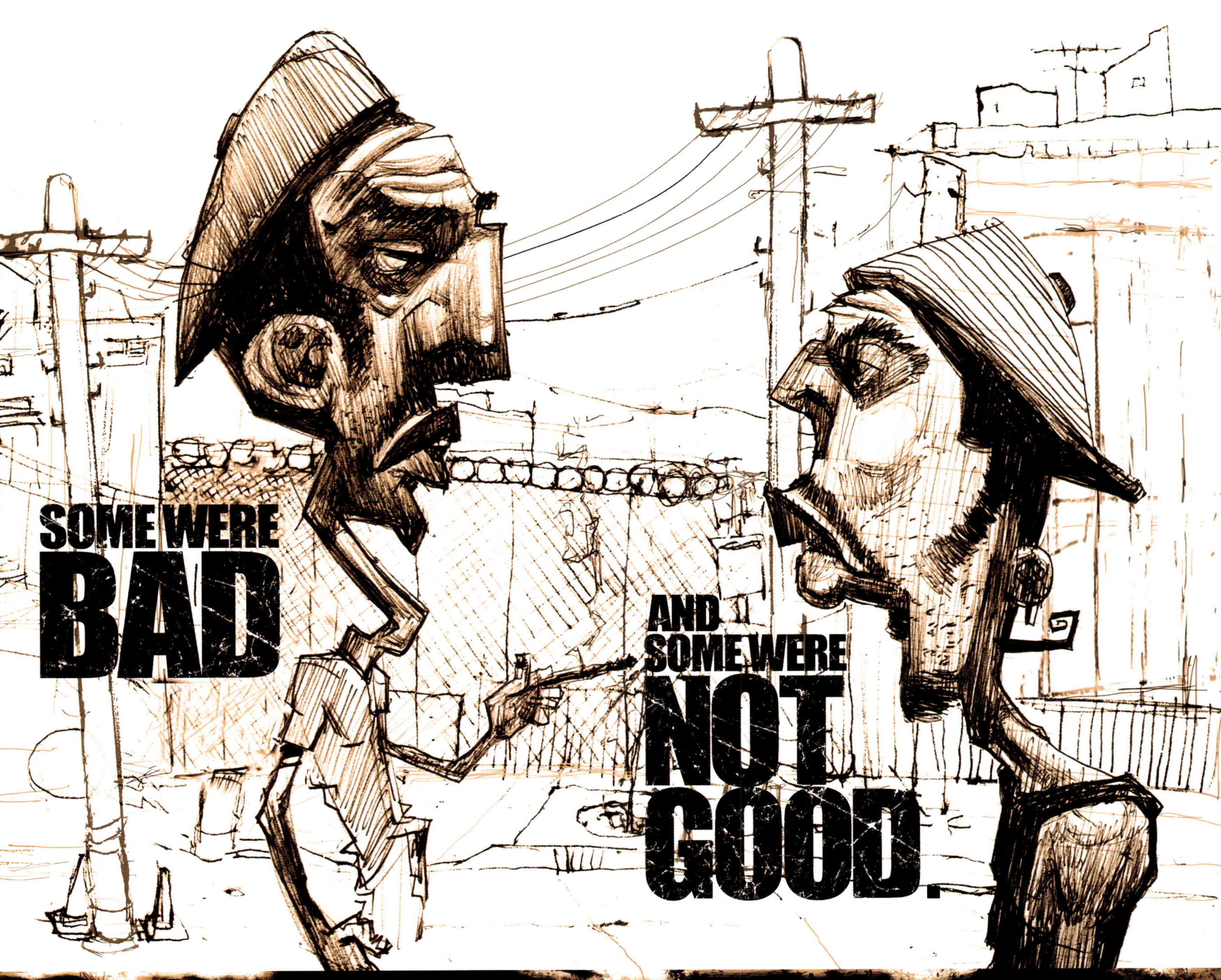
SOME WERE
BAD
AND
SOME WERE
NOT
GOOD.

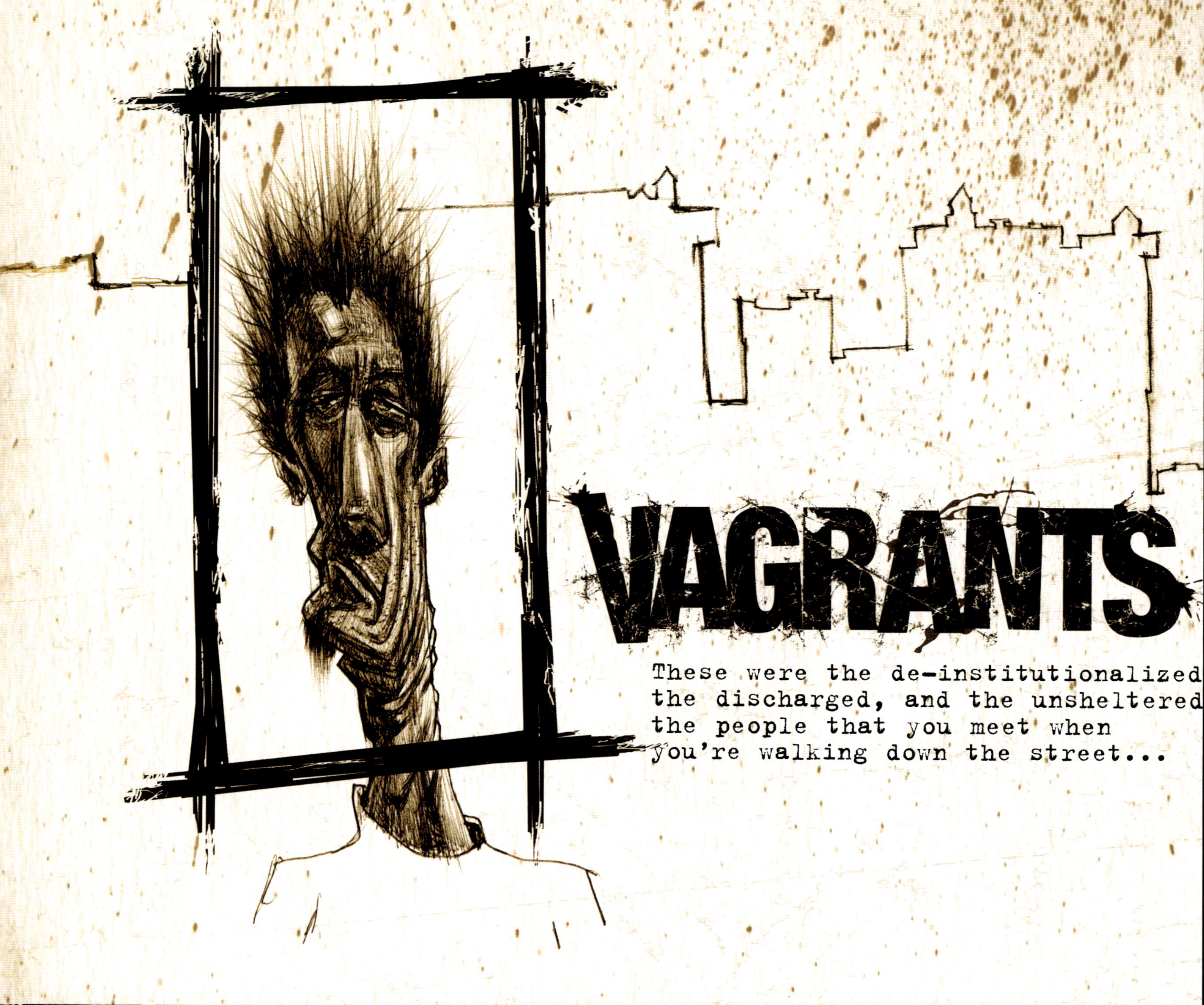

VAGRANTS

These were the de-institutionalized the discharged, and the unsheltered the people that you meet when you're walking down the street...

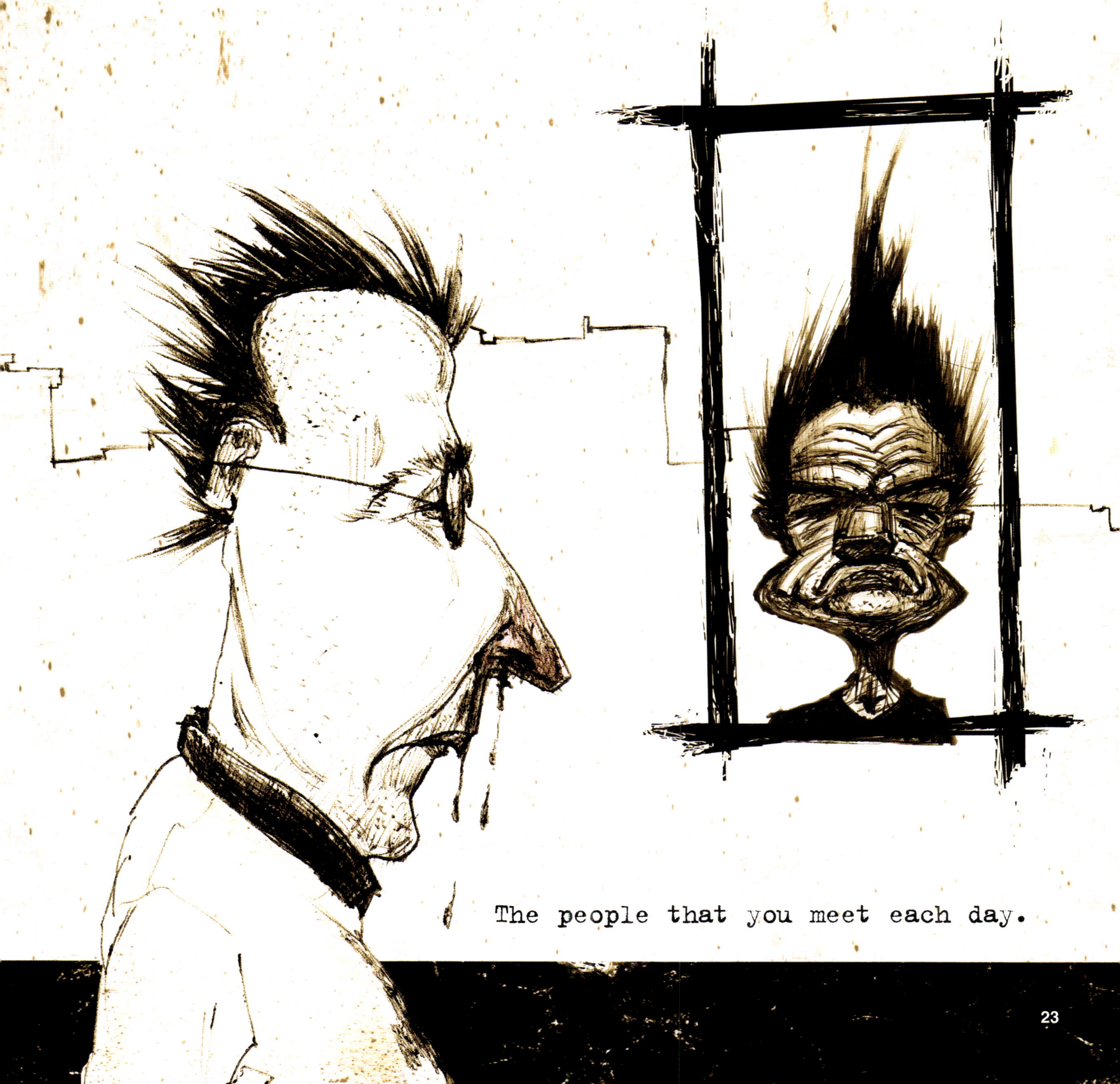

The people that you meet each day.

The Baller

If I wasn't hangin' out in front of the welfare hotel, I was at the Douglas or Dykeman Projects chillin' with my friends or checking out the B-Boys breaking at Rocksteady Park. I watched the powerful faces and attitudes of the ballers ballin' down at Riverside Park and the graf writers bombin' the 1 and 2 subway lines. This was my world. I studied, I observed the characters of my surroundings.

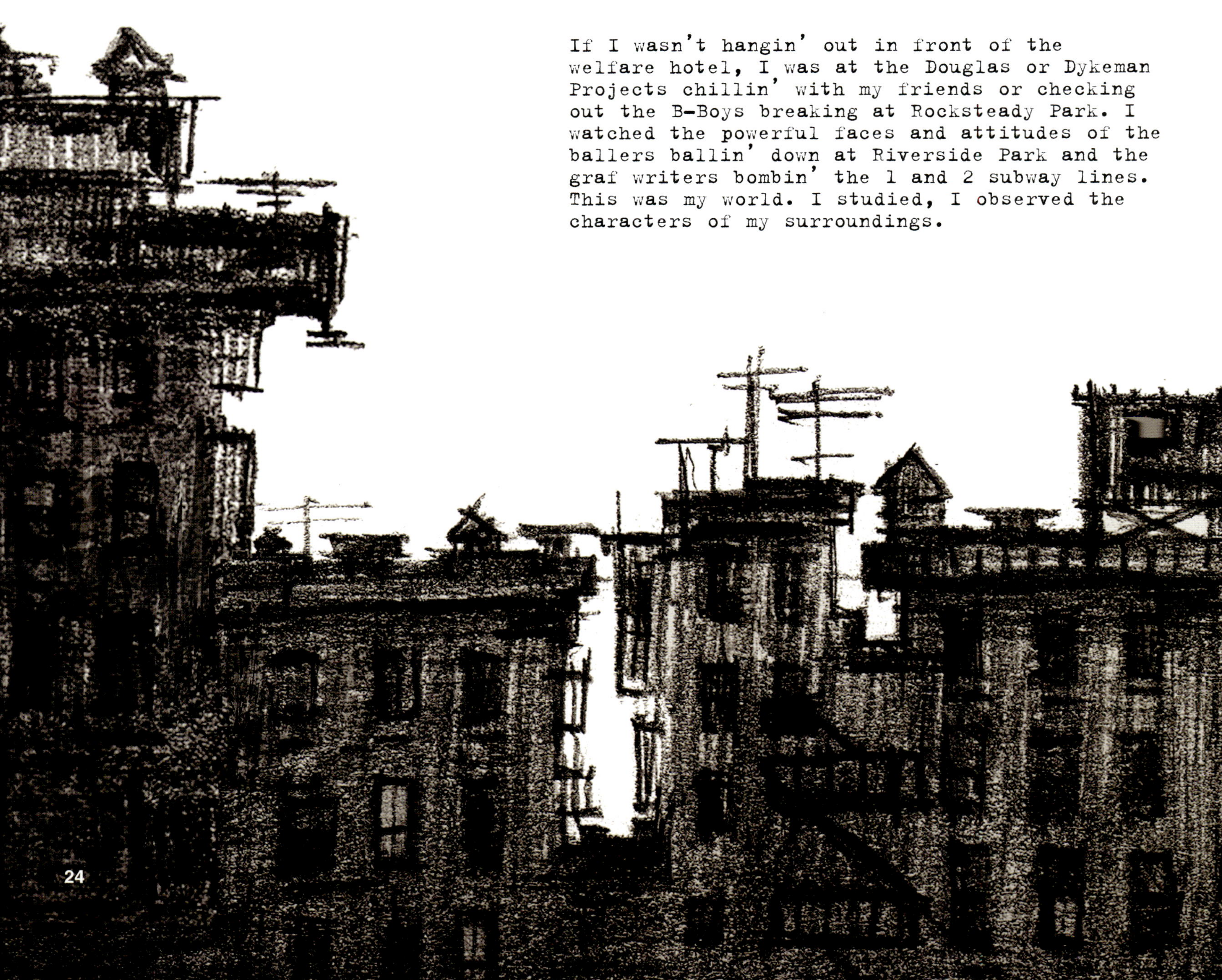

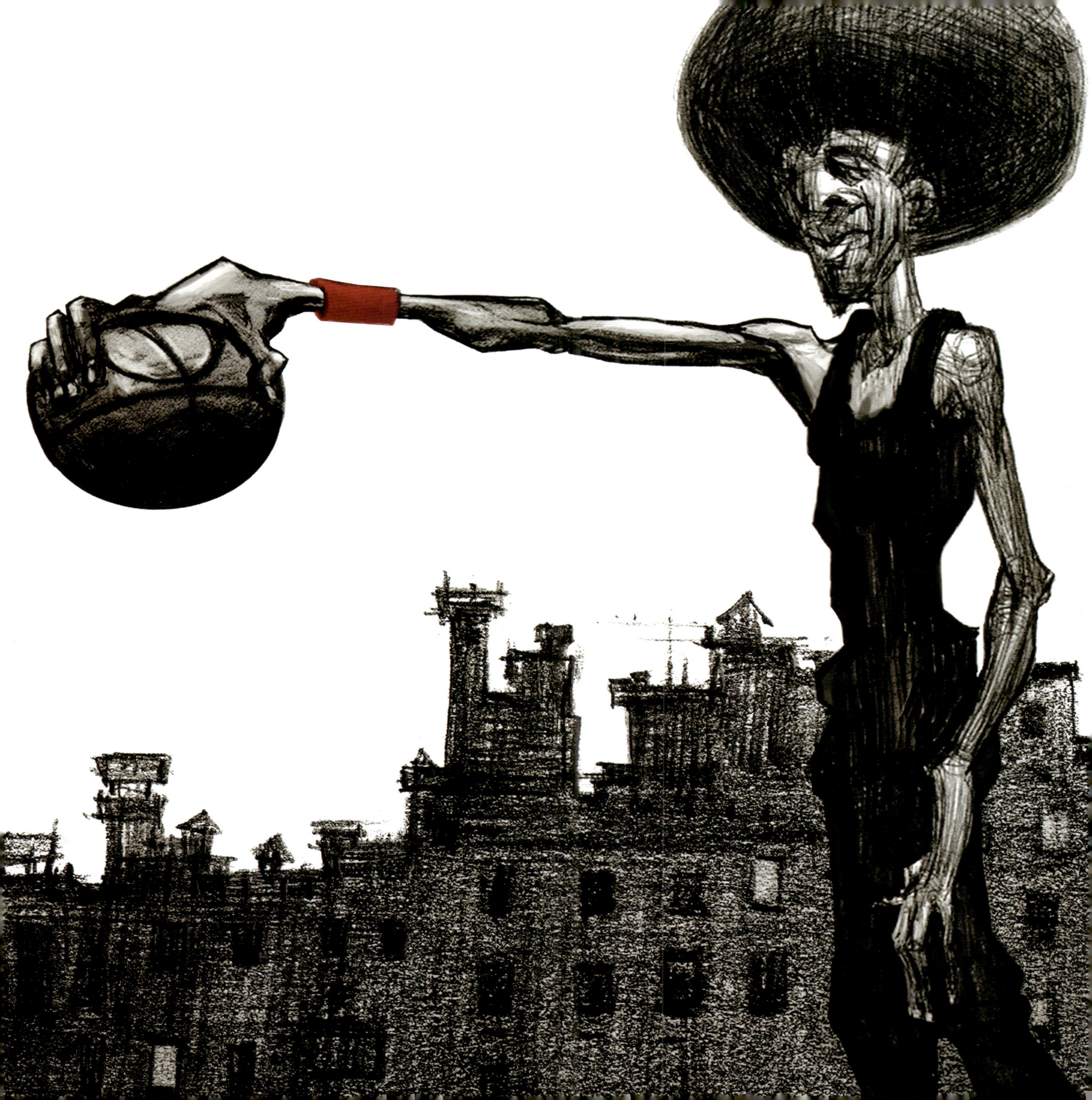

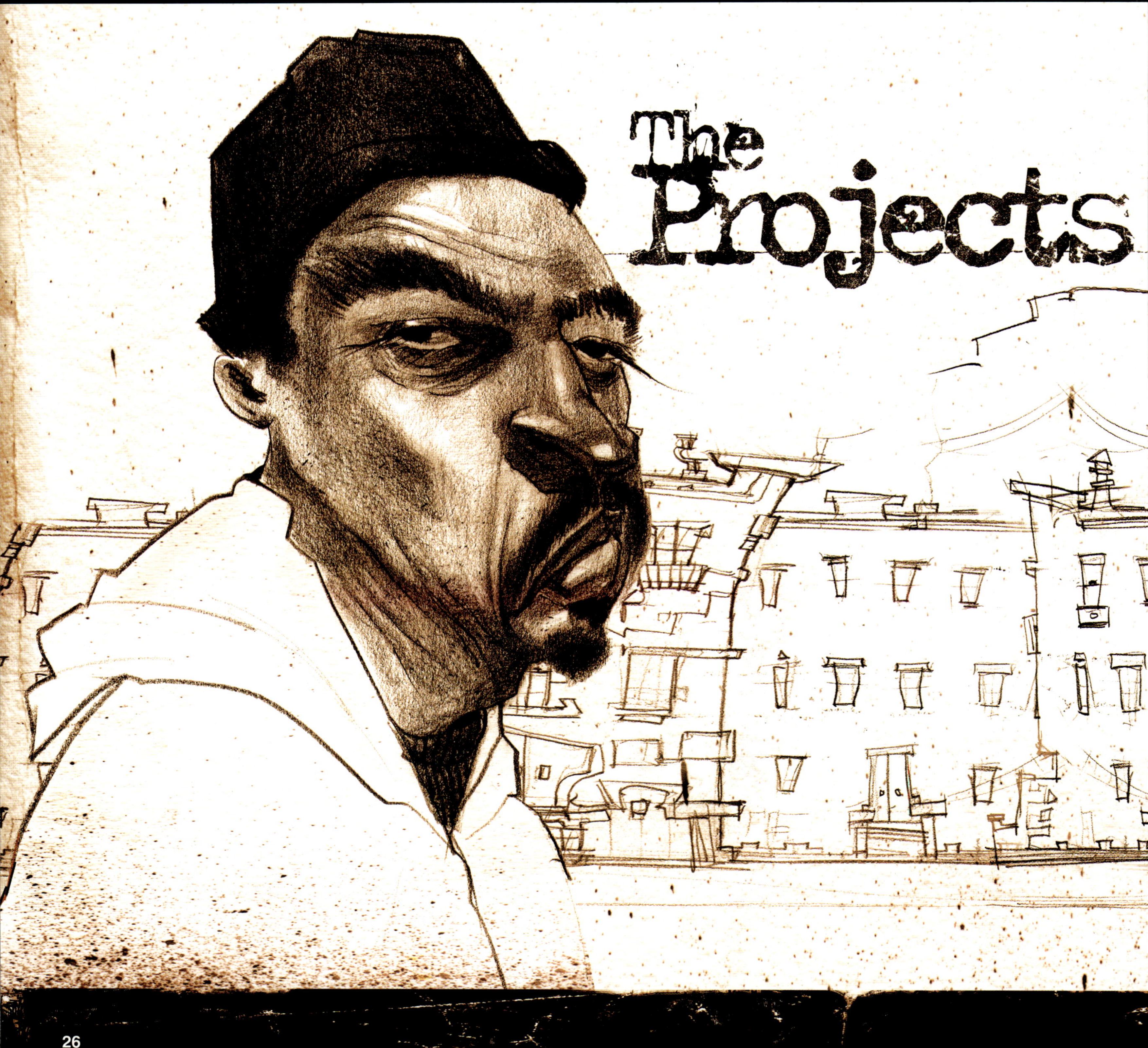

The Projects

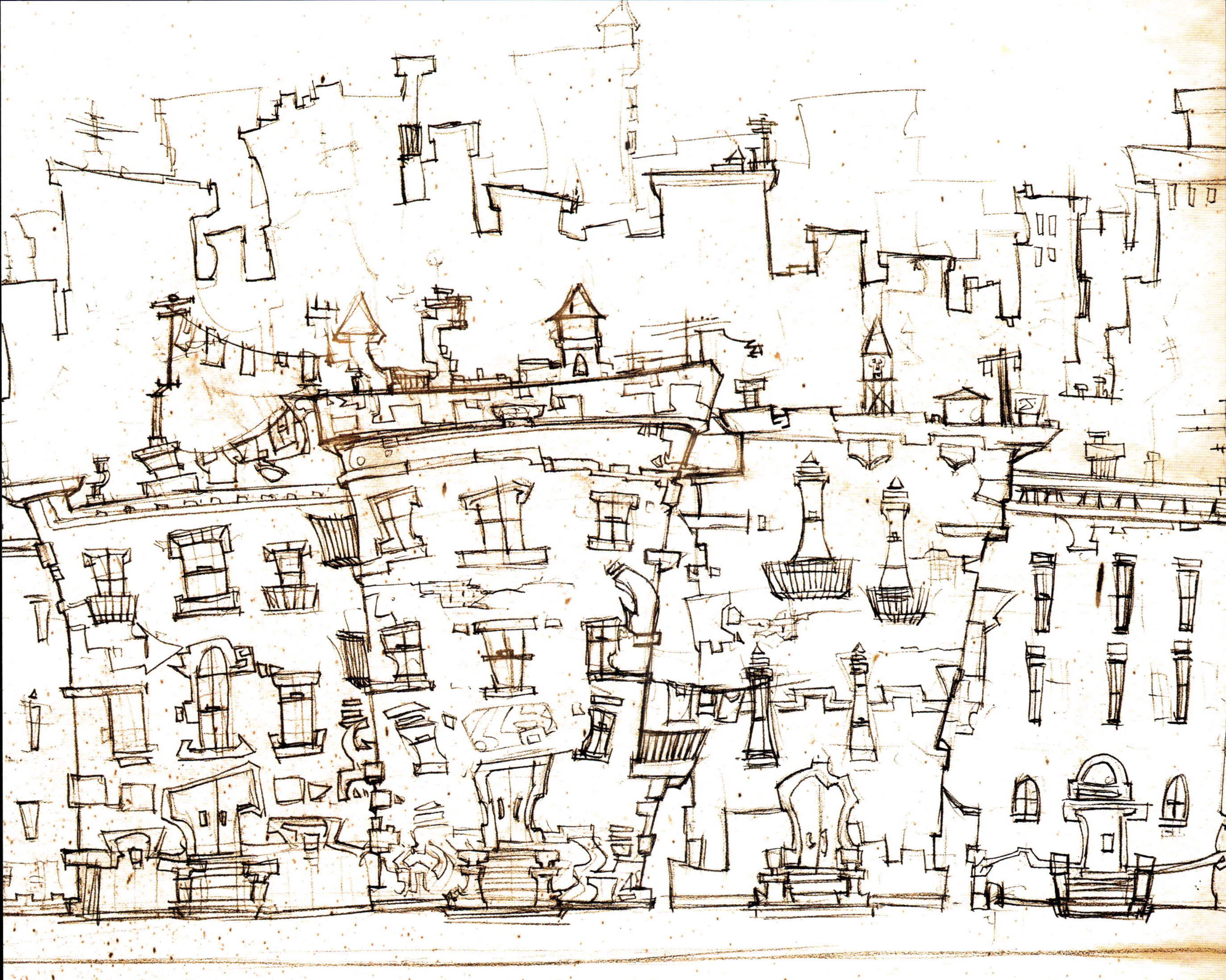

Spanish Harlem

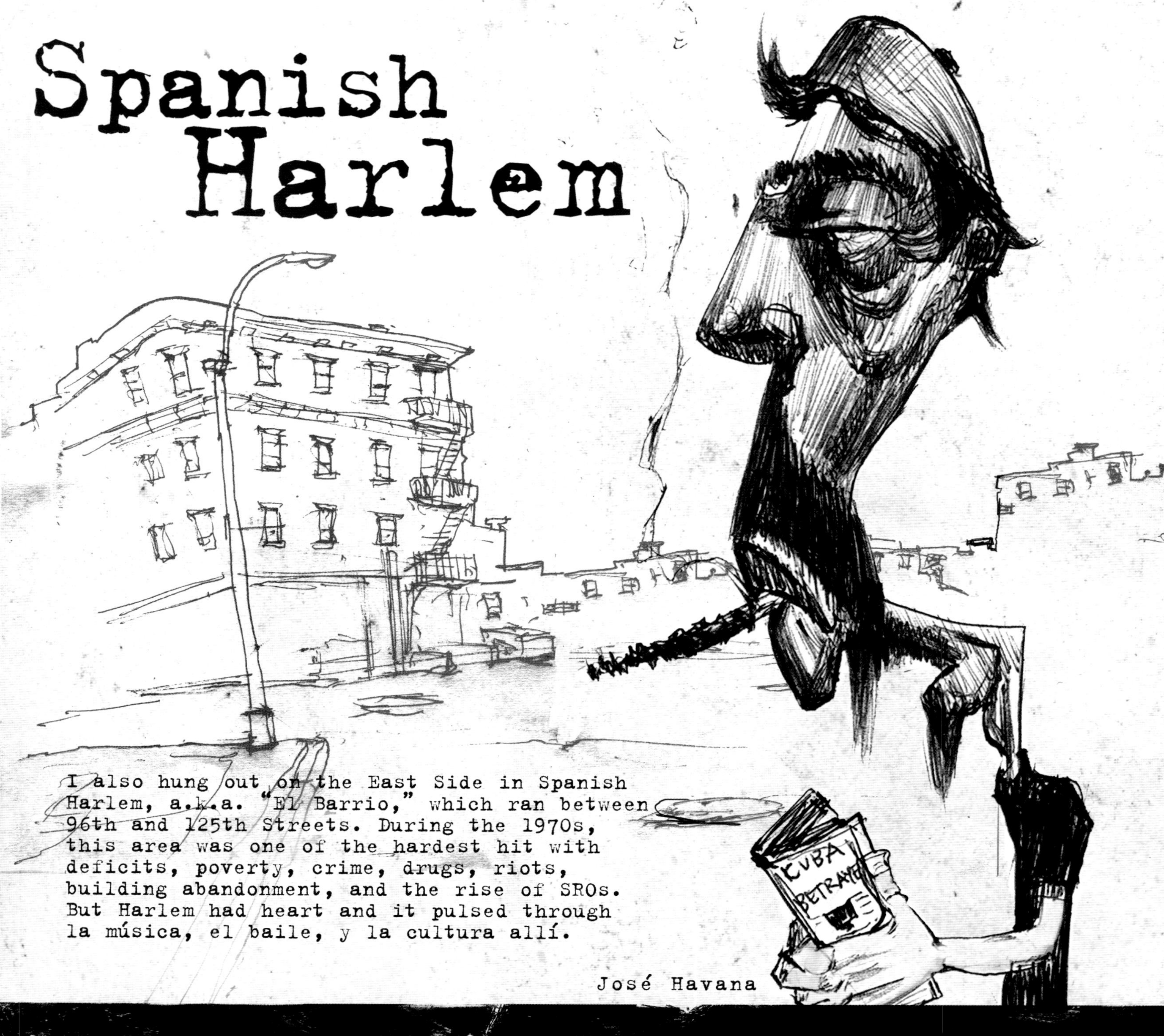

I also hung out on the East Side in Spanish Harlem, a.k.a. "El Barrio," which ran between 96th and 125th Streets. During the 1970s, this area was one of the hardest hit with deficits, poverty, crime, drugs, riots, building abandonment, and the rise of SROs. But Harlem had heart and it pulsed through la música, el baile, y la cultura allí.

José Havana

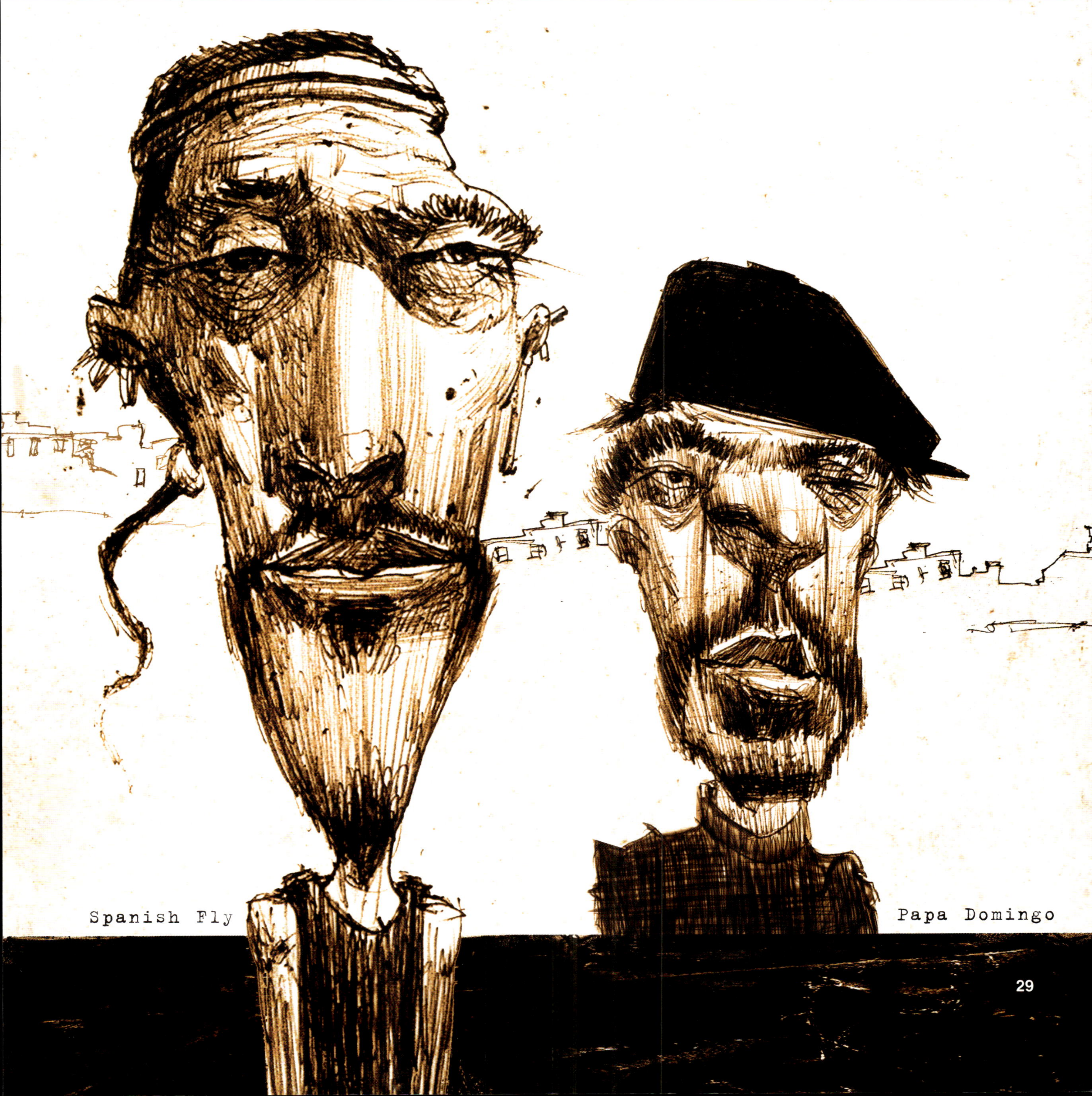
Spanish Fly
Papa Domingo

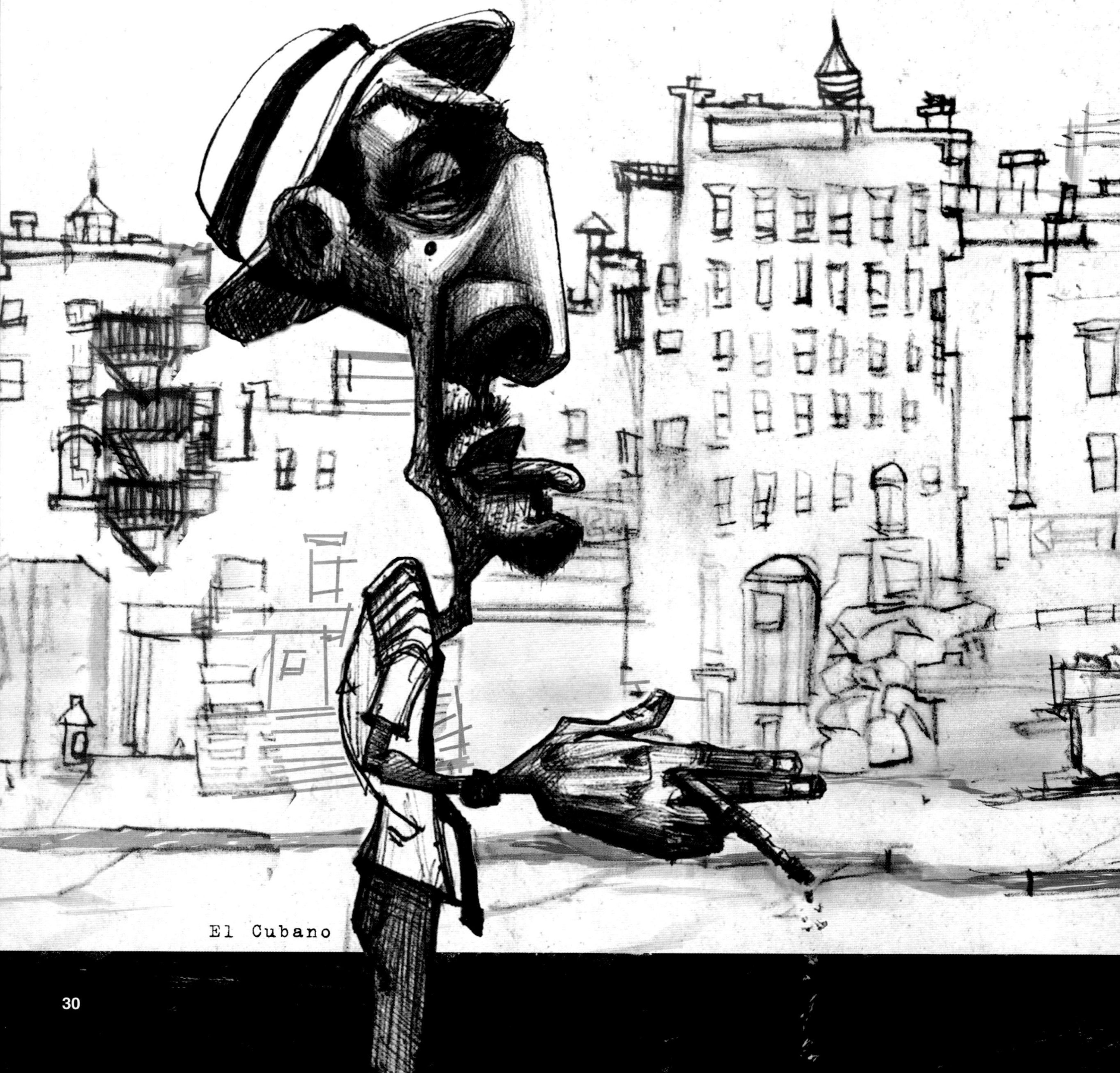

El Cubano

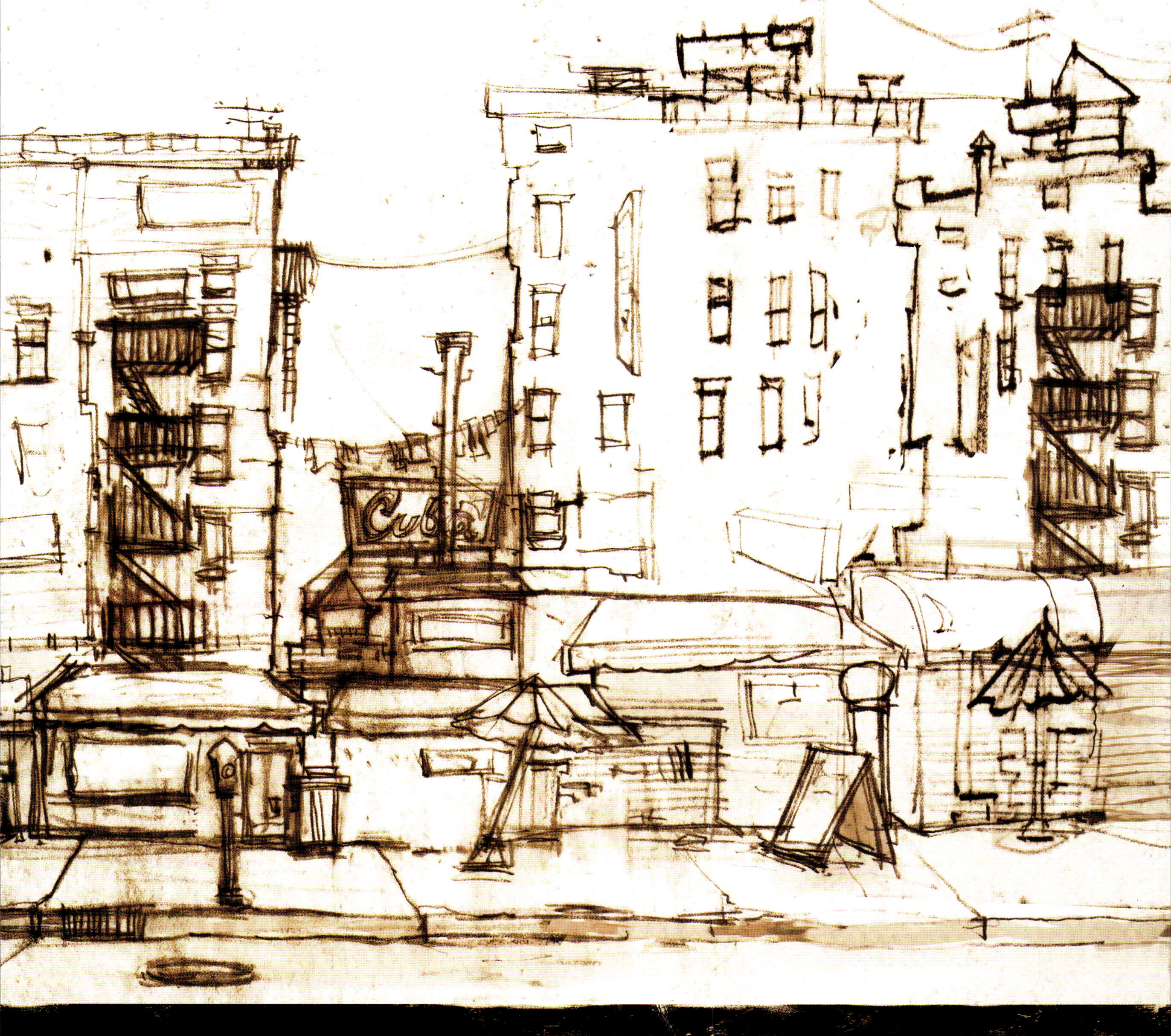
Cuba

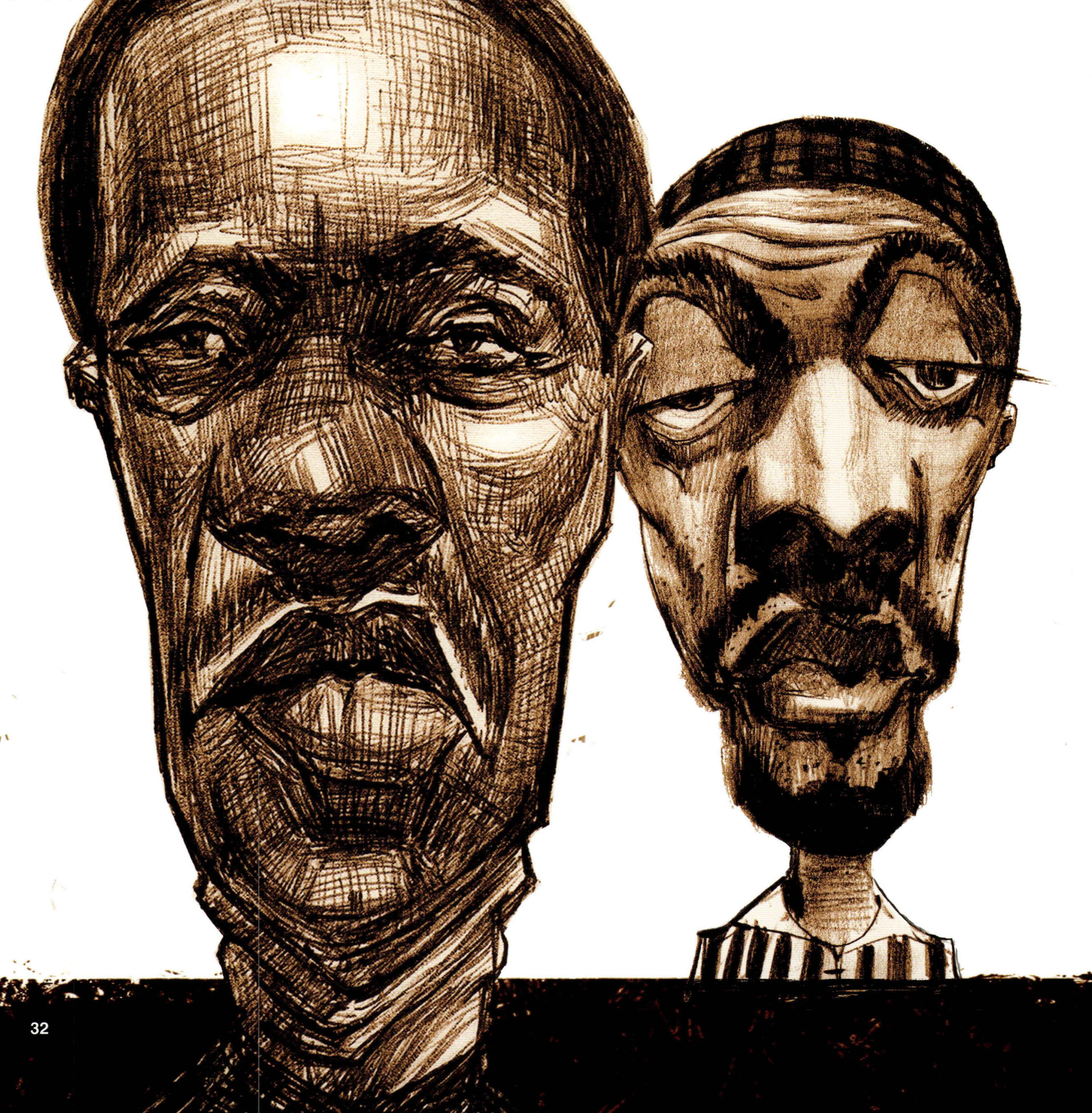

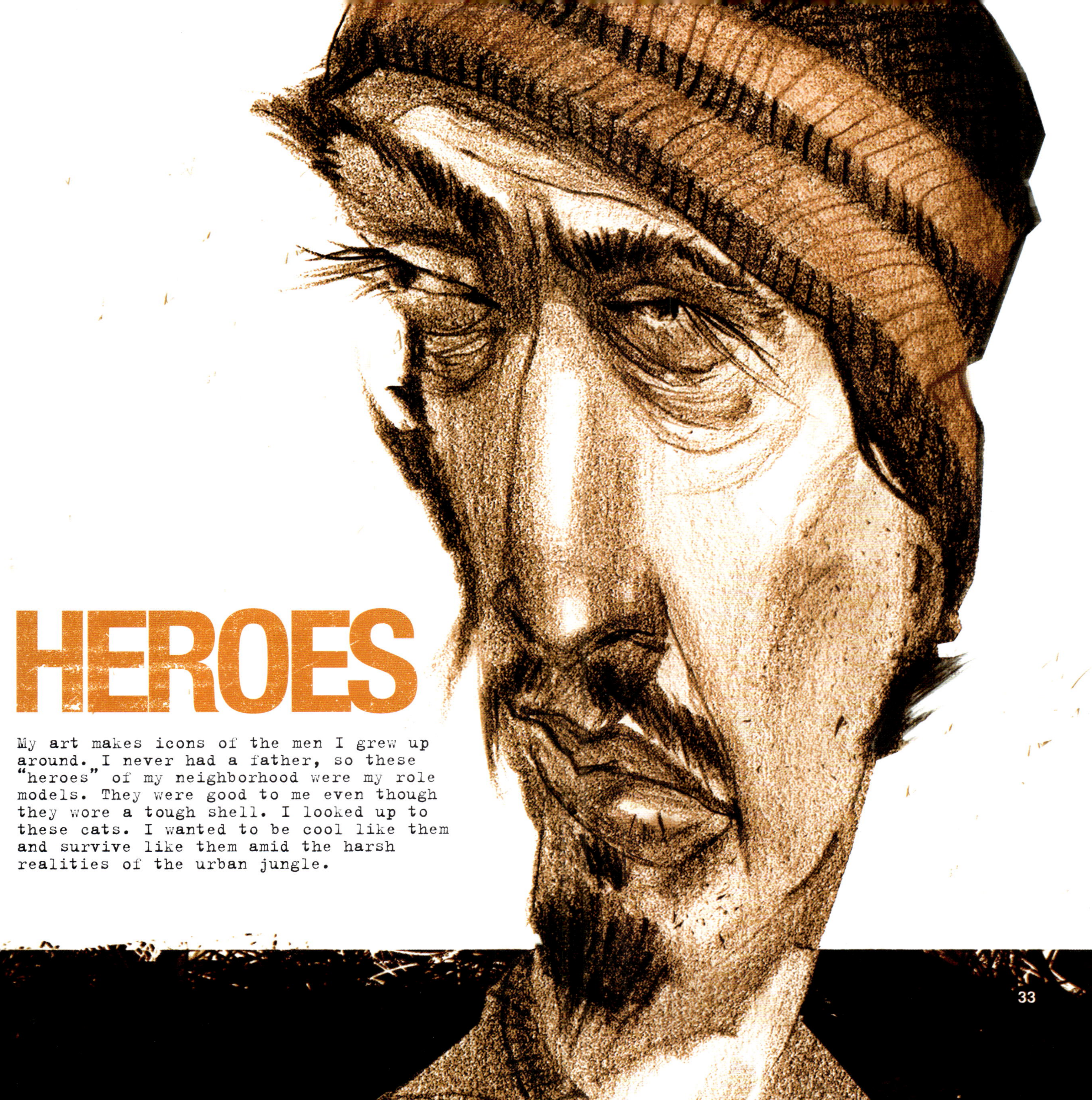

HEROES

My art makes icons of the men I grew up around. I never had a father, so these "heroes" of my neighborhood were my role models. They were good to me even though they wore a tough shell. I looked up to these cats. I wanted to be cool like them and survive like them amid the harsh realities of the urban jungle.

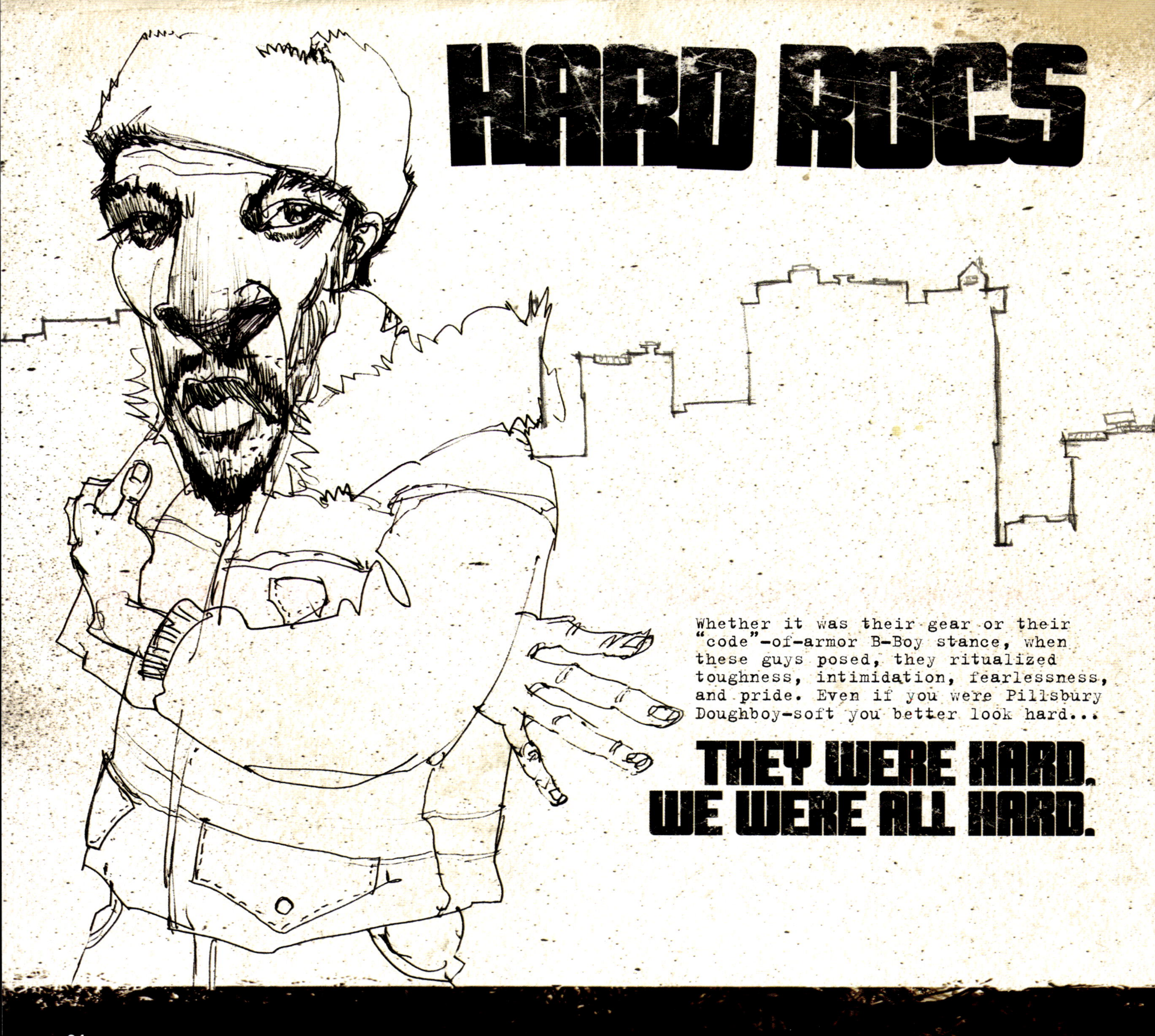

HARD ROCS

Whether it was their gear or their "code"-of-armor B-Boy stance, when these guys posed, they ritualized toughness, intimidation, fearlessness, and pride. Even if you were Pillsbury Doughboy-soft you better look hard...

THEY WERE HARD. WE WERE ALL HARD.

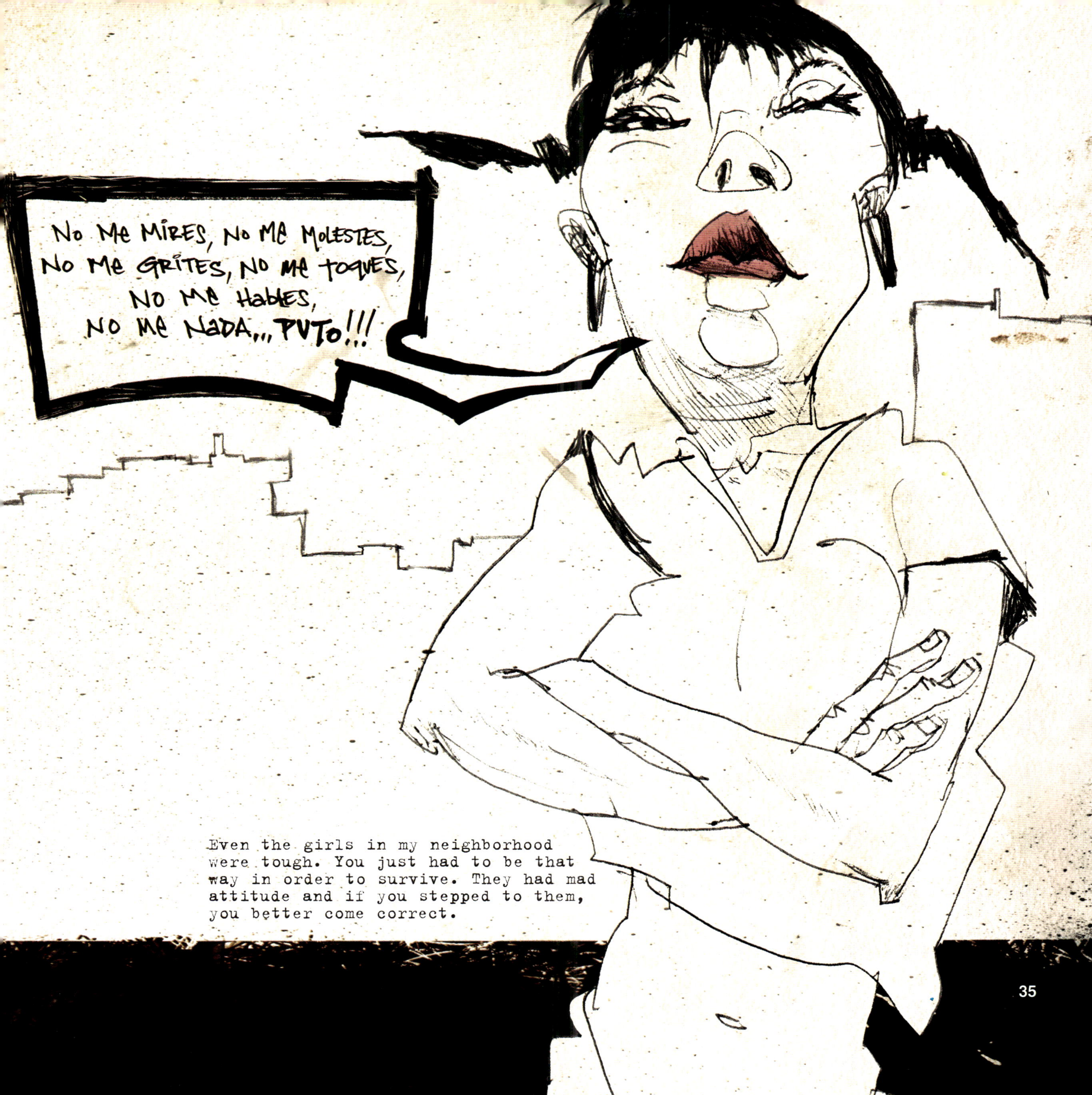

Even the girls in my neighborhood were tough. You just had to be that way in order to survive. They had mad attitude and if you stepped to them, you better come correct.

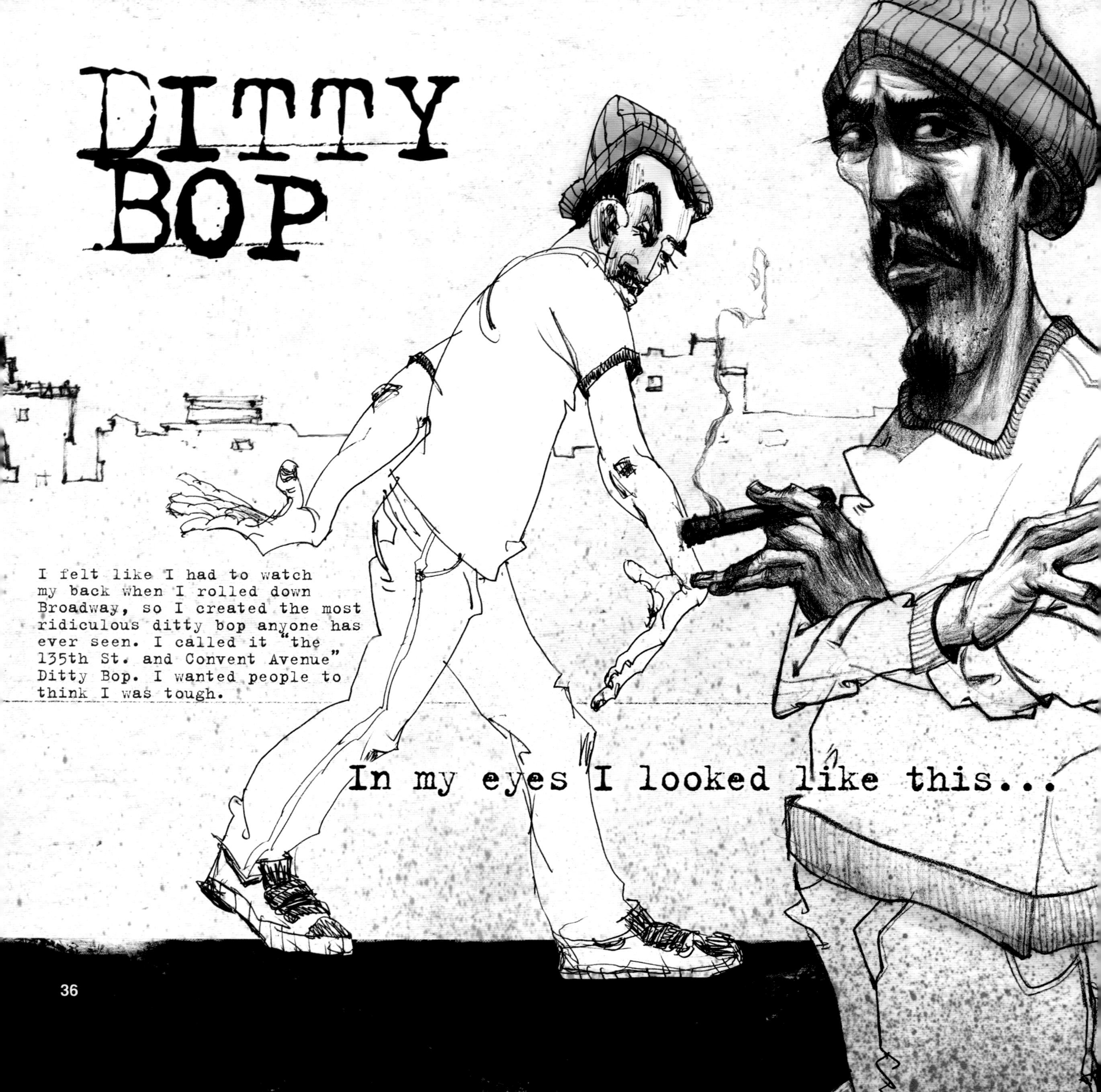
DITTY BOP
I felt like I had to watch my back when I rolled down Broadway, so I created the most ridiculous ditty bop anyone has ever seen. I called it "the 135th St. and Convent Avenue" Ditty Bop. I wanted people to think I was tough.
In my eyes I looked like this...

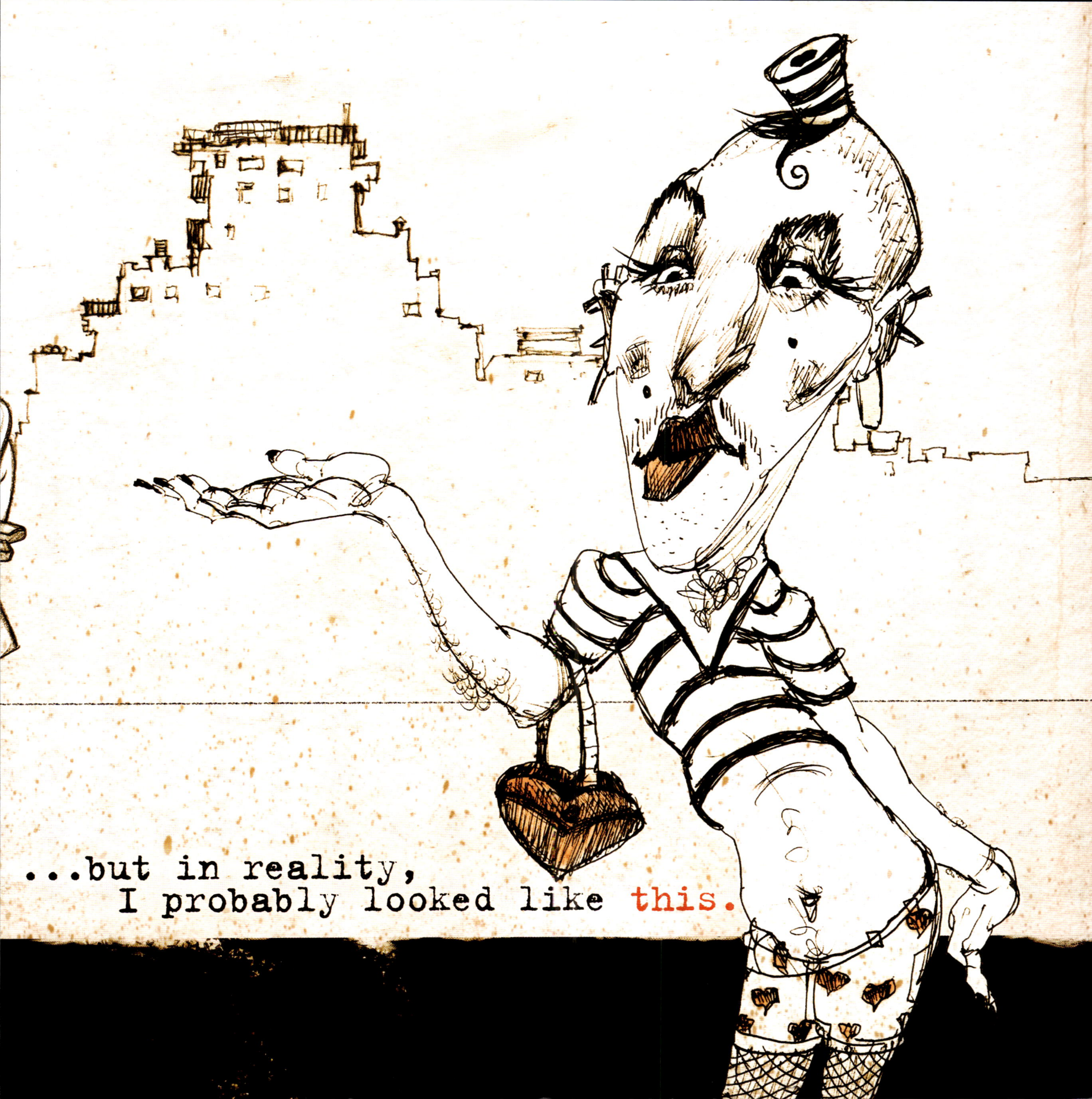
...but in reality,
I probably looked like this.

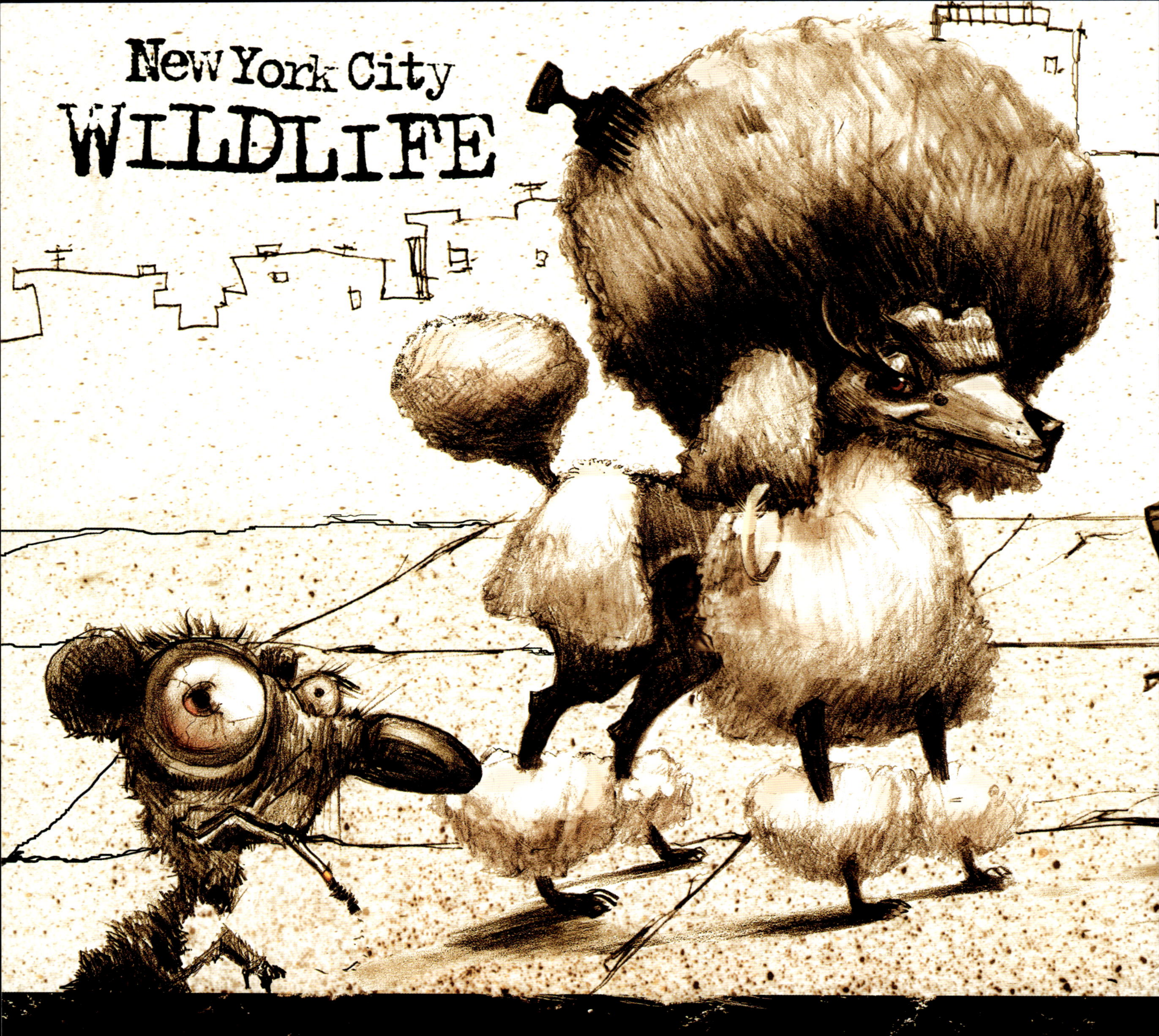
New York City
WILDLIFE

Even the plants and animals had attitude and a drive to survive.

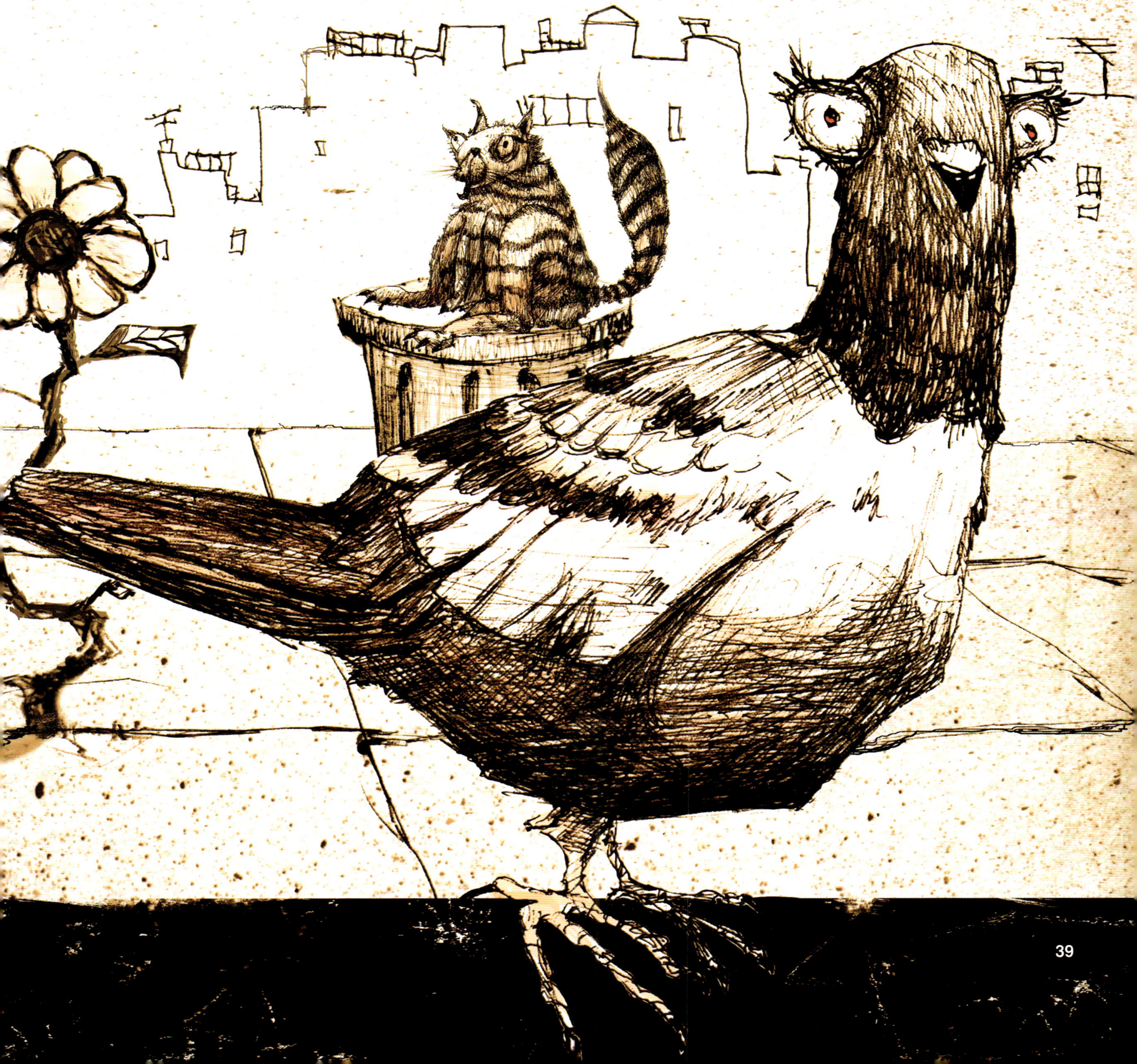

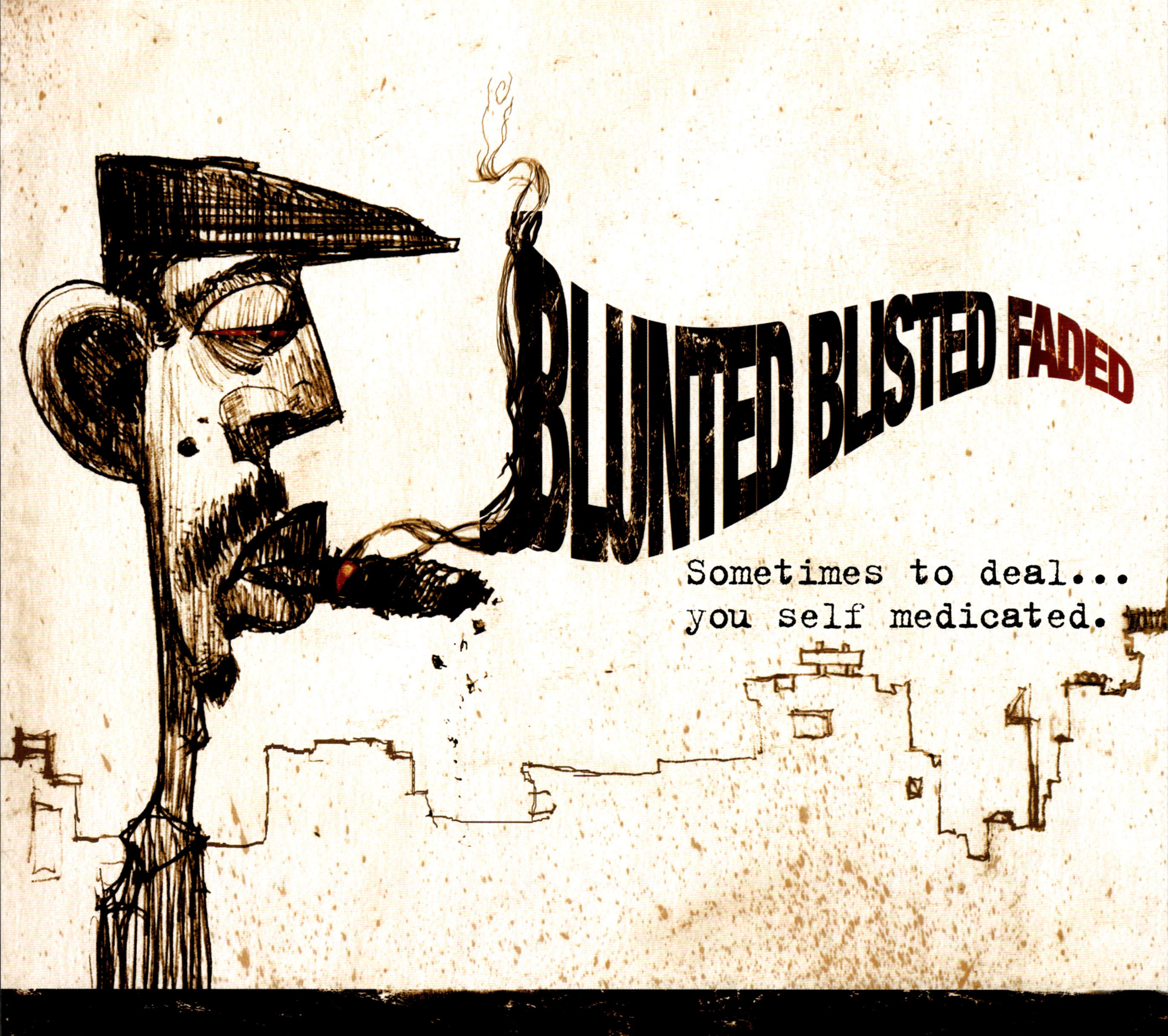
BLUNTED BLISTED FADED
Sometimes to deal...
you self medicated.

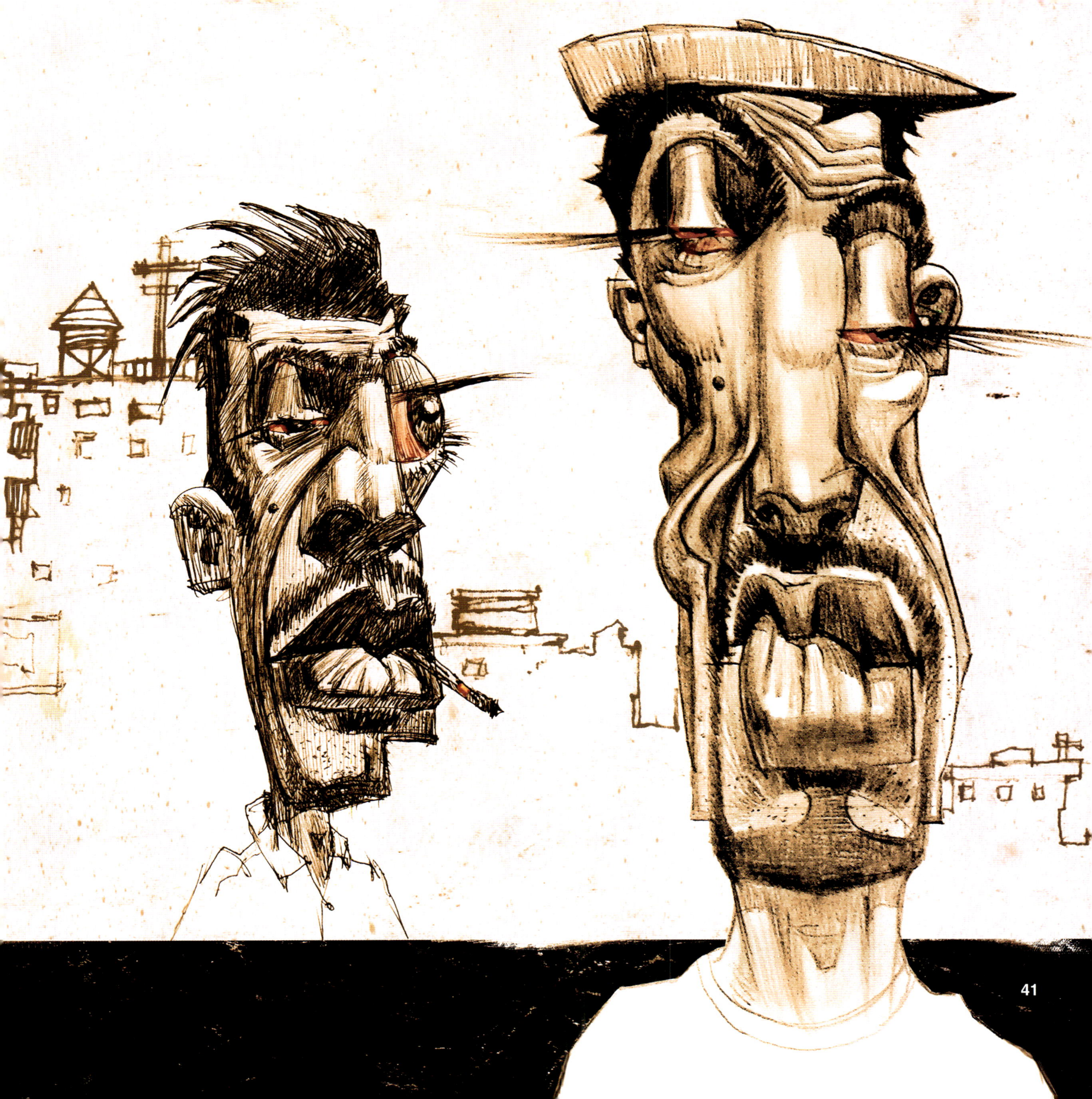

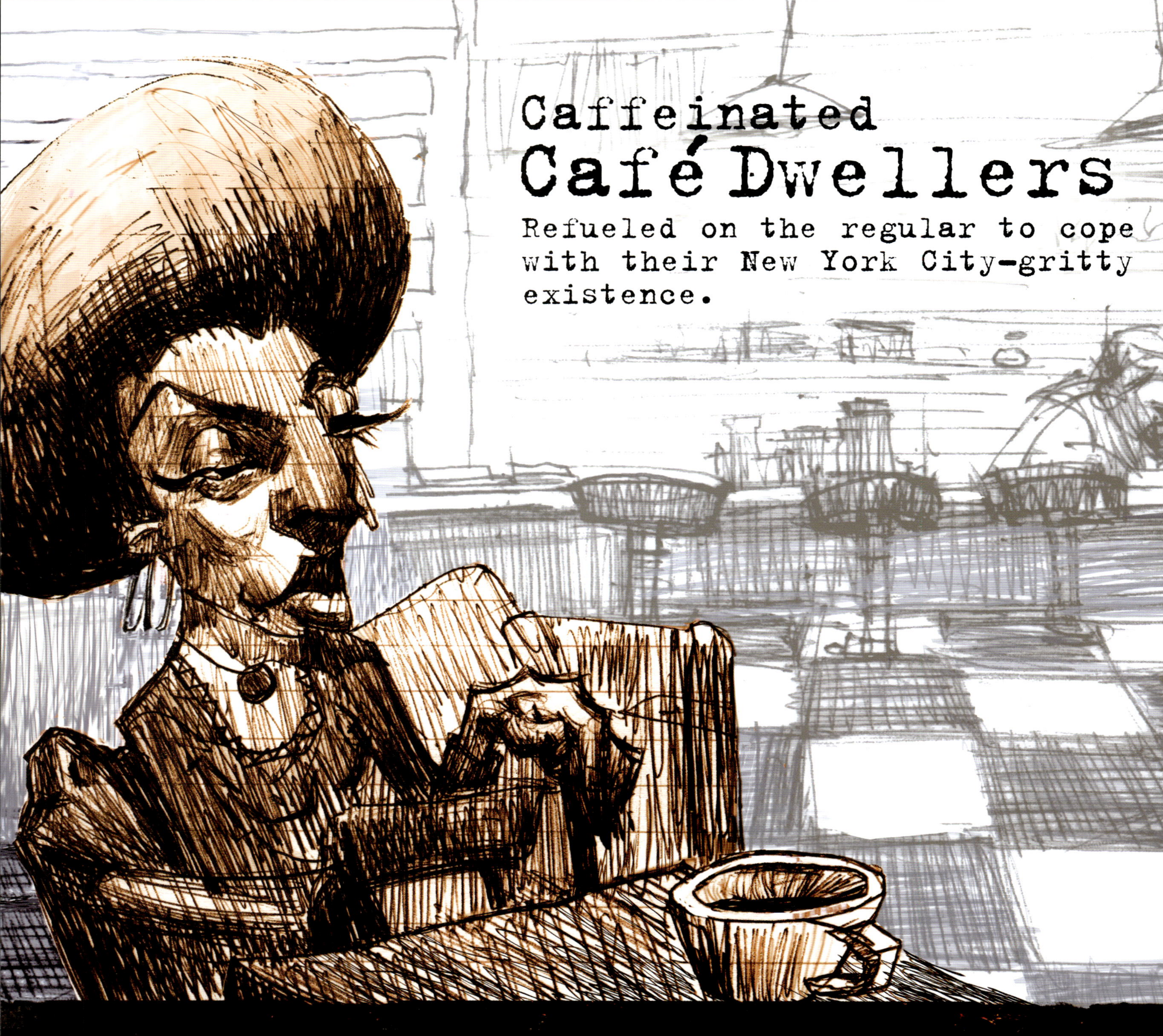

Caffeinated Café Dwellers

Refueled on the regular to cope with their New York City-gritty existence.

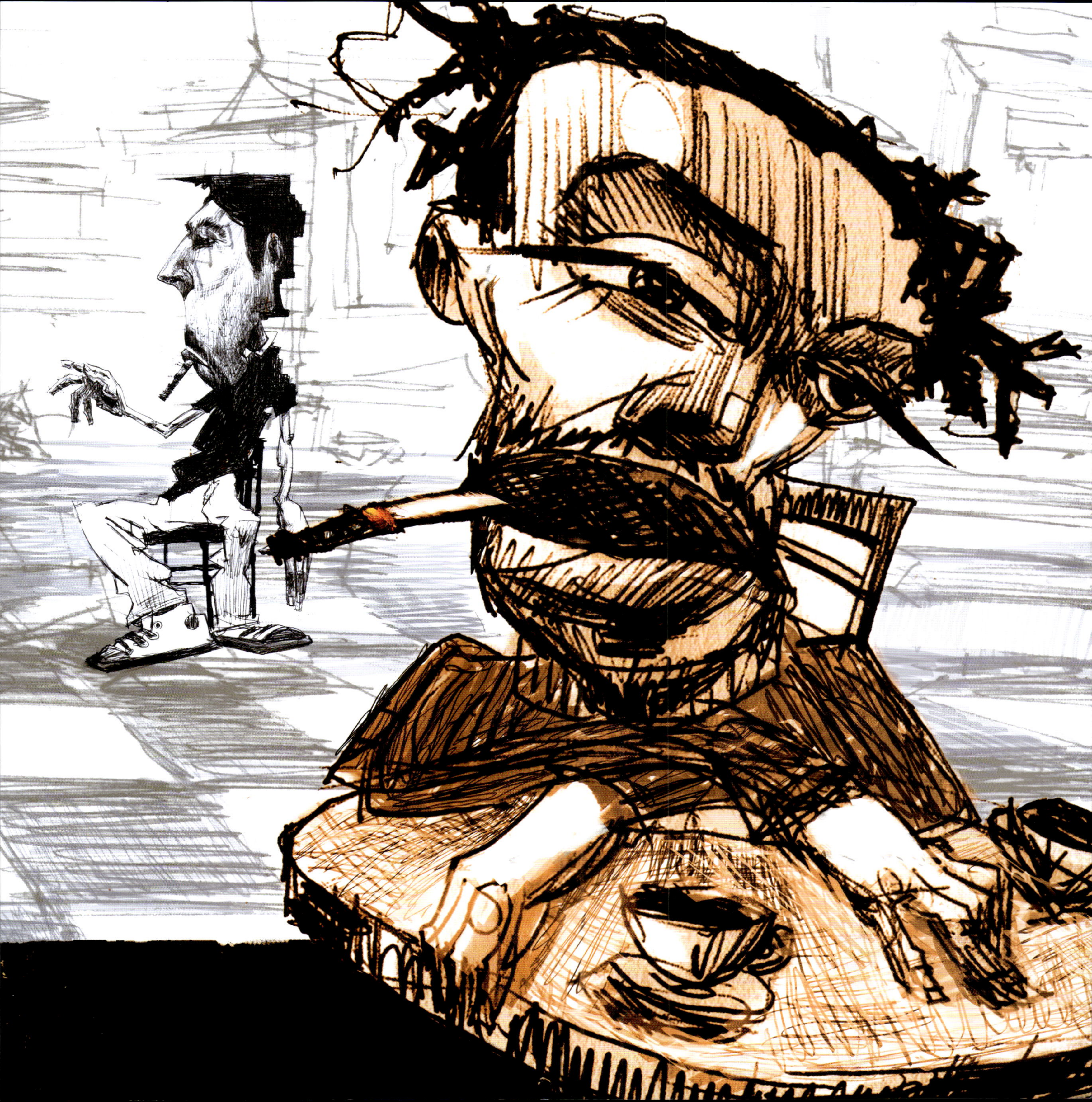

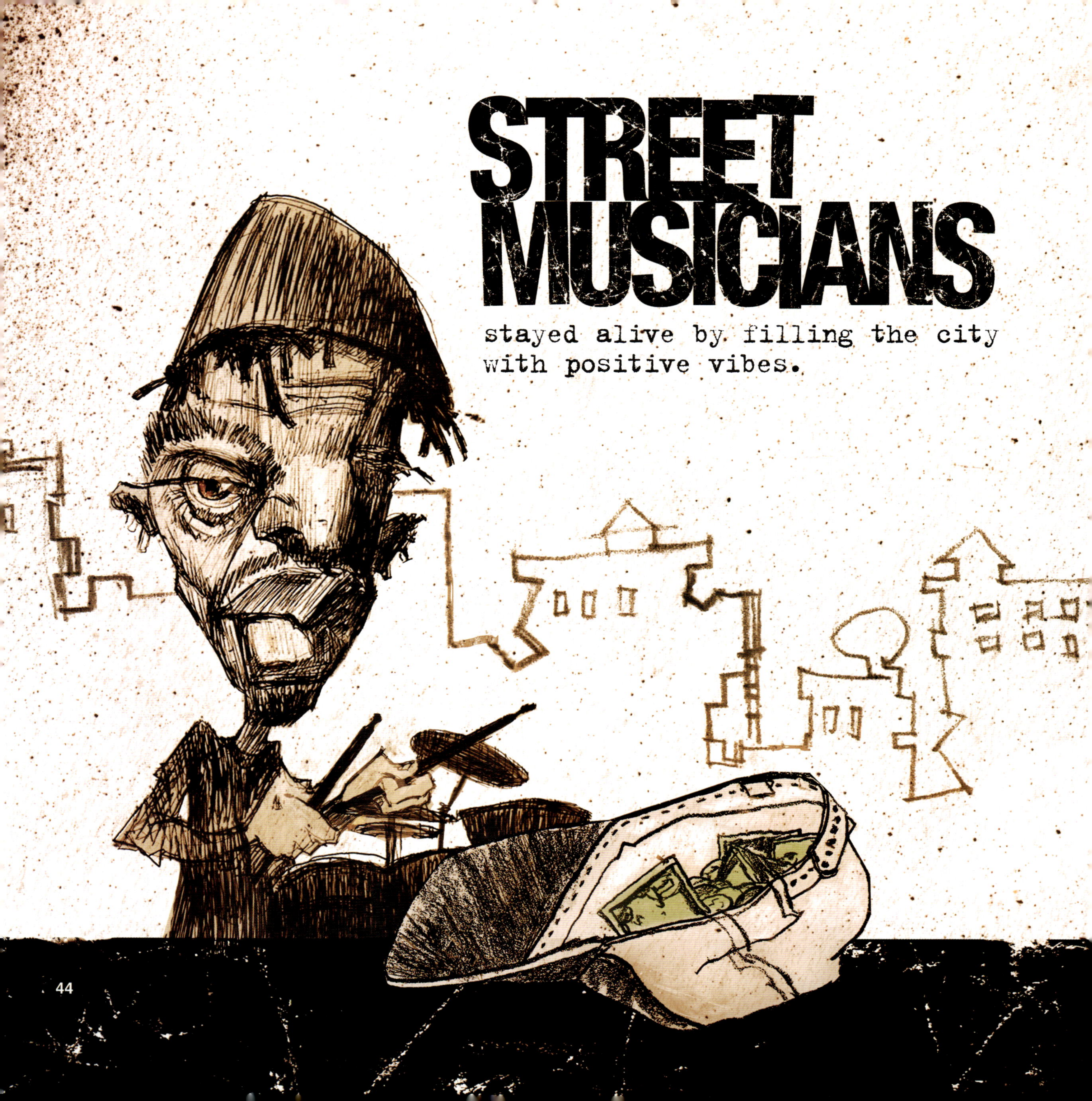
STREET MUSICIANS
stayed alive by filling the city
with positive vibes.

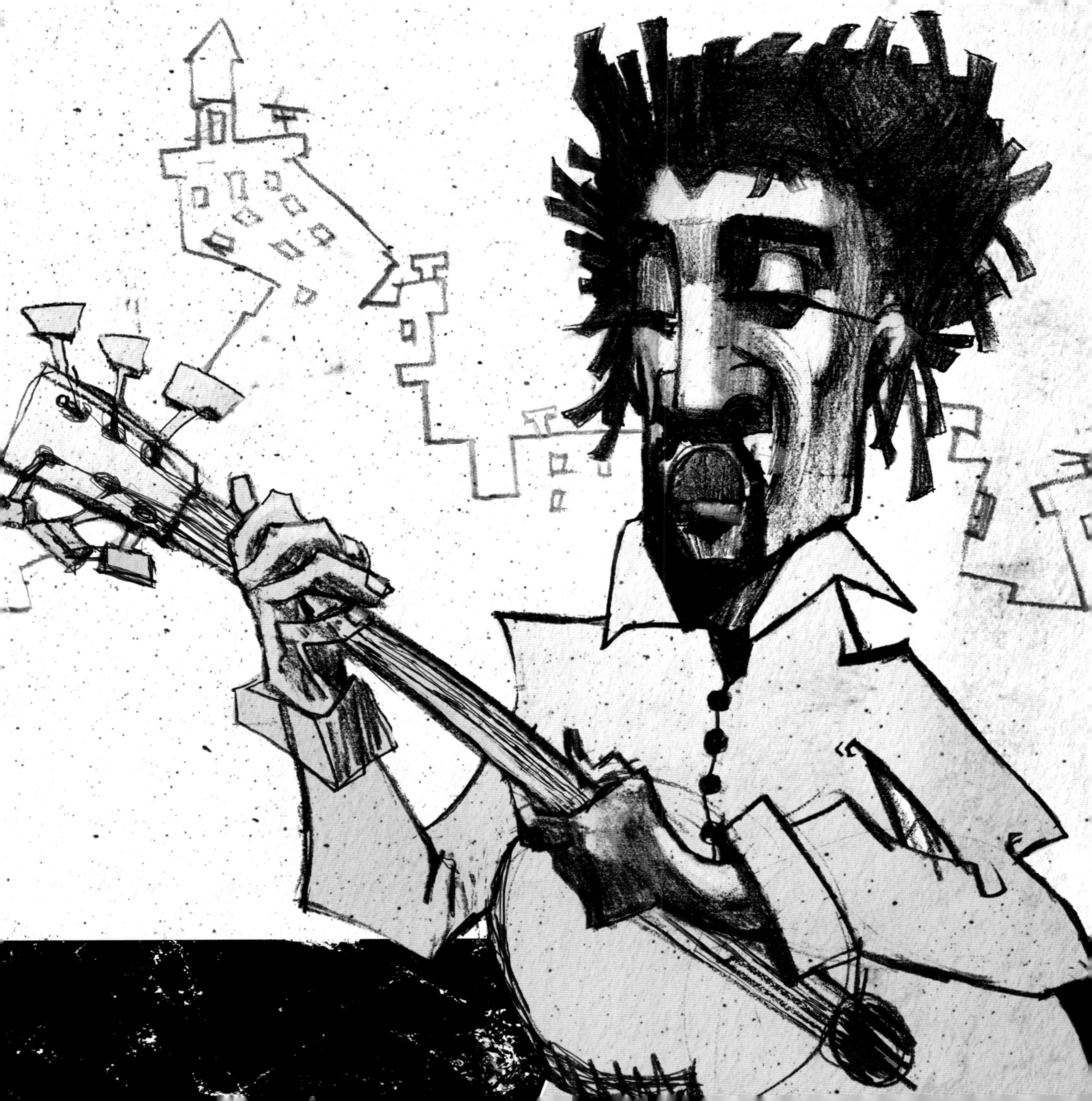

And then there were the
POETS
pulling prose
from within
to awaken those
without.

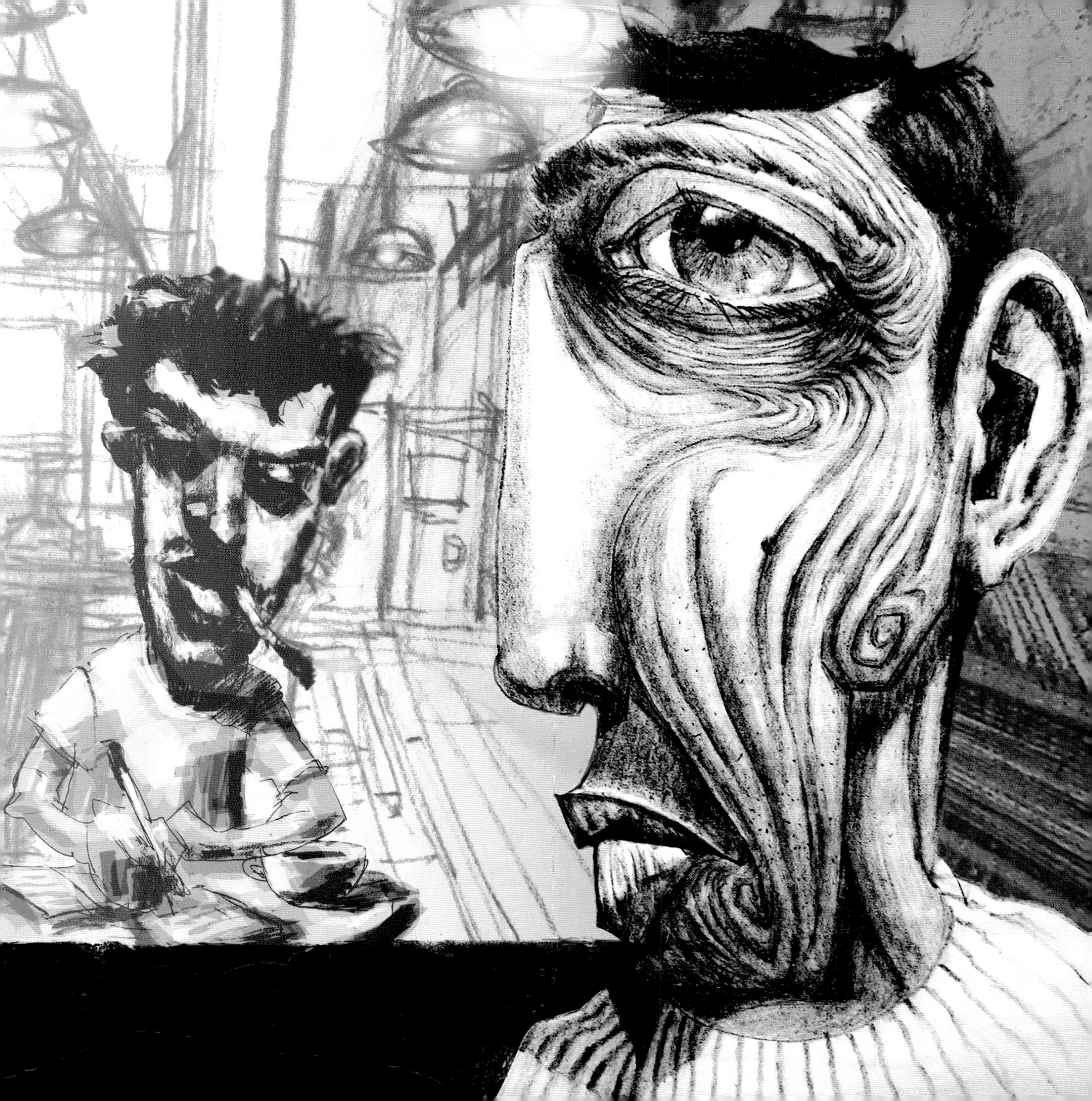

THE BIRTH OF HIP-HOP

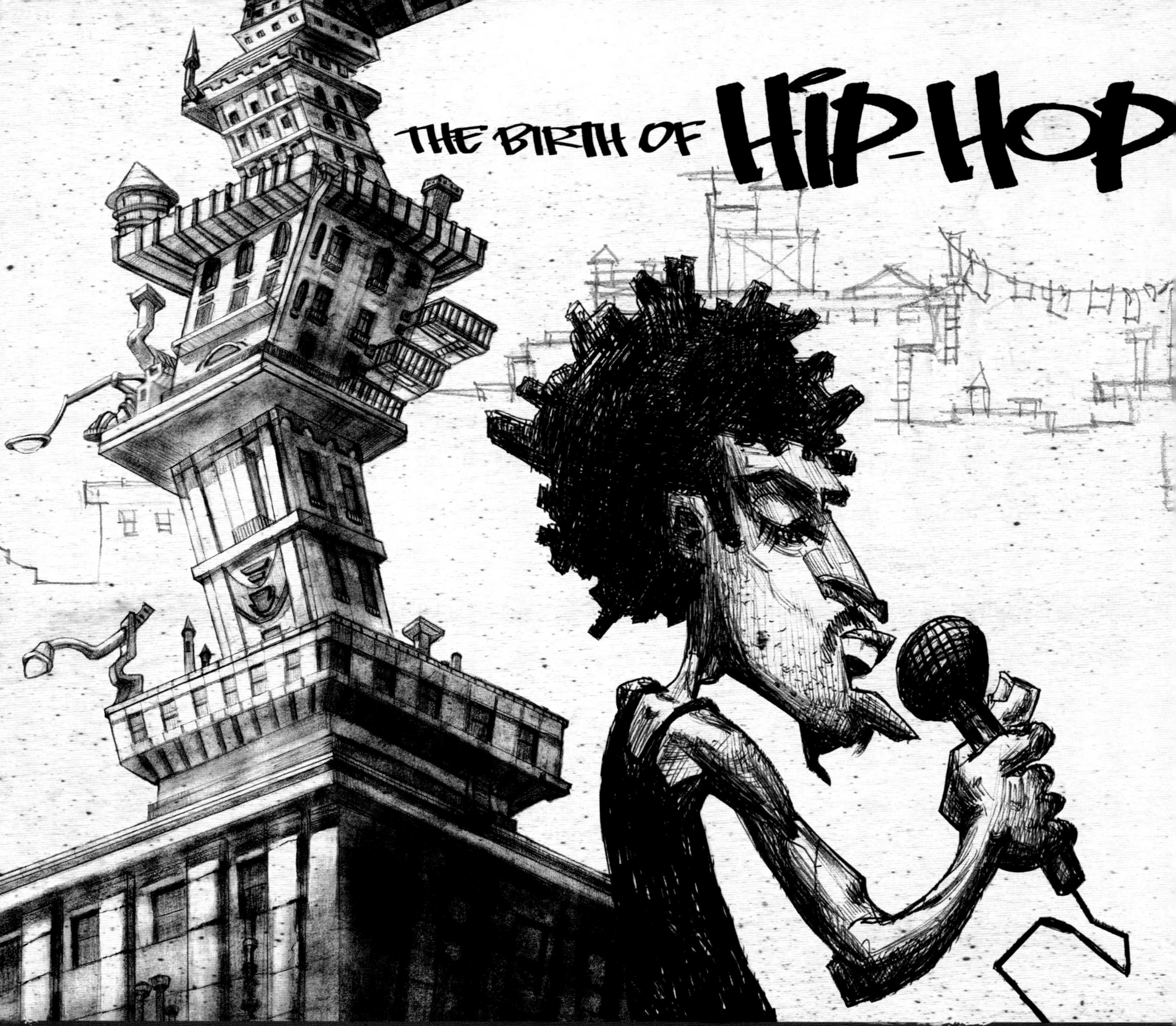

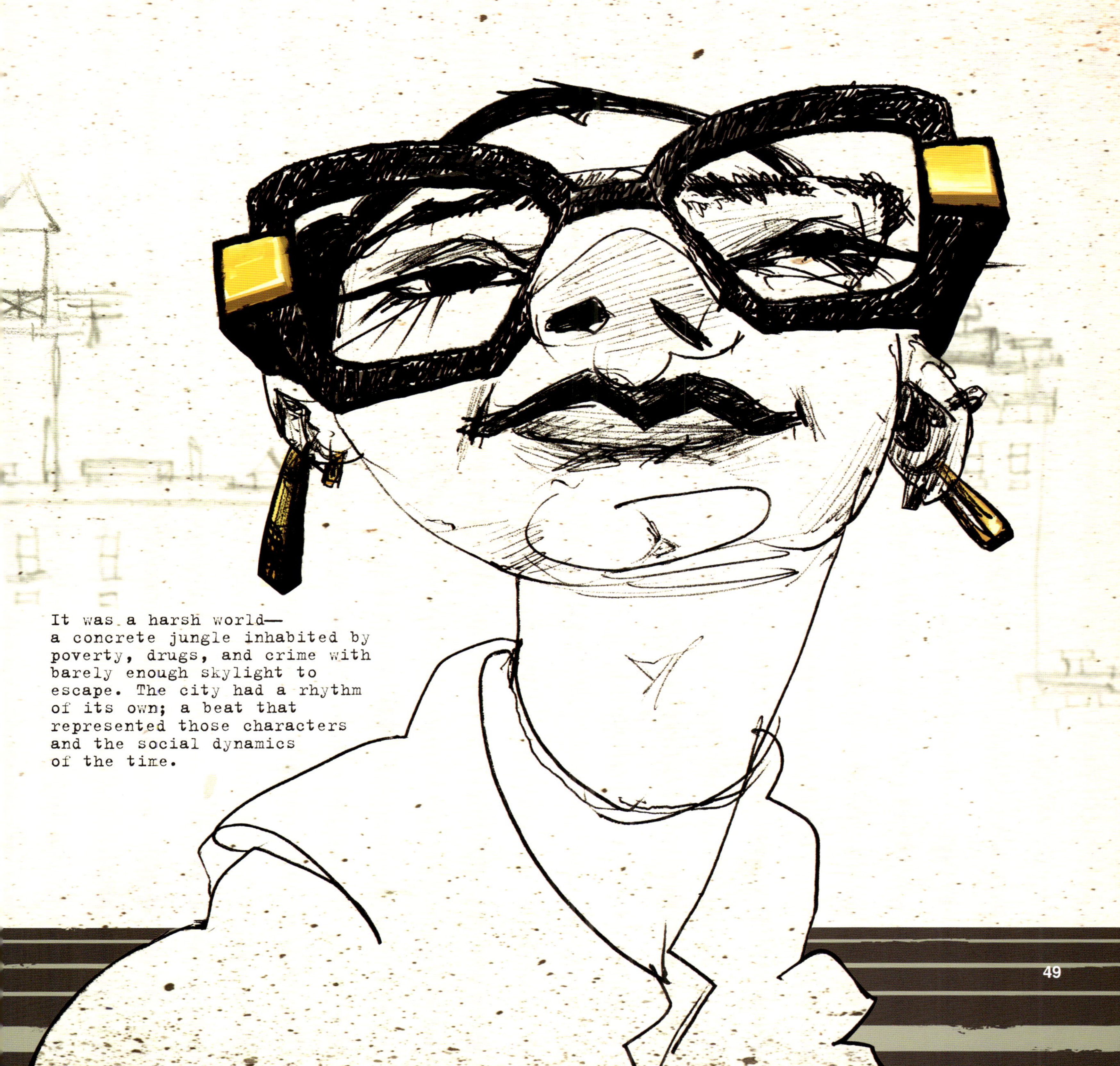

It was a harsh world—
a concrete jungle inhabited by poverty, drugs, and crime with barely enough skylight to escape. The city had a rhythm of its own; a beat that represented those characters and the social dynamics of the time.

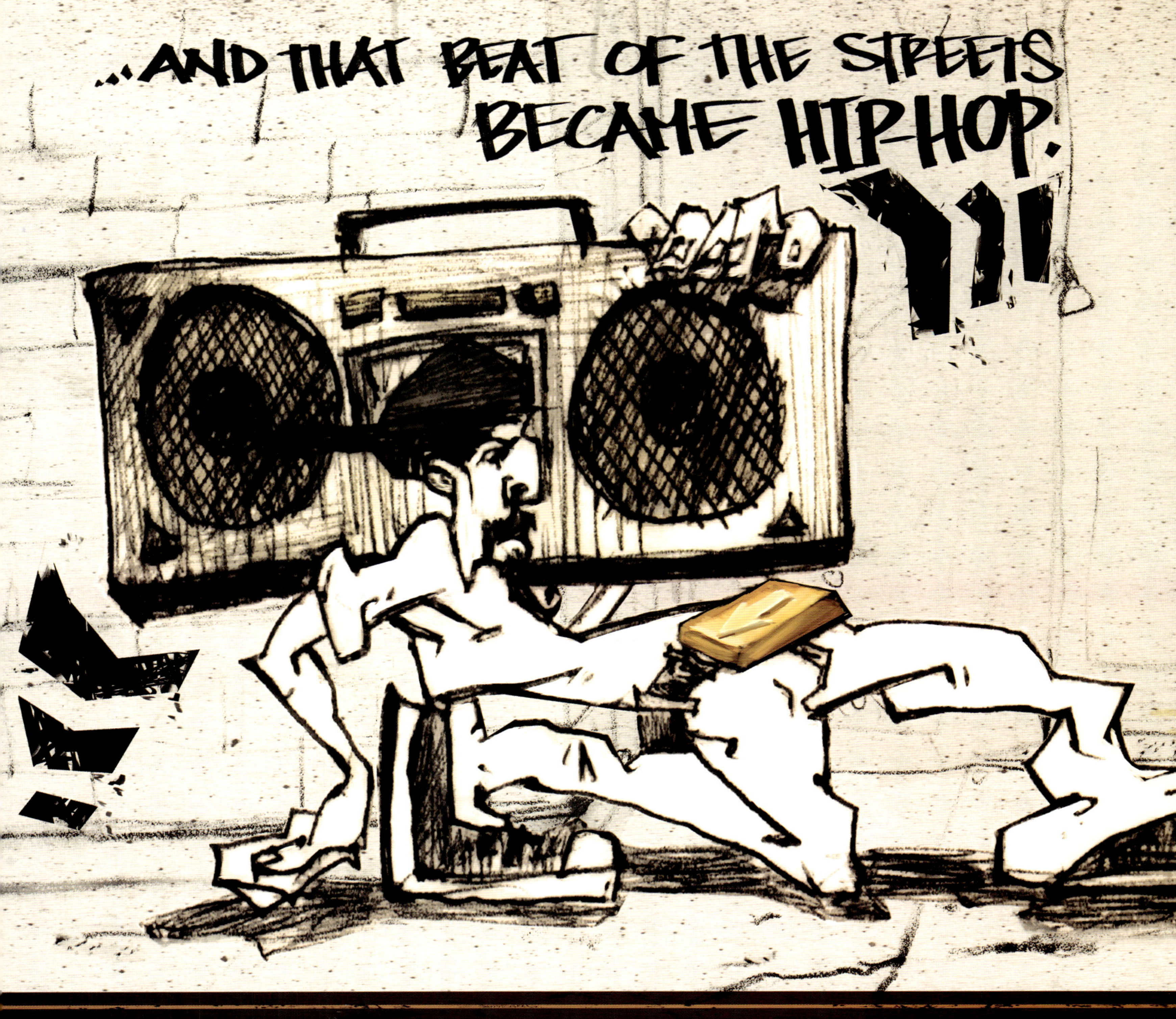
...AND THAT BEAT OF THE STREETS
BECAME HIP-HOP.

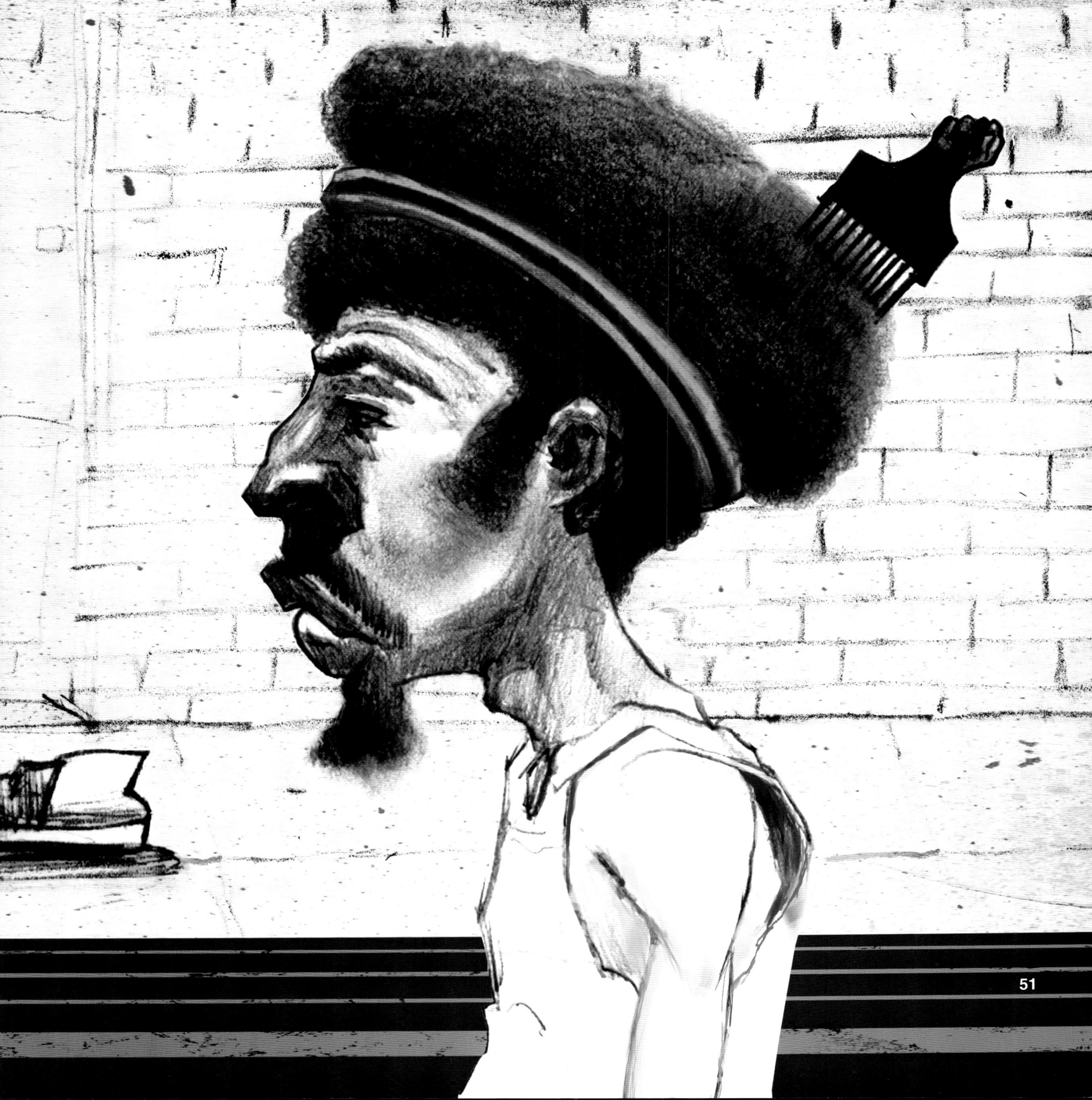

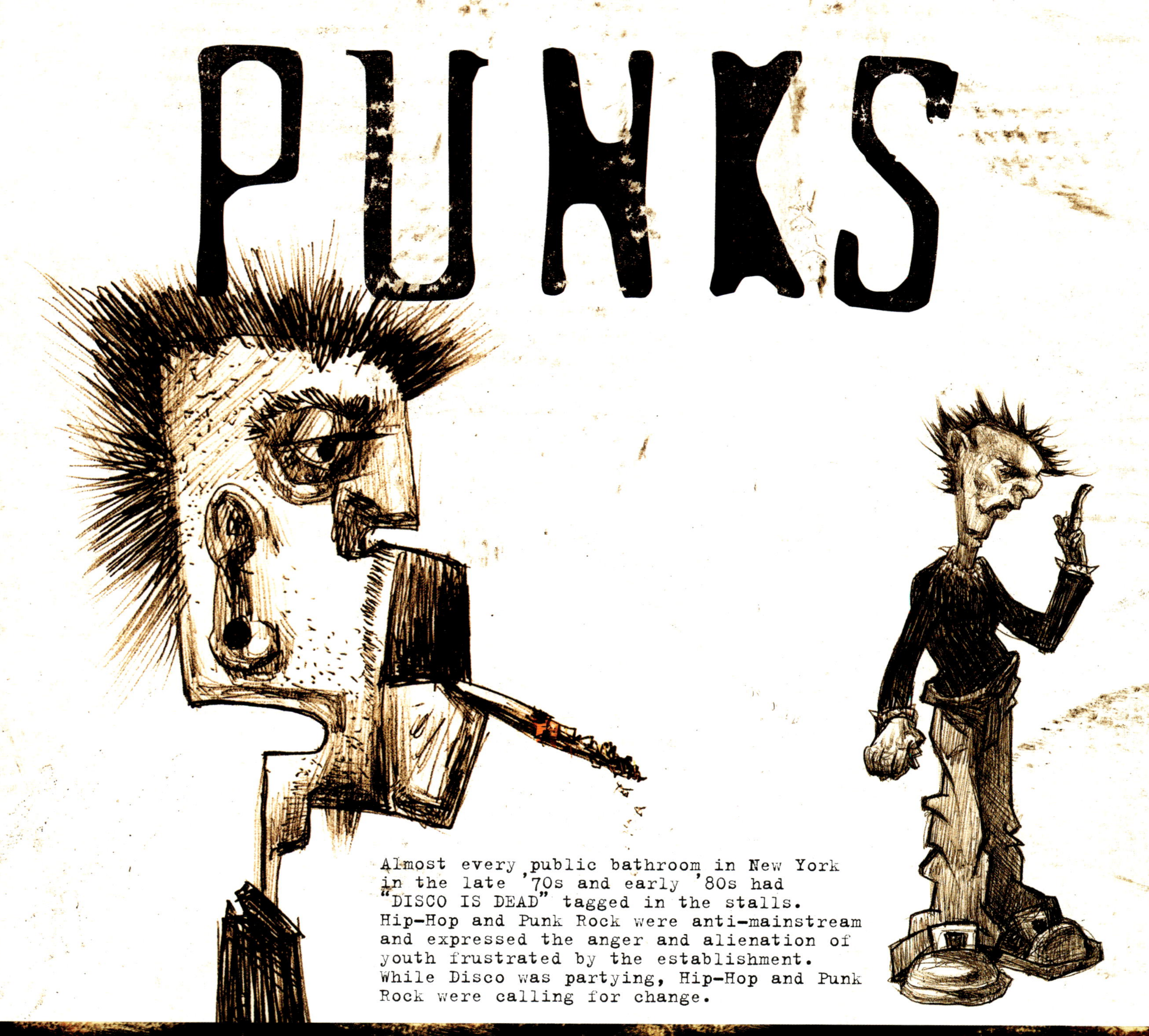
PUNKS
Almost every public bathroom in New York in the late '70s and early '80s had "DISCO IS DEAD" tagged in the stalls. Hip-Hop and Punk Rock were anti-mainstream and expressed the anger and alienation of youth frustrated by the establishment. While Disco was partying, Hip-Hop and Punk Rock were calling for change.

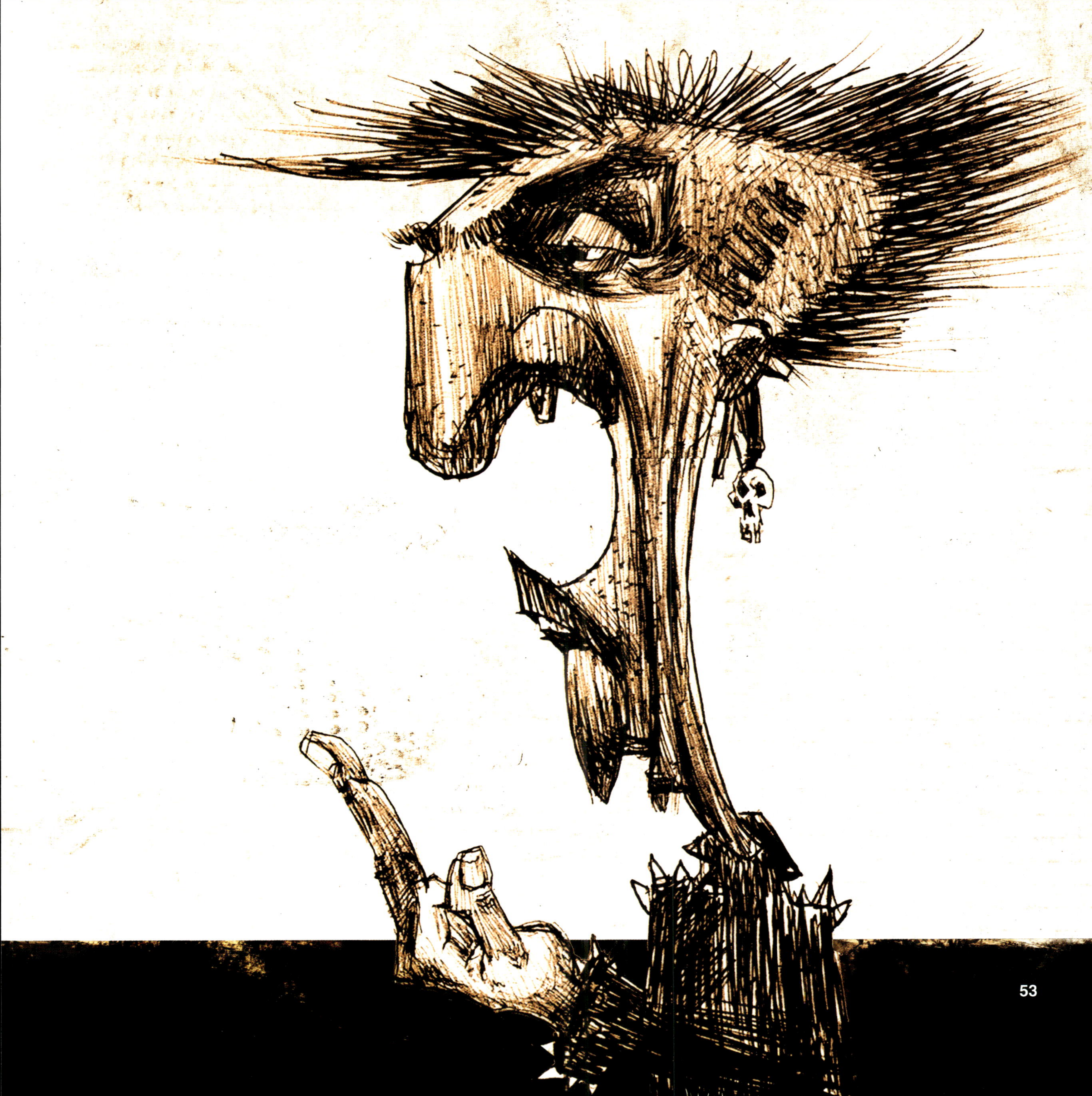

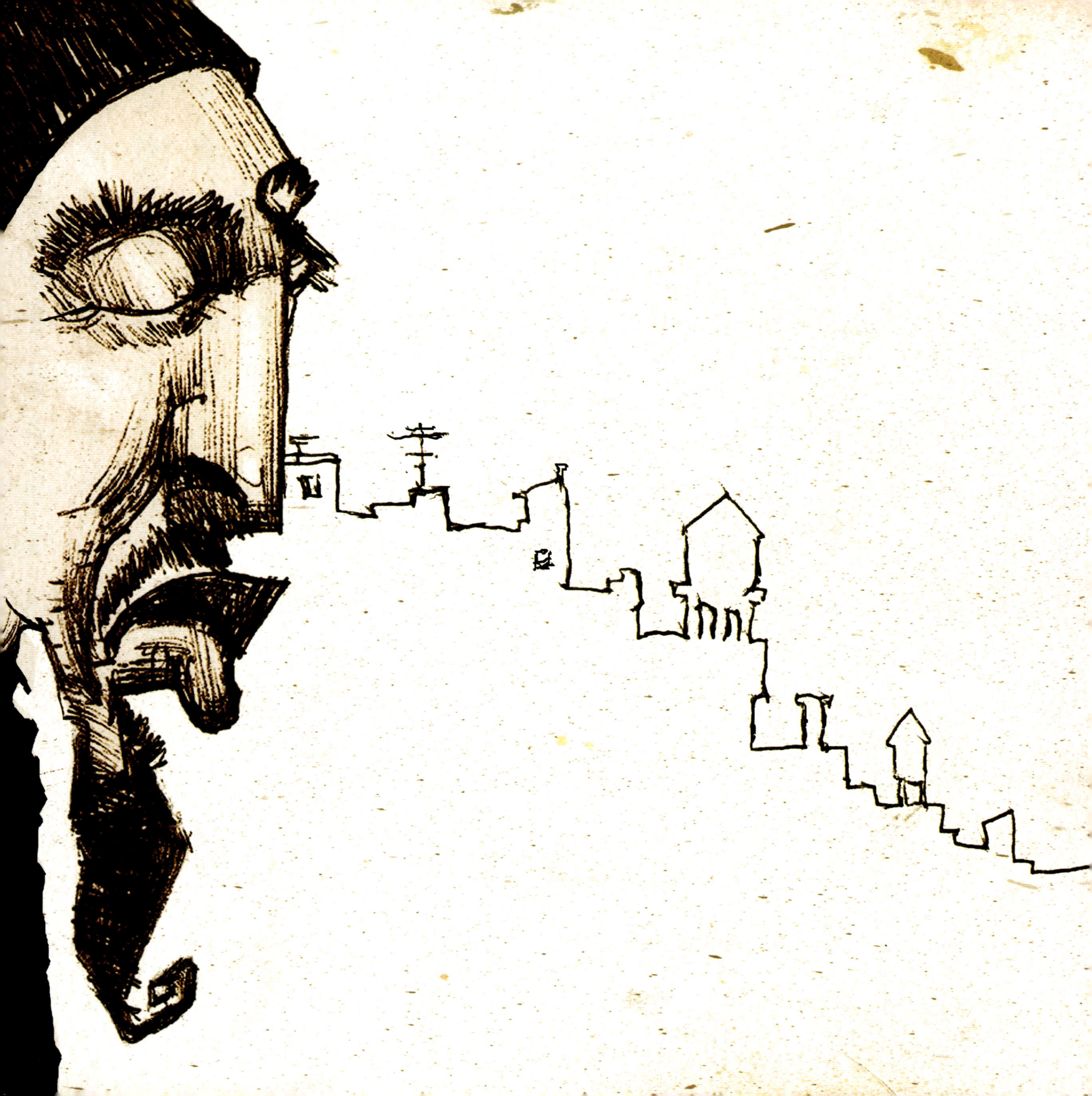

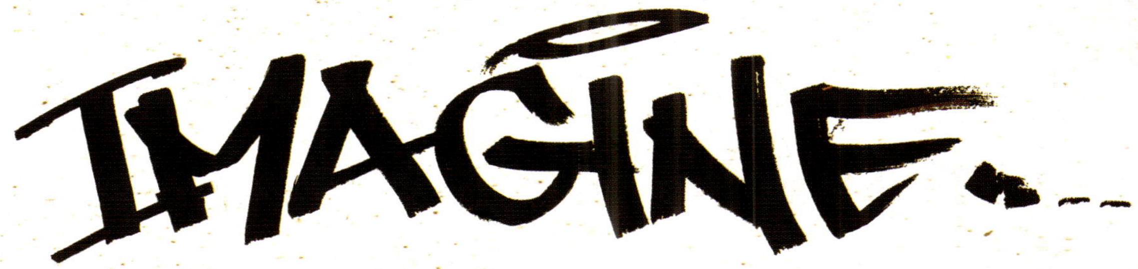

Anger and frustration turned into determination and inspiration. The Hip-Hop movement was an outlet for pure creative expression. The first time I saw popping, B-Boying, and graffiti, they were magical to me. I knew I had to be a part of it.

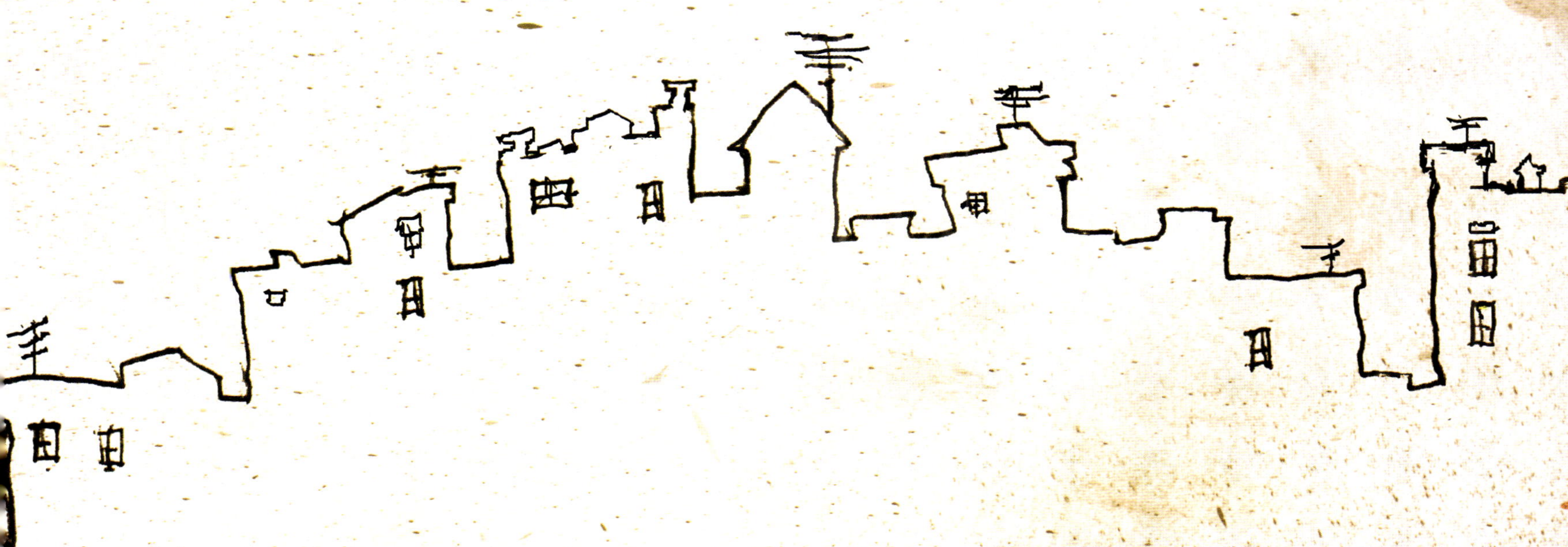

B-BOYIN' WAS MY LIFE.

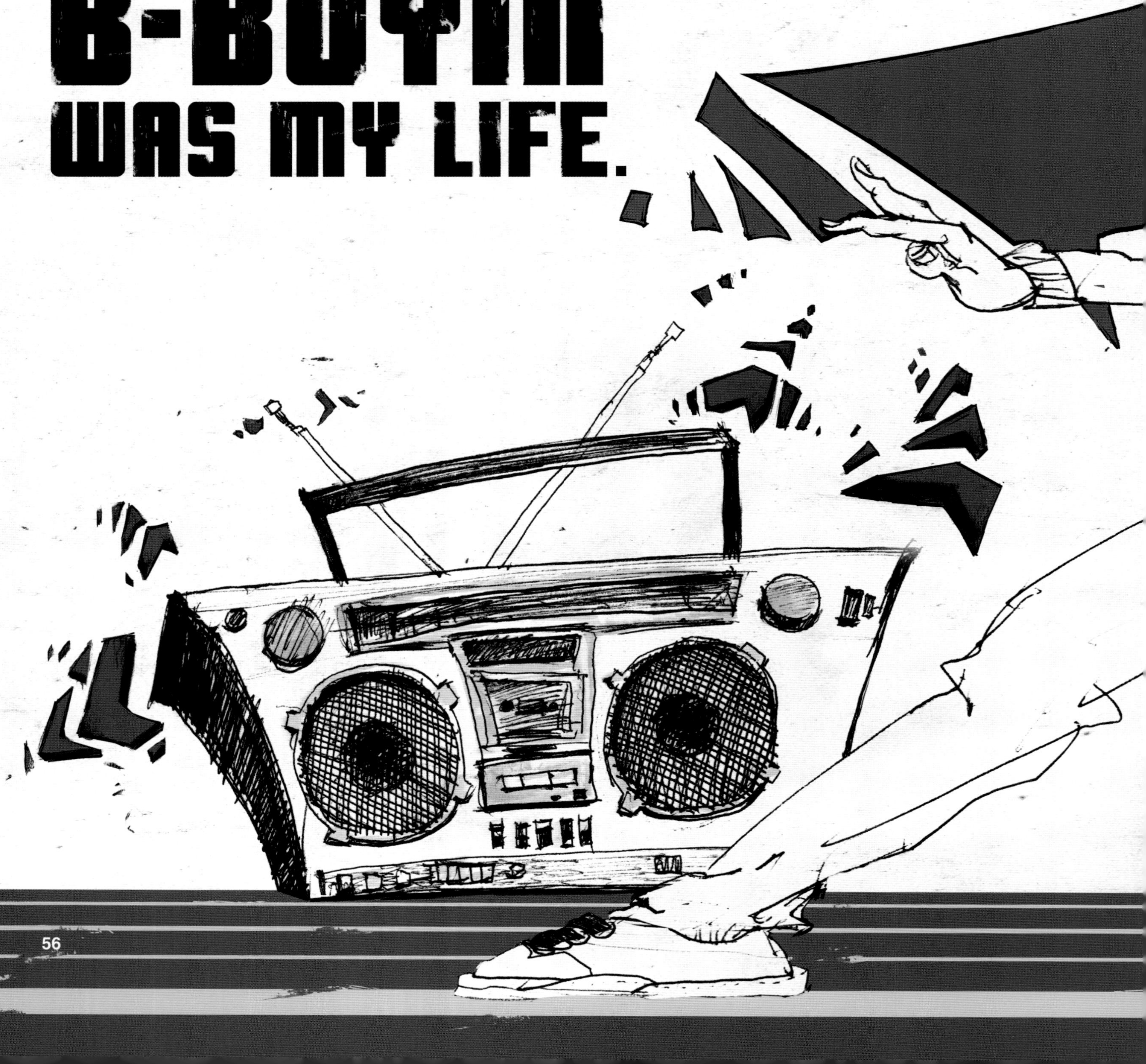

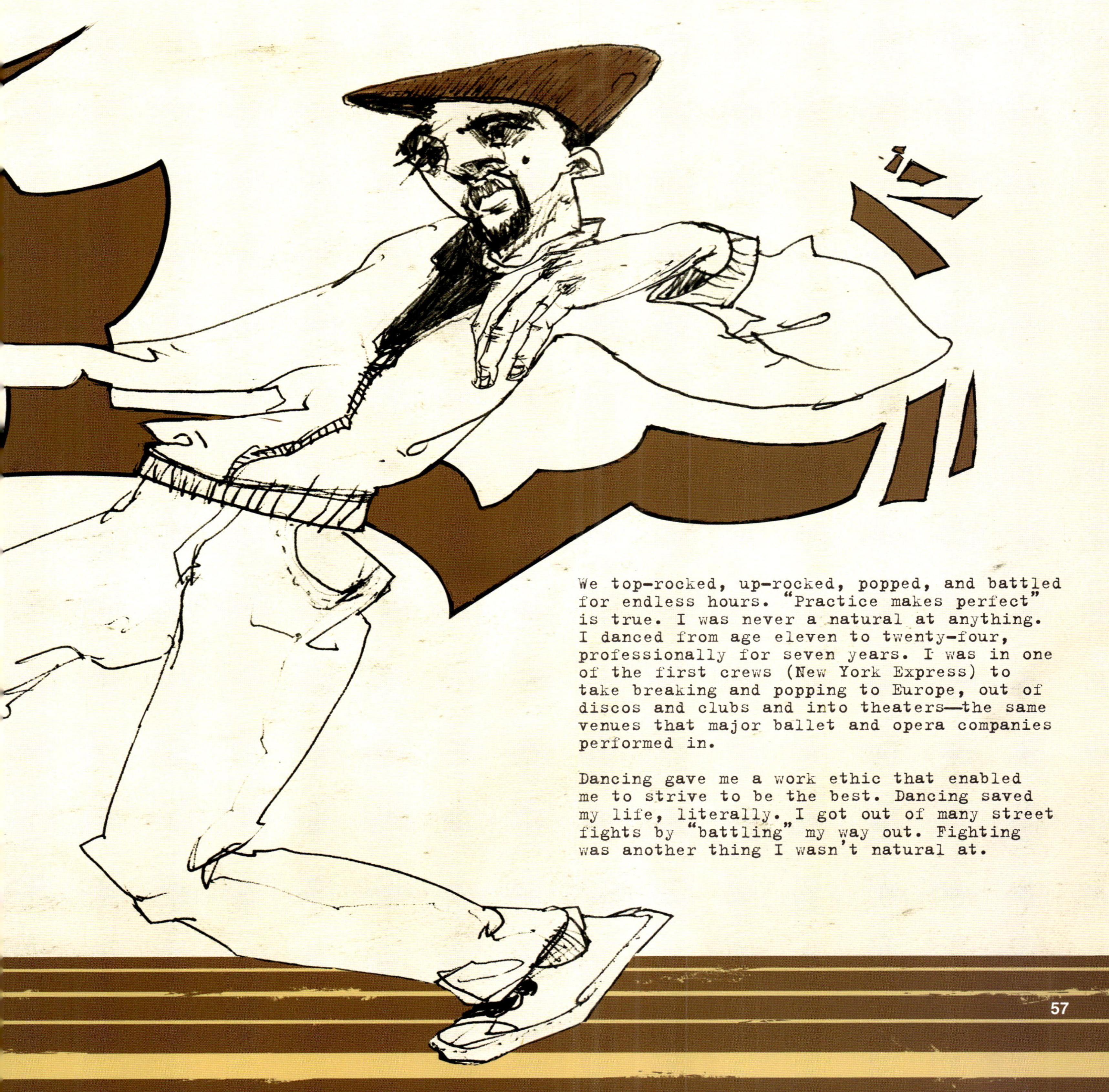

We top-rocked, up-rocked, popped, and battled for endless hours. “Practice makes perfect” is true. I was never a natural at anything. I danced from age eleven to twenty-four, professionally for seven years. I was in one of the first crews (New York Express) to take breaking and popping to Europe, out of discos and clubs and into theaters—the same venues that major ballet and opera companies performed in.

Dancing gave me a work ethic that enabled me to strive to be the best. Dancing saved my life, literally. I got out of many street fights by “battling” my way out. Fighting was another thing I wasn’t natural at.

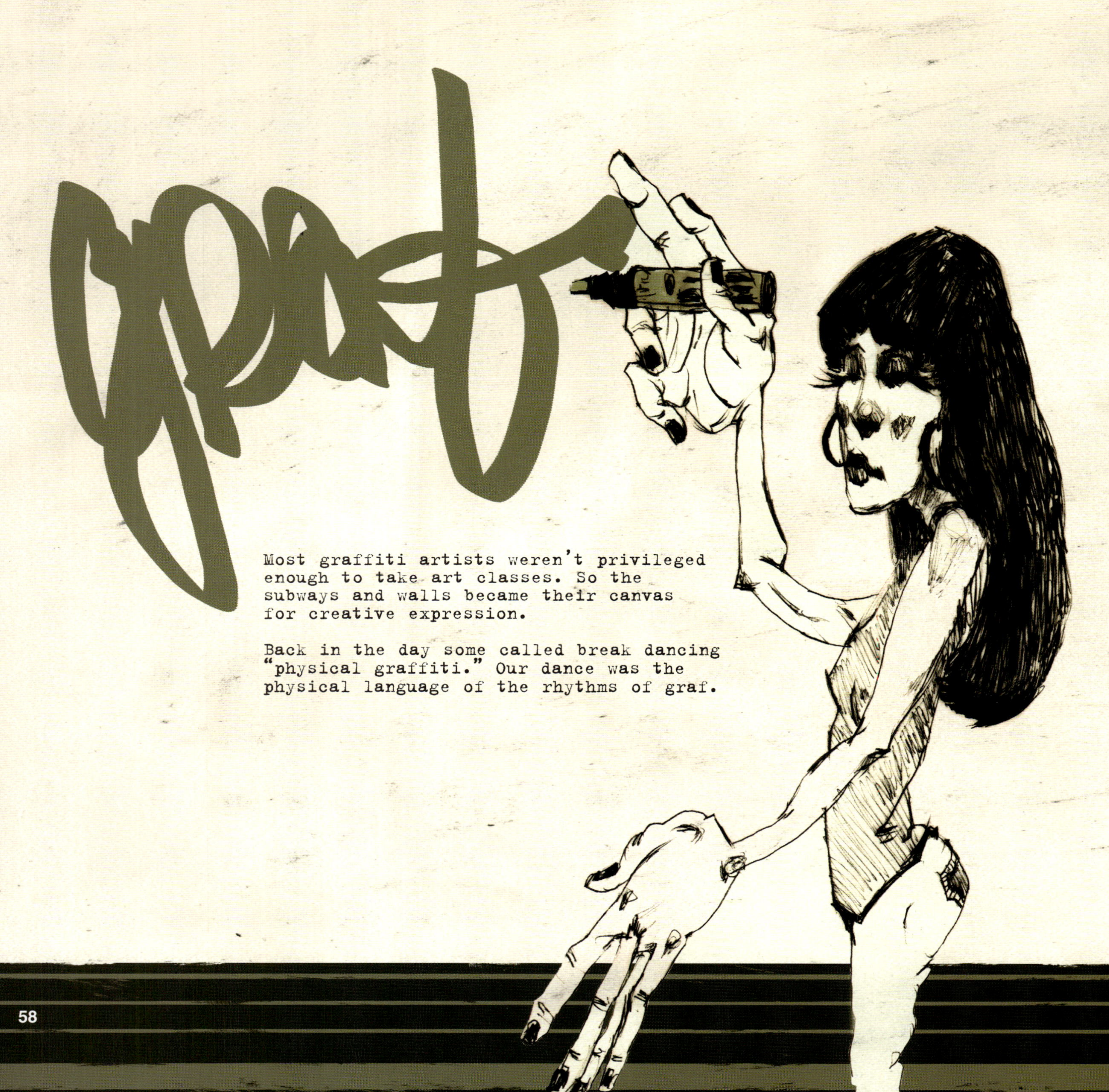

Most graffiti artists weren't privileged enough to take art classes. So the subways and walls became their canvas for creative expression.

Back in the day some called break dancing "physical graffiti." Our dance was the physical language of the rhythms of graf.

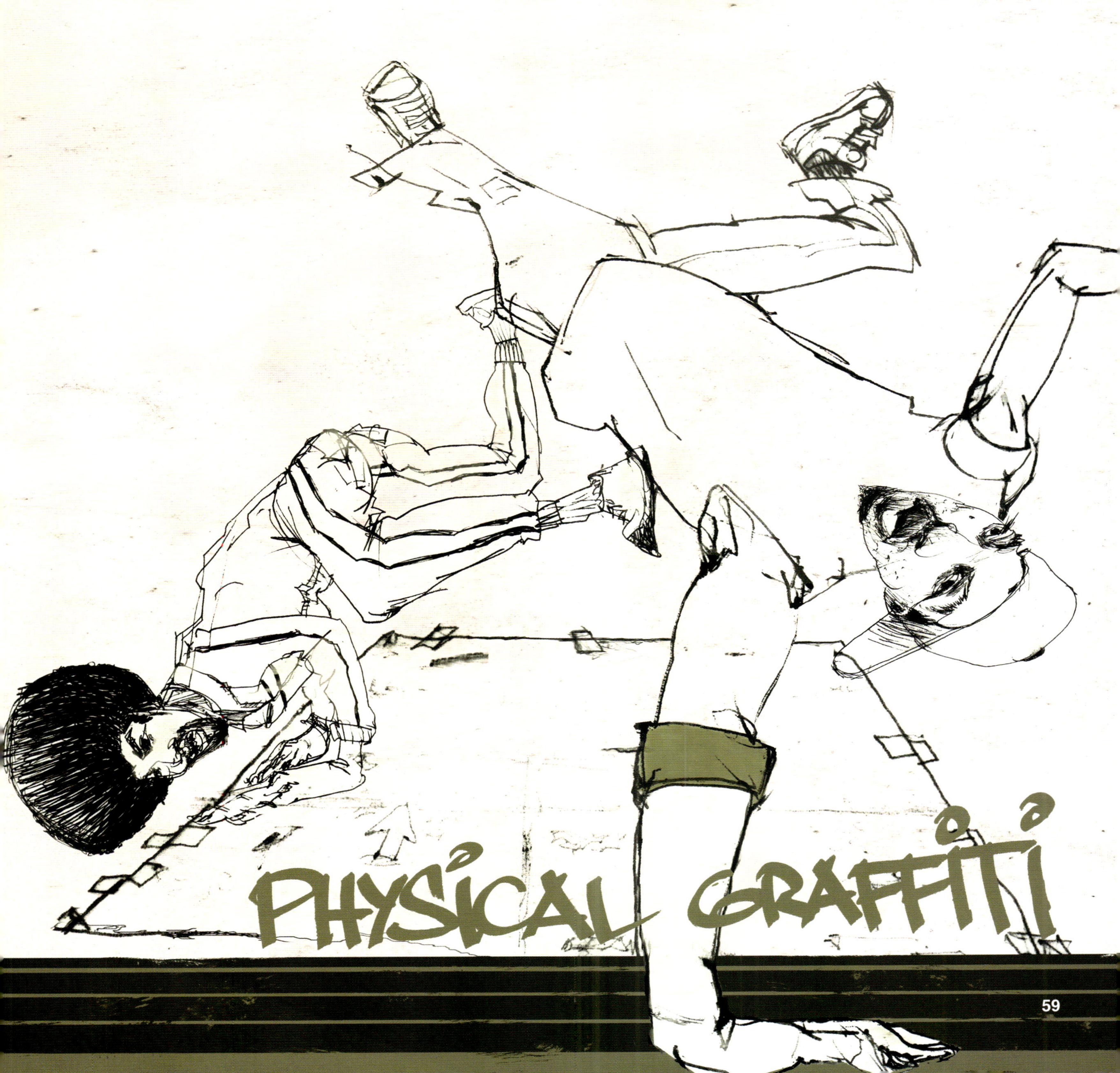

PHYSICAL GRAFFITI

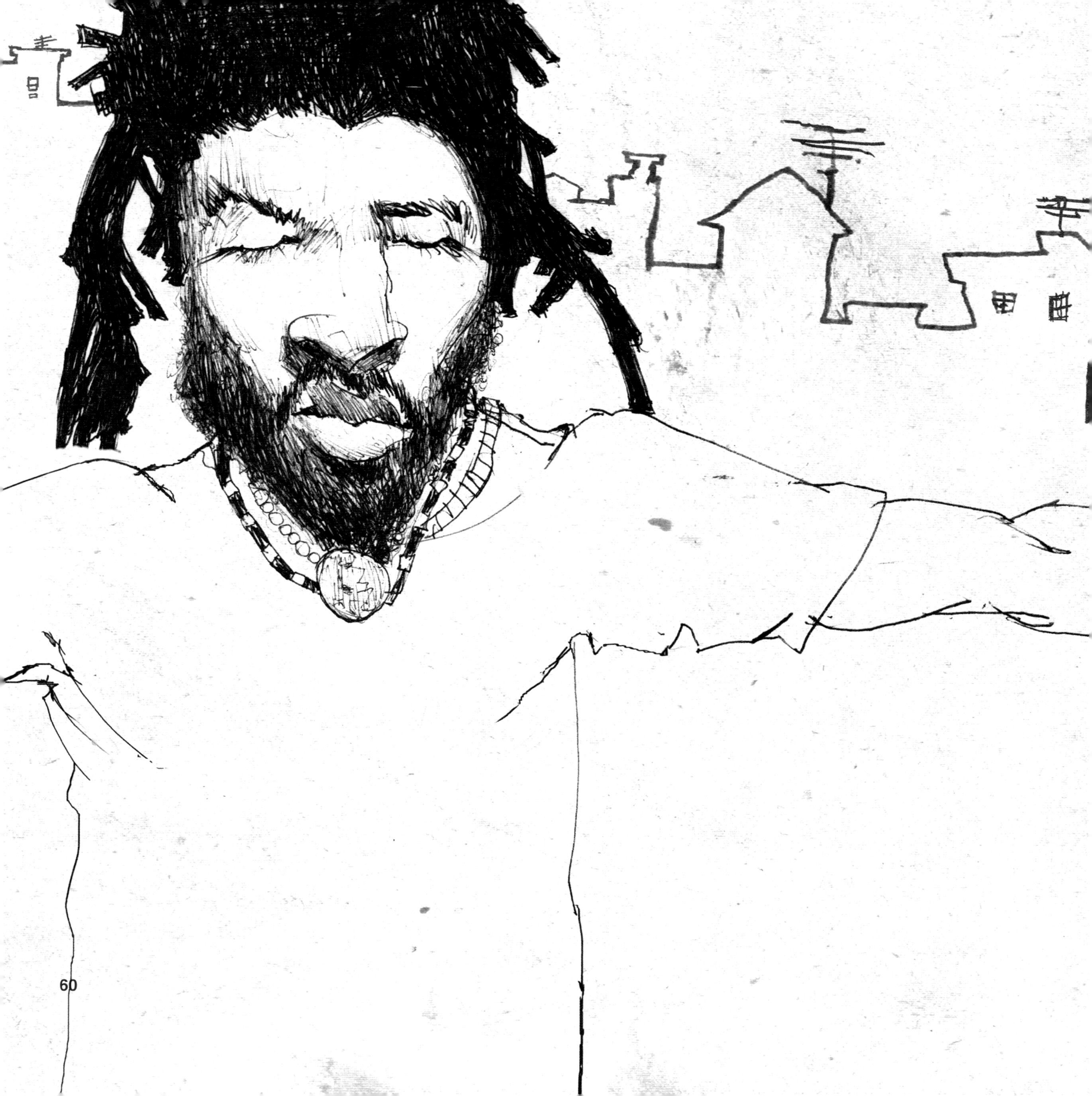

GRATITUDE..

Through the discipline of our art, we found peace. Hip-Hop heads believed, were aware, and had a responsibility to overcome adversity. Hip-Hop gave us a way of life that empowered us with a philosophy to rise above negativity. Hip-Hop gave us the strengths to endure challenges.

Hip-Hop is hope. Hip-Hop is truth. Hip-Hop is ONE.

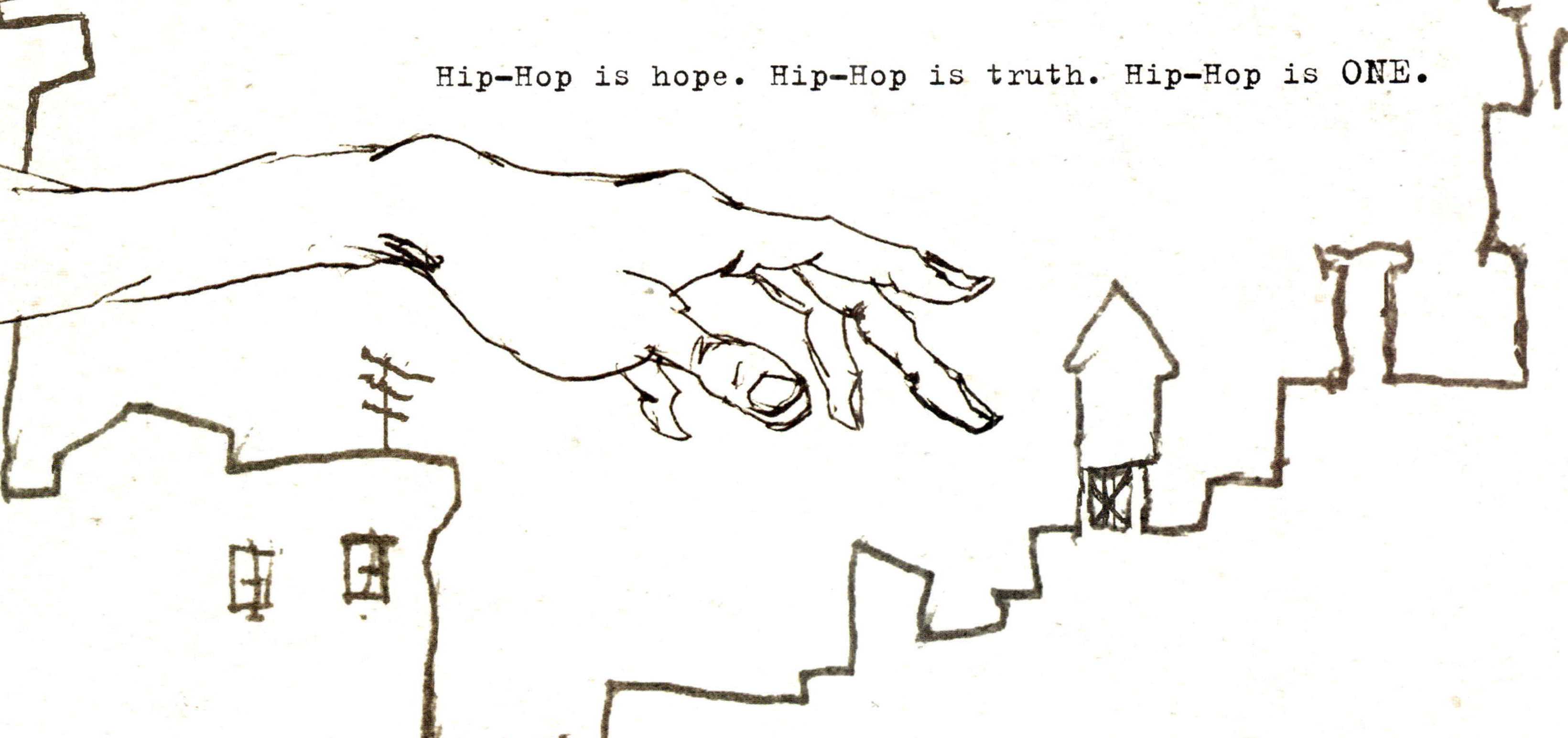

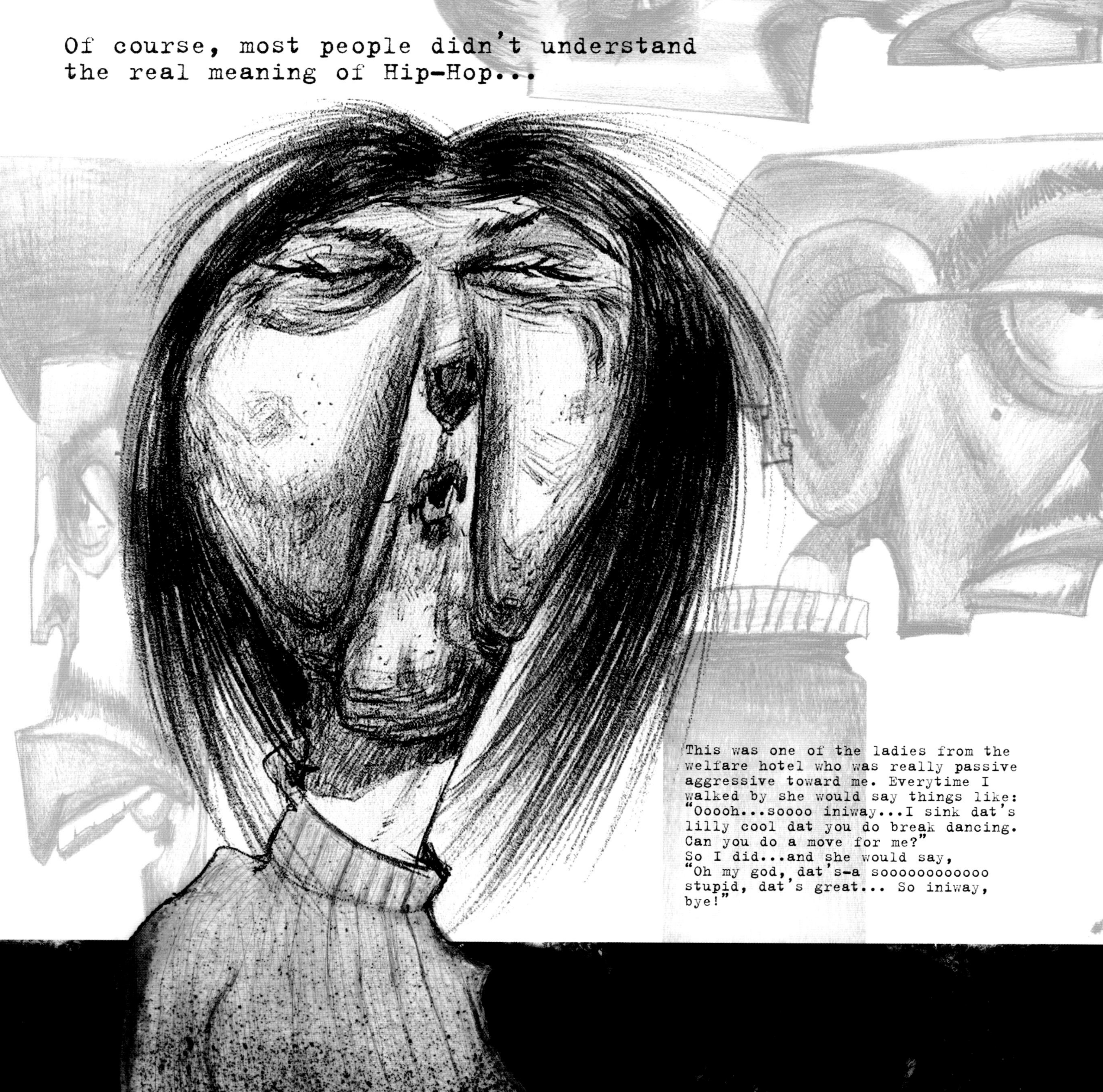
Of course, most people didn't understand the real meaning of Hip-Hop...
This was one of the ladies from the welfare hotel who was really passive aggressive toward me. Everytime I walked by she would say things like: "Ooooh...soooo iniway...I sink dat's lilly cool dat you do break dancing. Can you do a move for me?"
So I did...and she would say,
"Oh my god, dat's-a sooooooooooooo stupid, dat's great... So iniway, bye!"

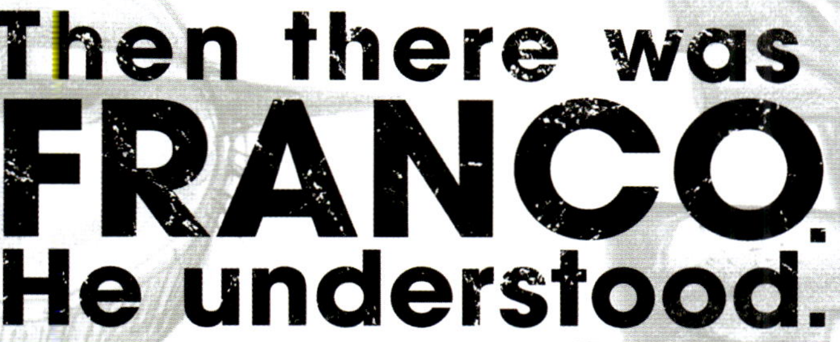

Then there was FRANCO. He understood.

Franco lived at one of the SROs down my block. He was this German cat who was a prophetlike character. He spoke in Hip-Hop terminology 'cuz he loved the music from the '80s. He made rap lyrics part of his everyday vocabulary. He used to say stuff like: "Eet's like a jungle somtimes. Eet makes me vundah how I keep from going undah."

He was the first person to tell me Hip-Hop was going to break the barriers of the color of our skin and spread throughout the world. He once said:
"Zees whole heep-hop thing ees going to be huuuge man, zees 'heep-hop you don't stop rockeen' to zah bang bang boogie said up jump zah boogie to zah rhythm of zah boogie to beat,' man, you know? Eet vill go from New York, spread through zee suburbs and vun day even be in Germany from Fraudenschtat and Baden Baden to Stuttgart and even Nuremburg. Vun day even Germans vill be breakeen' and rappeen' man, you know? I'm telling you, BUXA, zaht's the vay eet's gonna be, you know, 'Eet's like zaht and zaht's zee vay eet ees.' Eet's gonna take zee vorld by stooorm and integrate races and make us vun uuurban race man. Mark my vooords! 'Do you see vaht I see?' Stay 'F.R.E.S.H., Fresh, Fresh, Fresh! Yo zaht's fresh.'"

It was true. Hip-Hop, the most powerful cultural movement of our time, birthed a concept of oneness that touched a city, then a nation, and then the world. Hip-Hop spread. Hip-Hop was deep. And Hip-Hop had an impact on Franco from Germany.

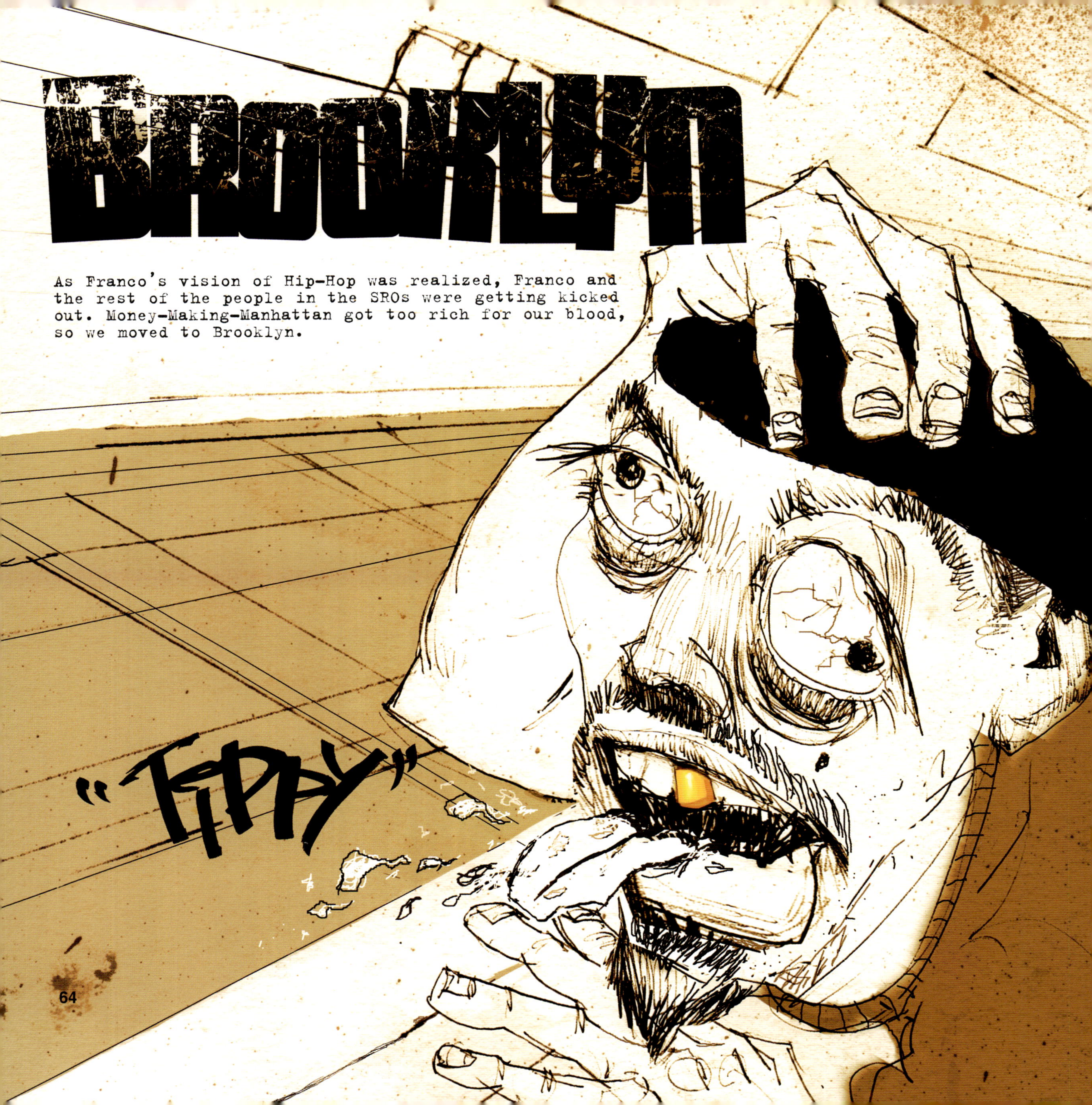
BROOKLYN
As Franco's vision of Hip-Hop was realized, Franco and the rest of the people in the SROs were getting kicked out. Money-Making-Manhattan got too rich for our blood, so we moved to Brooklyn.
"TIPPY"

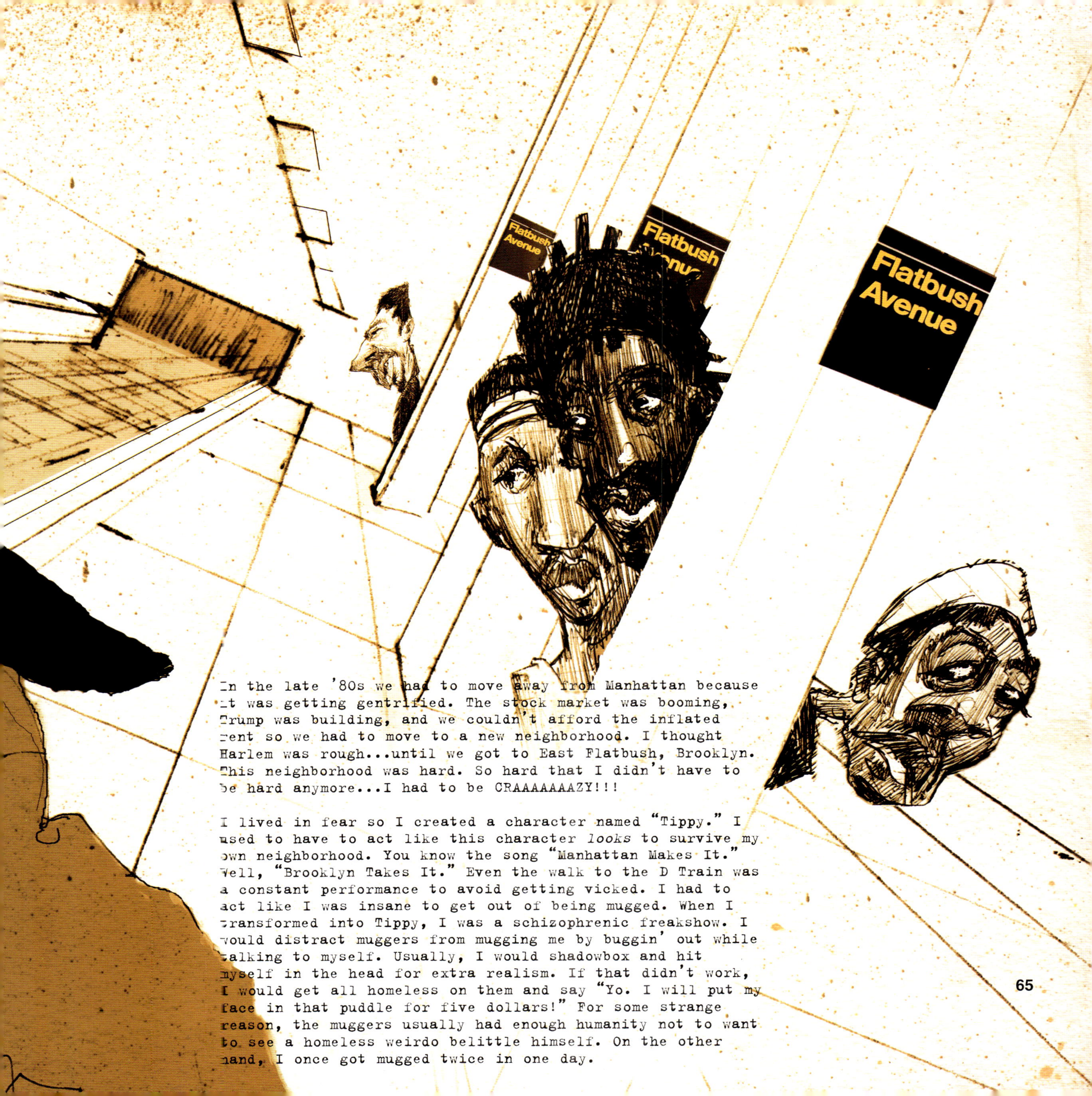

In the late '80s we had to move away from Manhattan because it was getting gentrified. The stock market was booming, Trump was building, and we couldn't afford the inflated rent so we had to move to a new neighborhood. I thought Harlem was rough...until we got to East Flatbush, Brooklyn. This neighborhood was hard. So hard that I didn't have to be hard anymore...I had to be CRAAAAAAAZY!!!

I lived in fear so I created a character named "Tippy." I used to have to act like this character *looks* to survive my own neighborhood. You know the song "Manhattan Makes It." Well, "Brooklyn Takes It." Even the walk to the D Train was a constant performance to avoid getting vicked. I had to act like I was insane to get out of being mugged. When I transformed into Tippy, I was a schizophrenic freakshow. I would distract muggers from mugging me by buggin' out while talking to myself. Usually, I would shadowbox and hit myself in the head for extra realism. If that didn't work, I would get all homeless on them and say "Yo. I will put my face in that puddle for five dollars!" For some strange reason, the muggers usually had enough humanity not to want to see a homeless weirdo belittle himself. On the other hand, I once got mugged twice in one day.

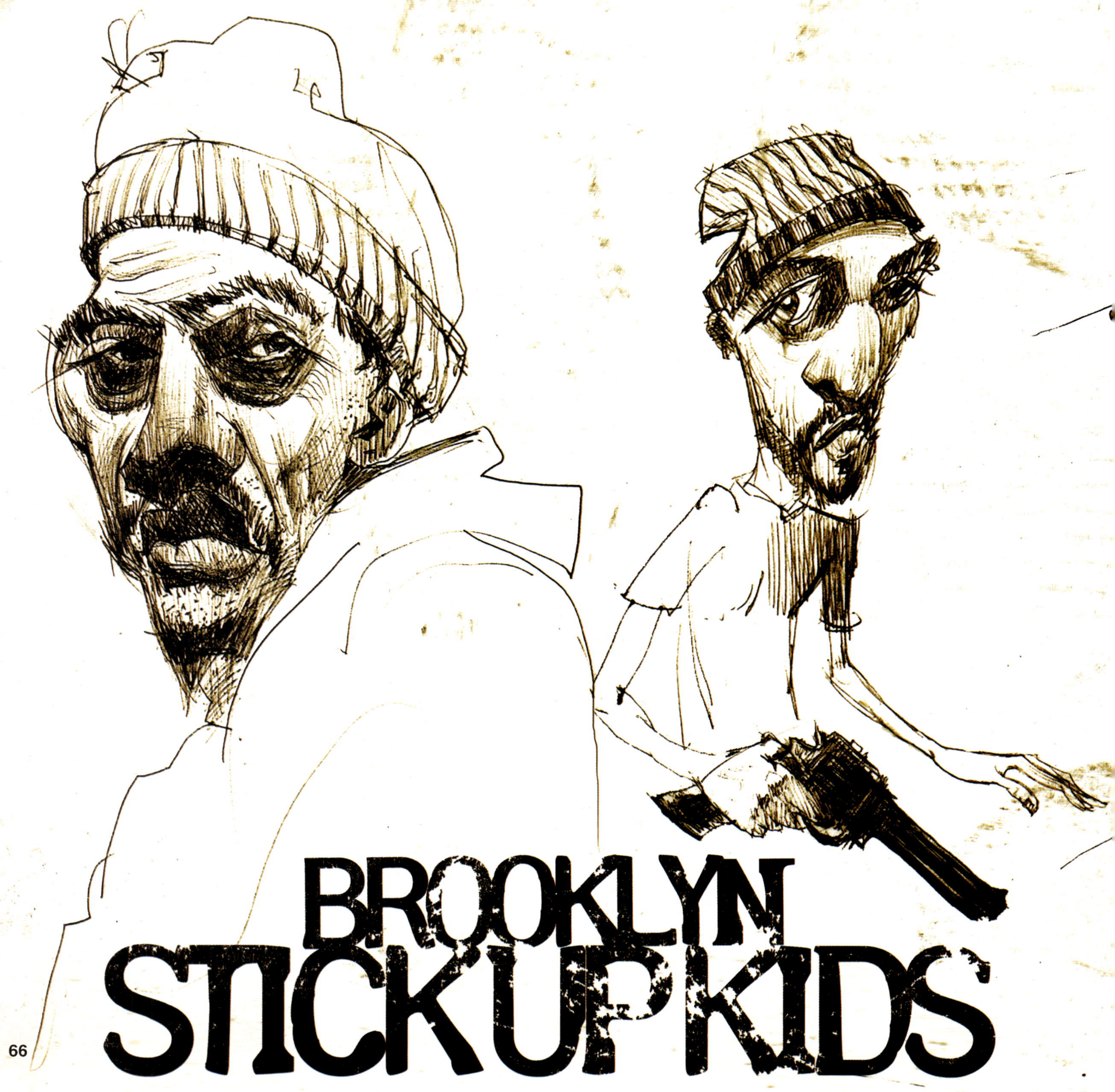

BROOKLYN STICK UP KIDS

were built like men and grew up fast.

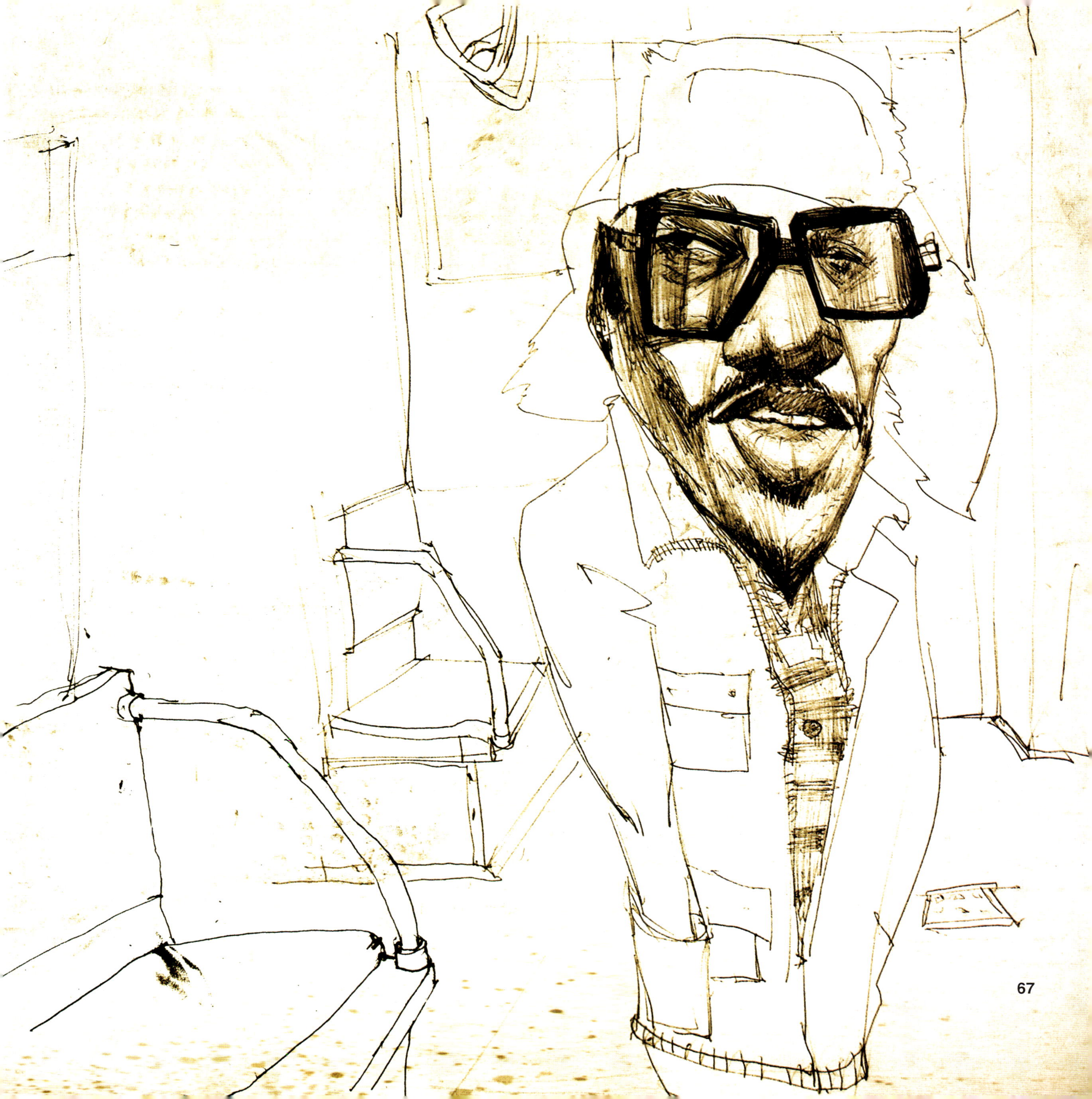

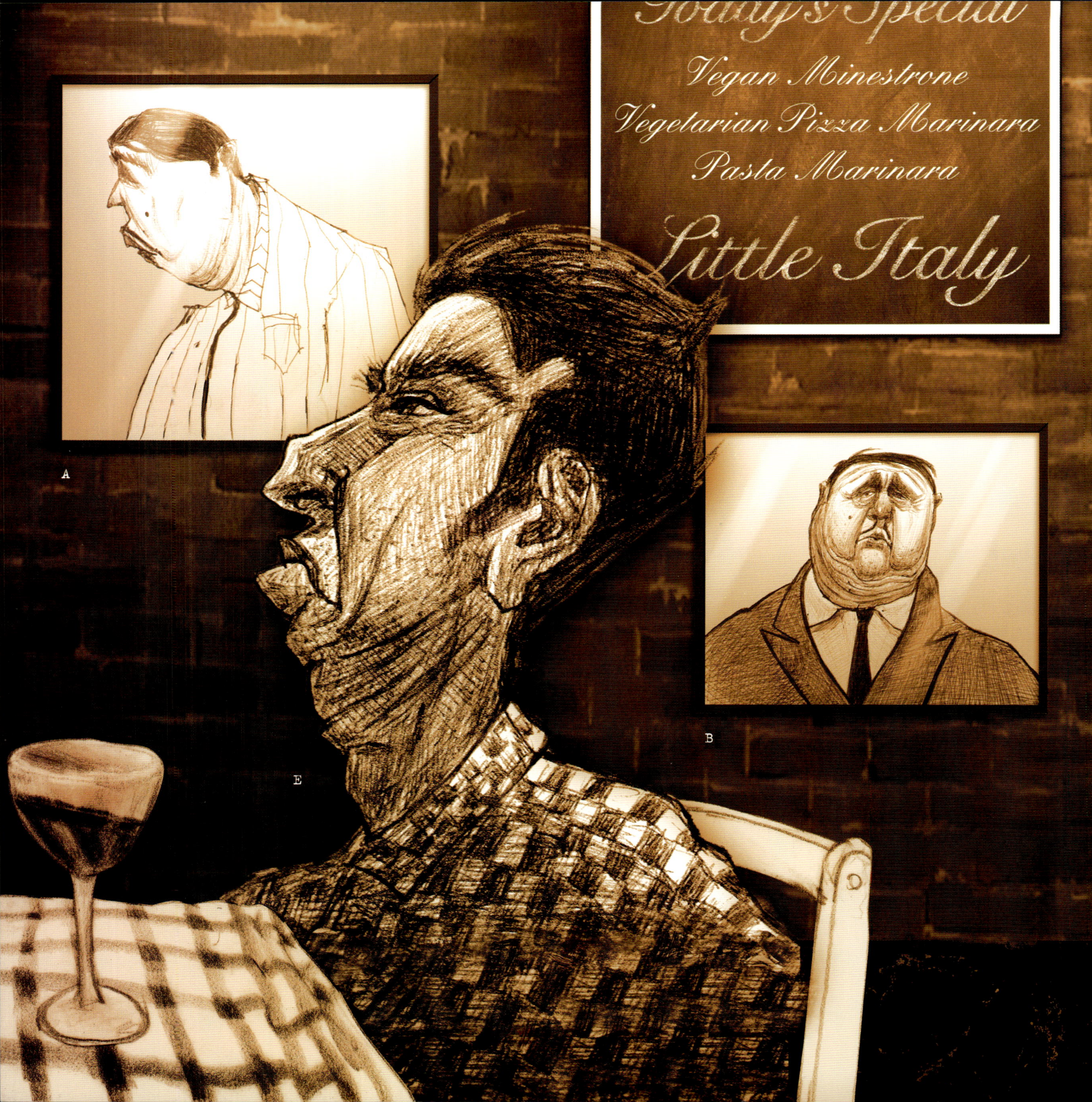
Vegan Minestrone
Vegetarian Pizza Marinara
Pasta Marinara
Little Italy

Life in Brooklyn was crazy. The journey home was rough, but at least we had a house and not a tiny NYC apartment. I didn't have to walk over my mom's bed in the living room to get to the kitchen anymore. Times had changed, but my mom and I still had the same dynamic. When she would tell me to take the garbage out, I would snap on her and say, "You take it out, you cooked it." My mom was a terrible cook so we would roll back to the city to eat. Our favorite restaurants were in Little Italy and Chinatown.

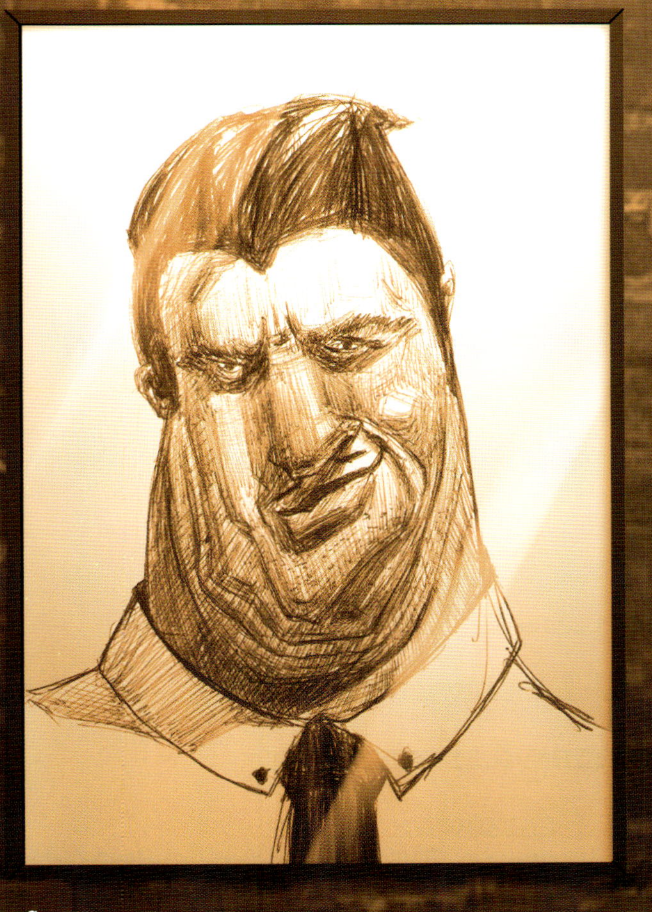

C

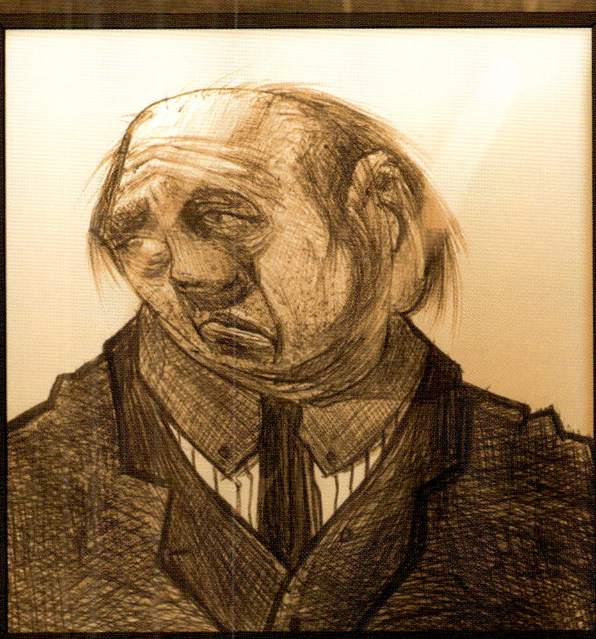

D

A.
Frankie Fuck You.

B.
Donny Ding Dongs also known as Tony Twinkies;formerly Ring Ding Ralph.

C.
Tony "I'm goin' to trow you out the window" Fugazzi.

D.
Charlie Chuckles, he's the life of the party.

E.
Vinny Squares

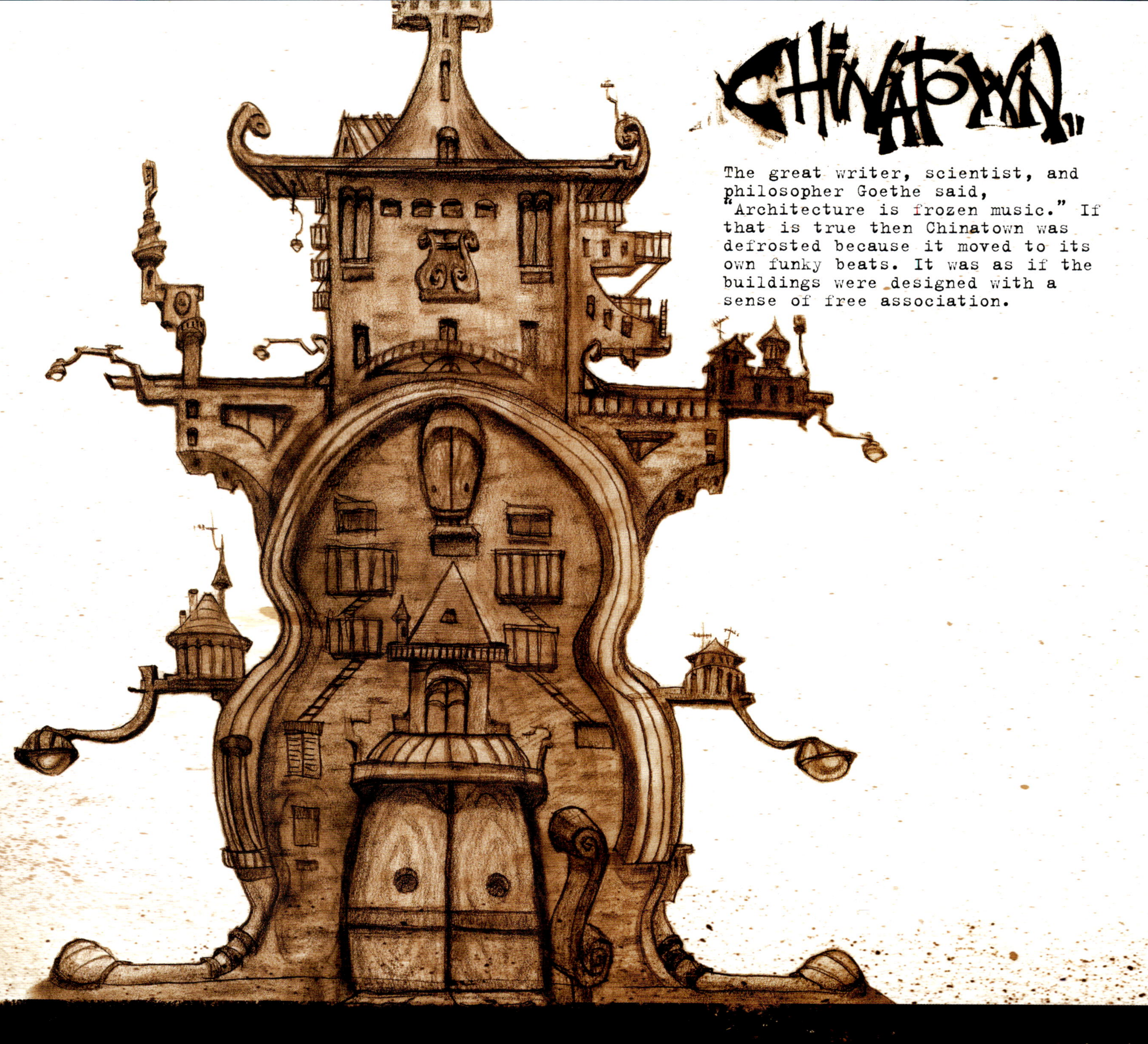

CHINATOWN

The great writer, scientist, and philosopher Goethe said, "Architecture is frozen music." If that is true then Chinatown was defrosted because it moved to its own funky beats. It was as if the buildings were designed with a sense of free association.

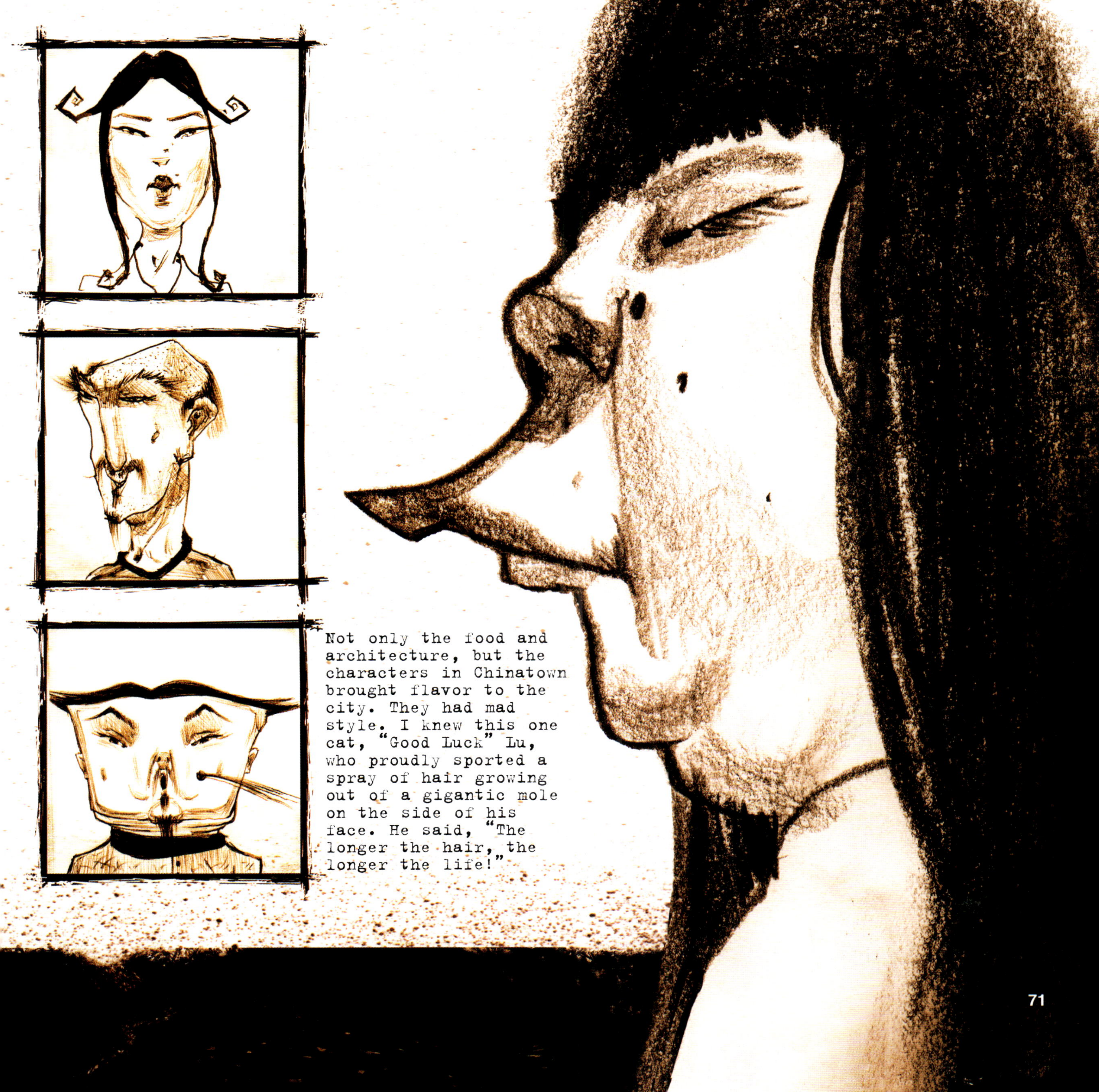
Not only the food and architecture, but the characters in Chinatown brought flavor to the city. They had mad style. I knew this one cat, "Good Luck" Lu, who proudly sported a spray of hair growing out of a gigantic mole on the side of his face. He said, "The longer the hair, the longer the life!"

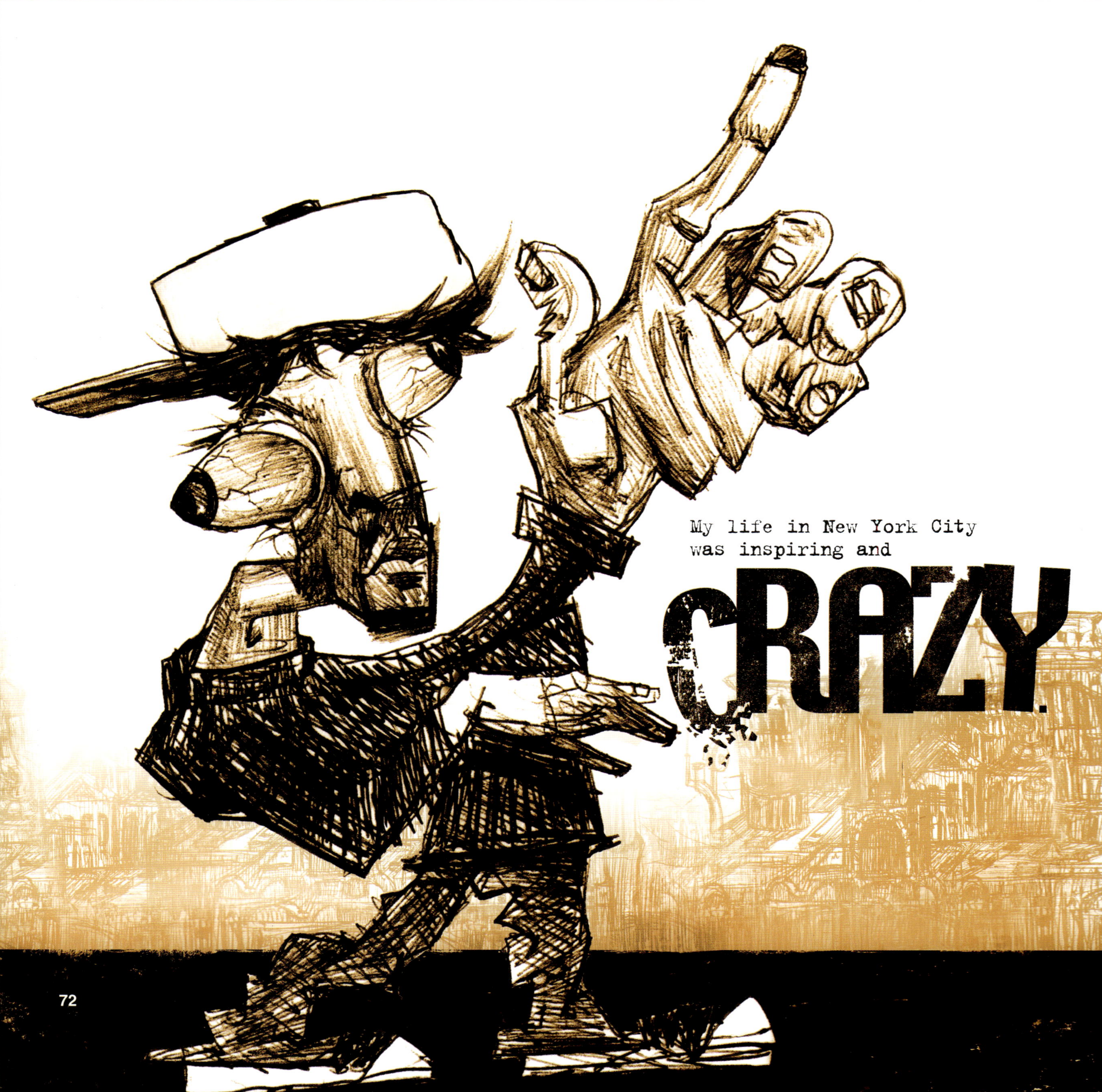
My life in New York City
was inspiring and
cRAZY.

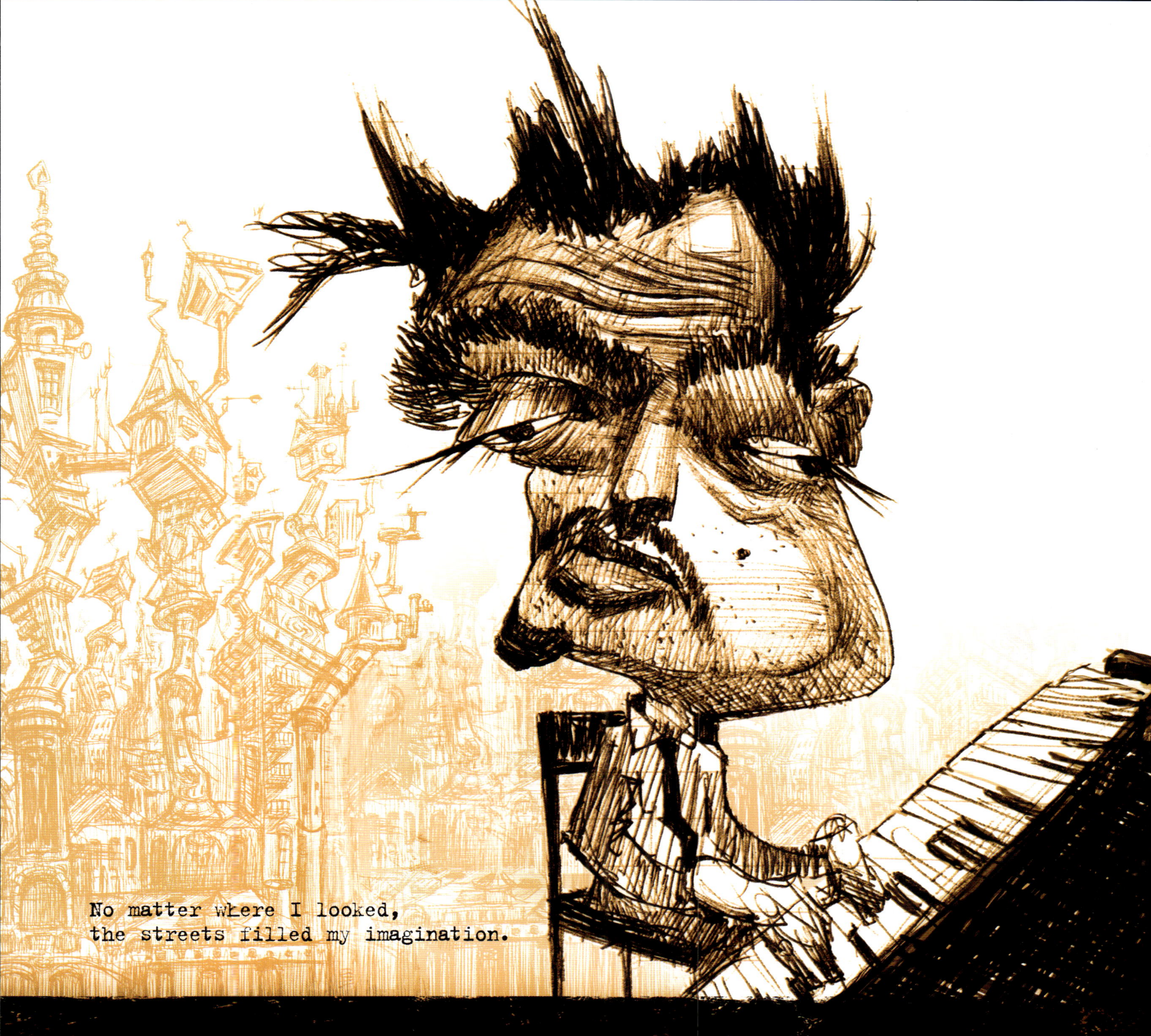
No matter where I looked,
the streets filled my imagination.

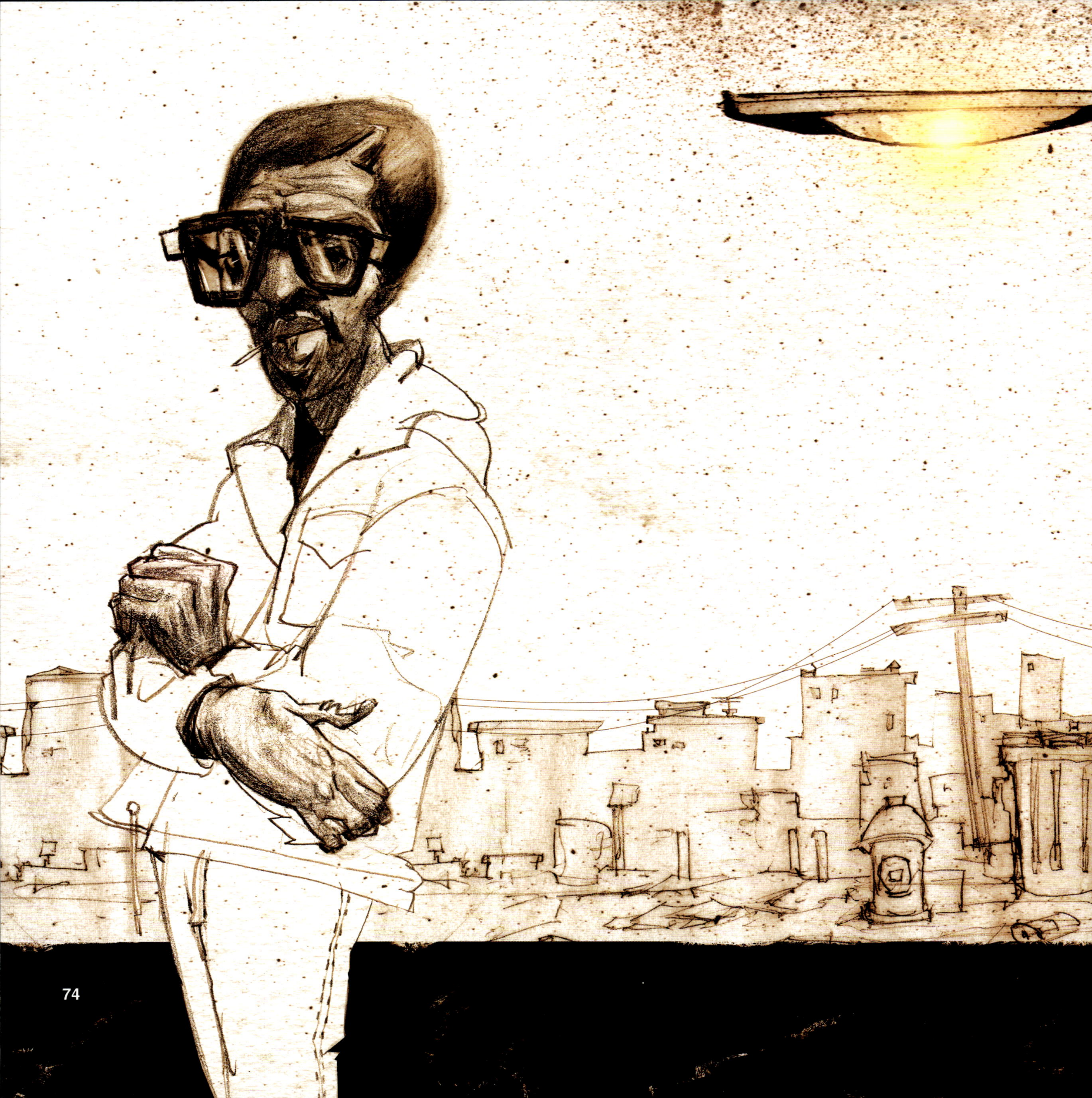

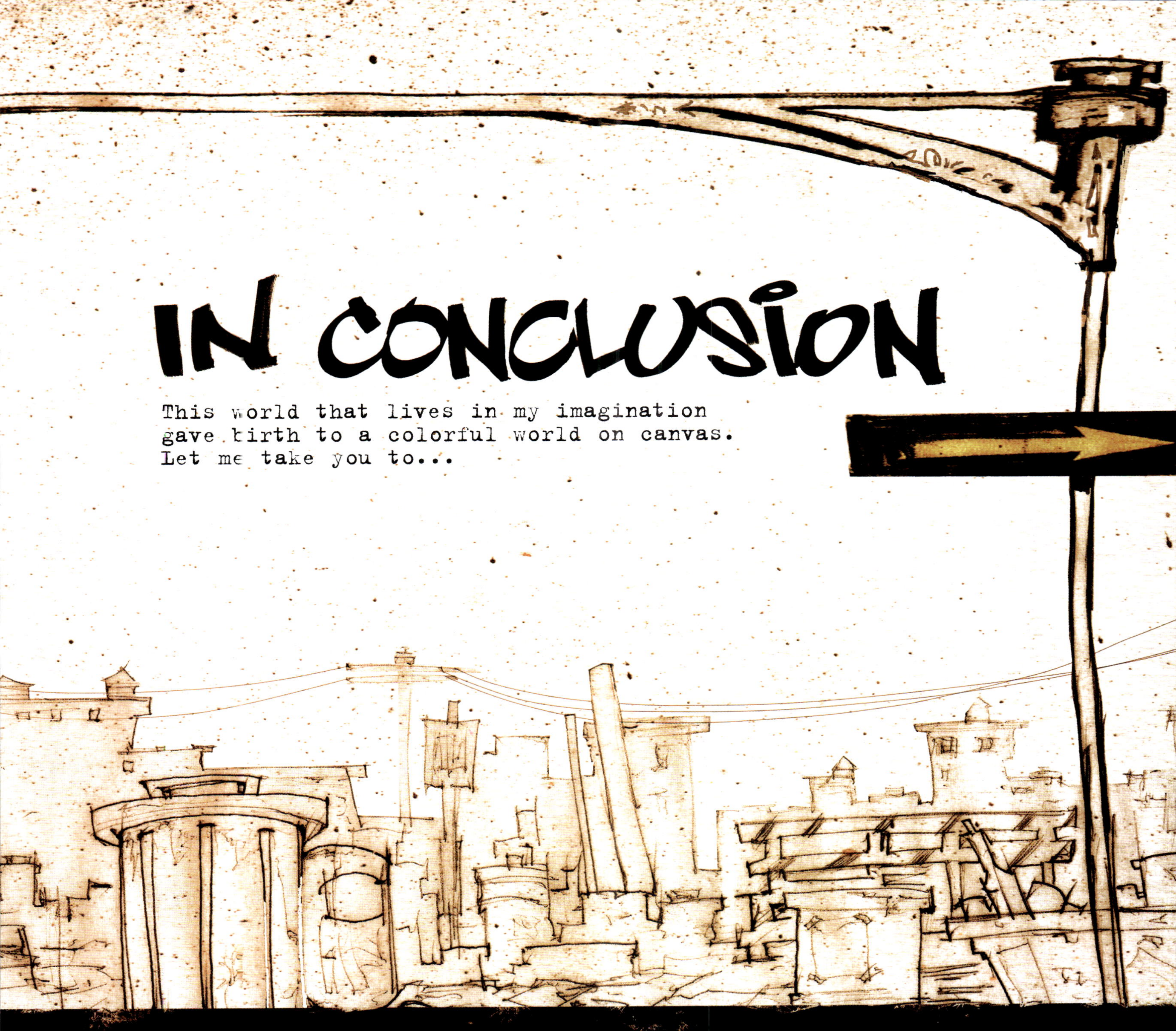
IN CONCLUSION
This world that lives in my imagination
gave birth to a colorful world on canvas.
Let me take you to...

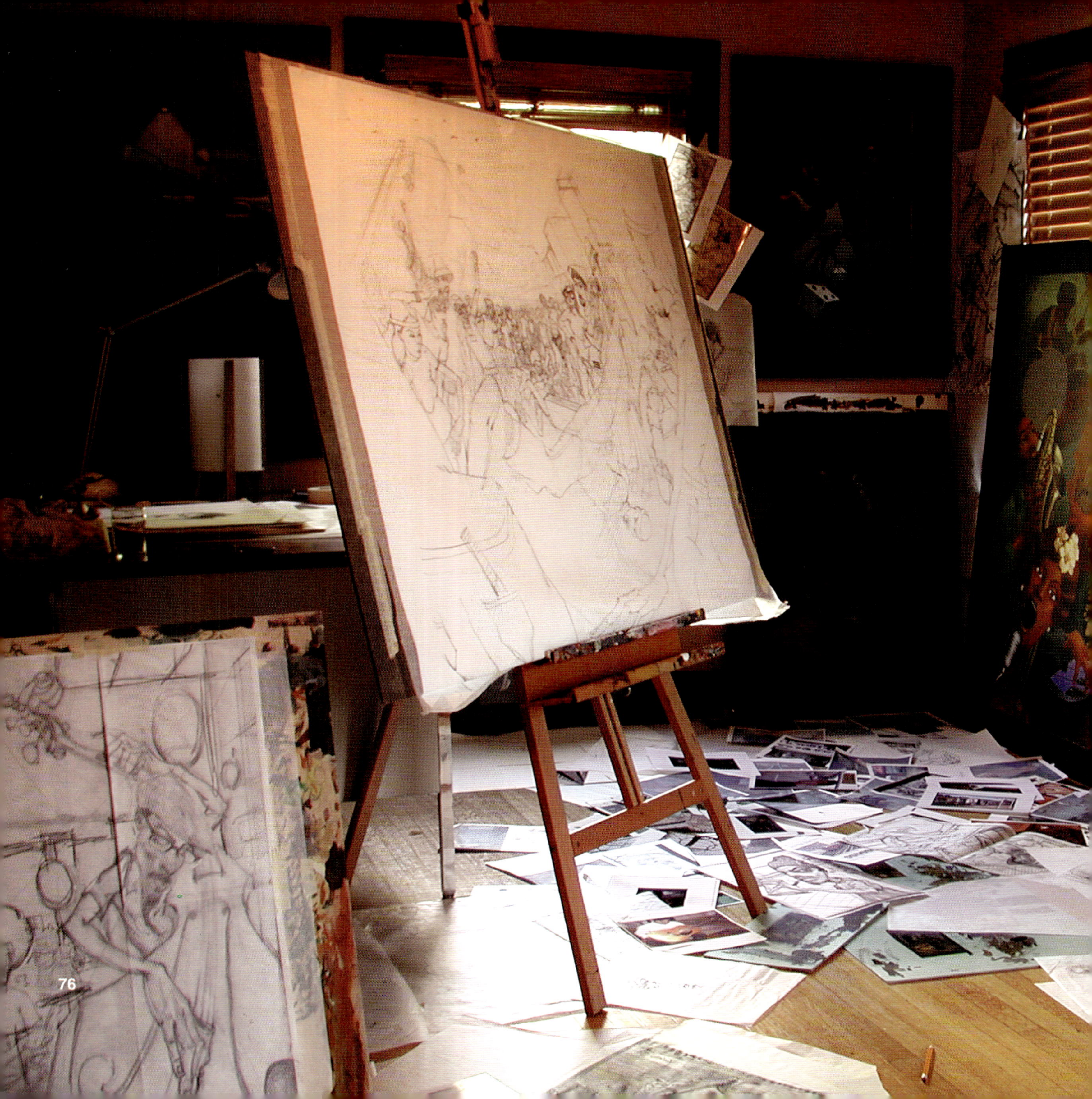

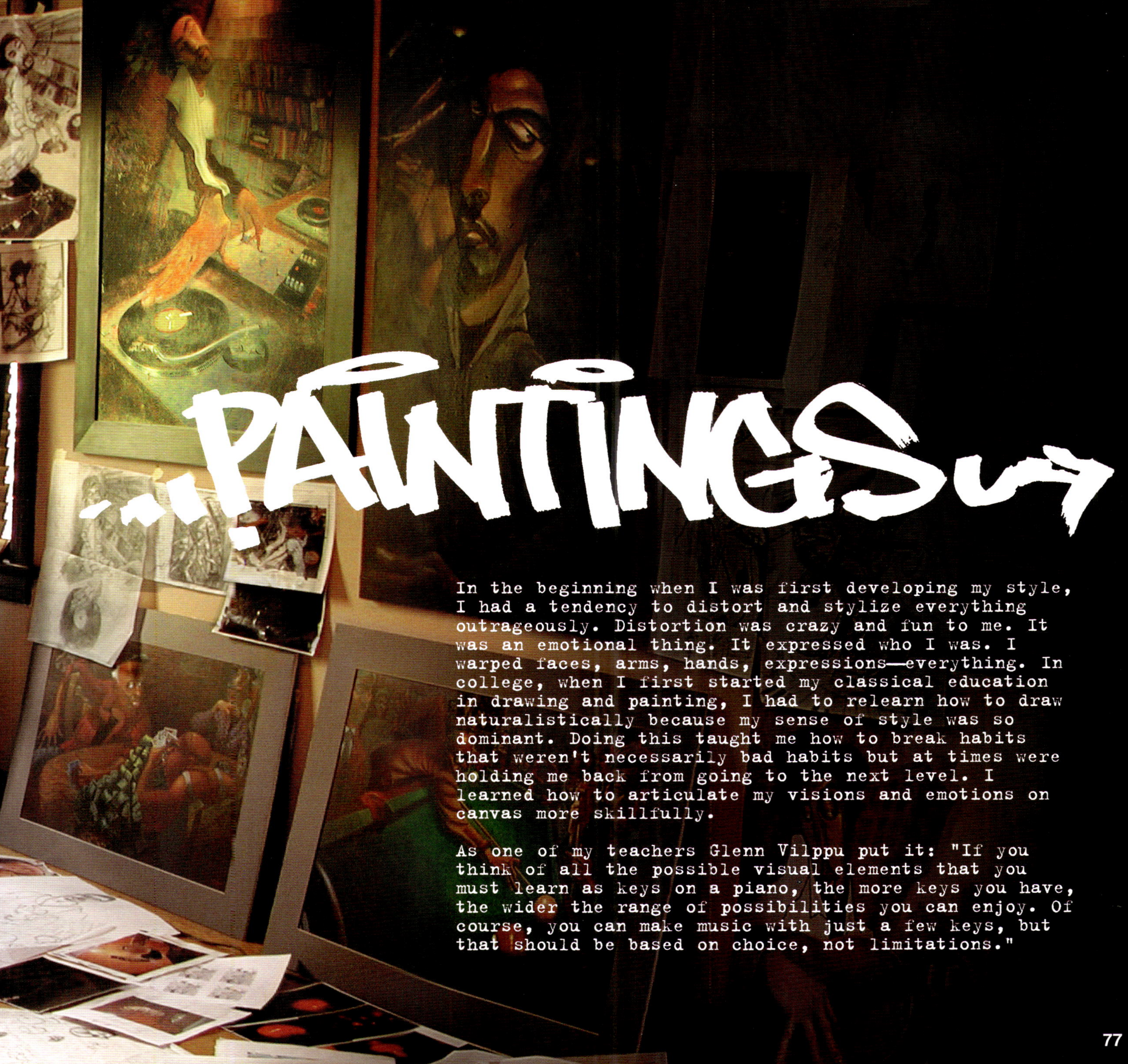

...PAINTINGS

In the beginning when I was first developing my style, I had a tendency to distort and stylize everything outrageously. Distortion was crazy and fun to me. It was an emotional thing. It expressed who I was. I warped faces, arms, hands, expressions—everything. In college, when I first started my classical education in drawing and painting, I had to relearn how to draw naturalistically because my sense of style was so dominant. Doing this taught me how to break habits that weren't necessarily bad habits but at times were holding me back from going to the next level. I learned how to articulate my visions and emotions on canvas more skillfully.

As one of my teachers Glenn Vilppu put it: "If you think of all the possible visual elements that you must learn as keys on a piano, the more keys you have, the wider the range of possibilities you can enjoy. Of course, you can make music with just a few keys, but that should be based on choice, not limitations."

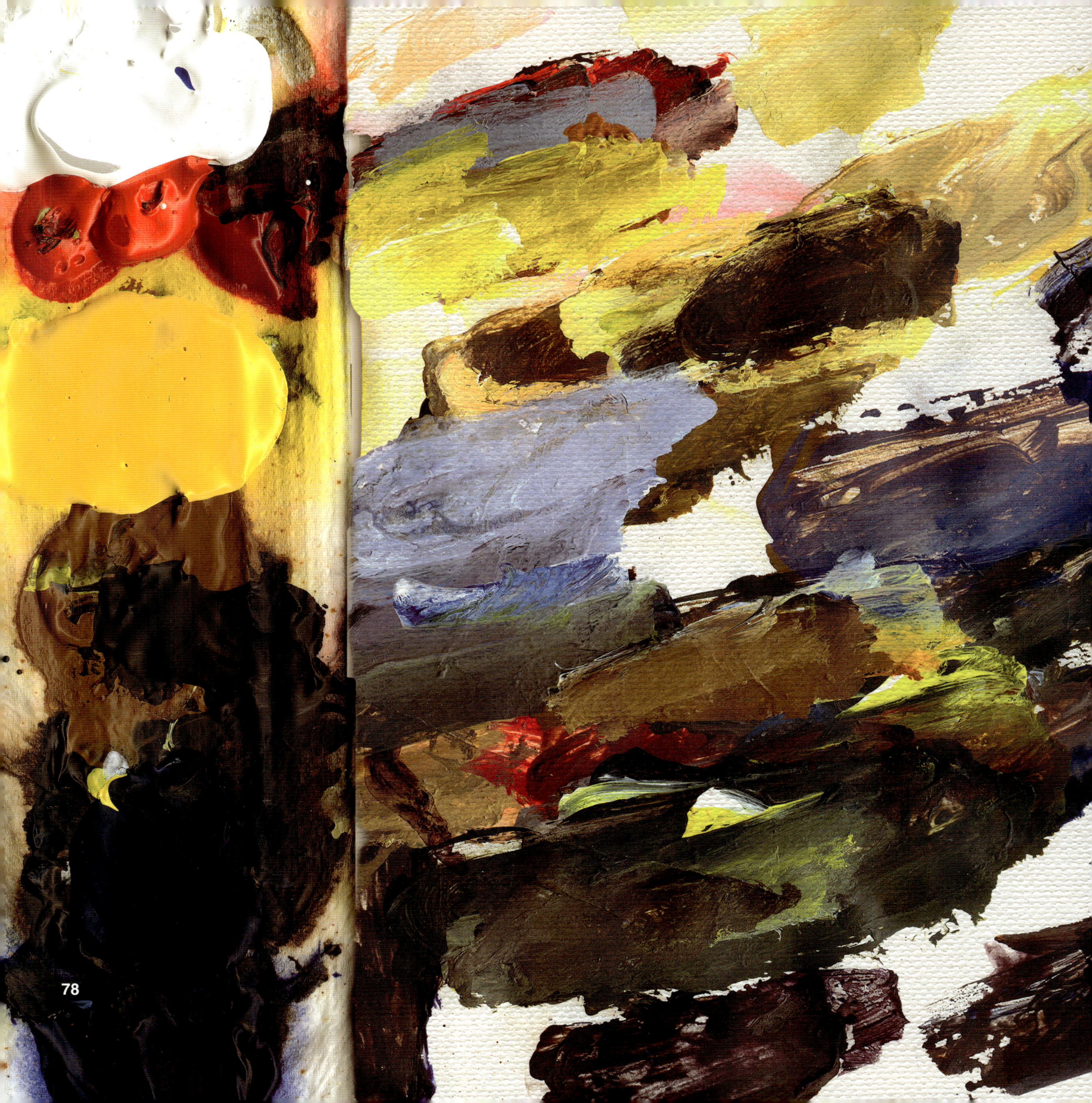

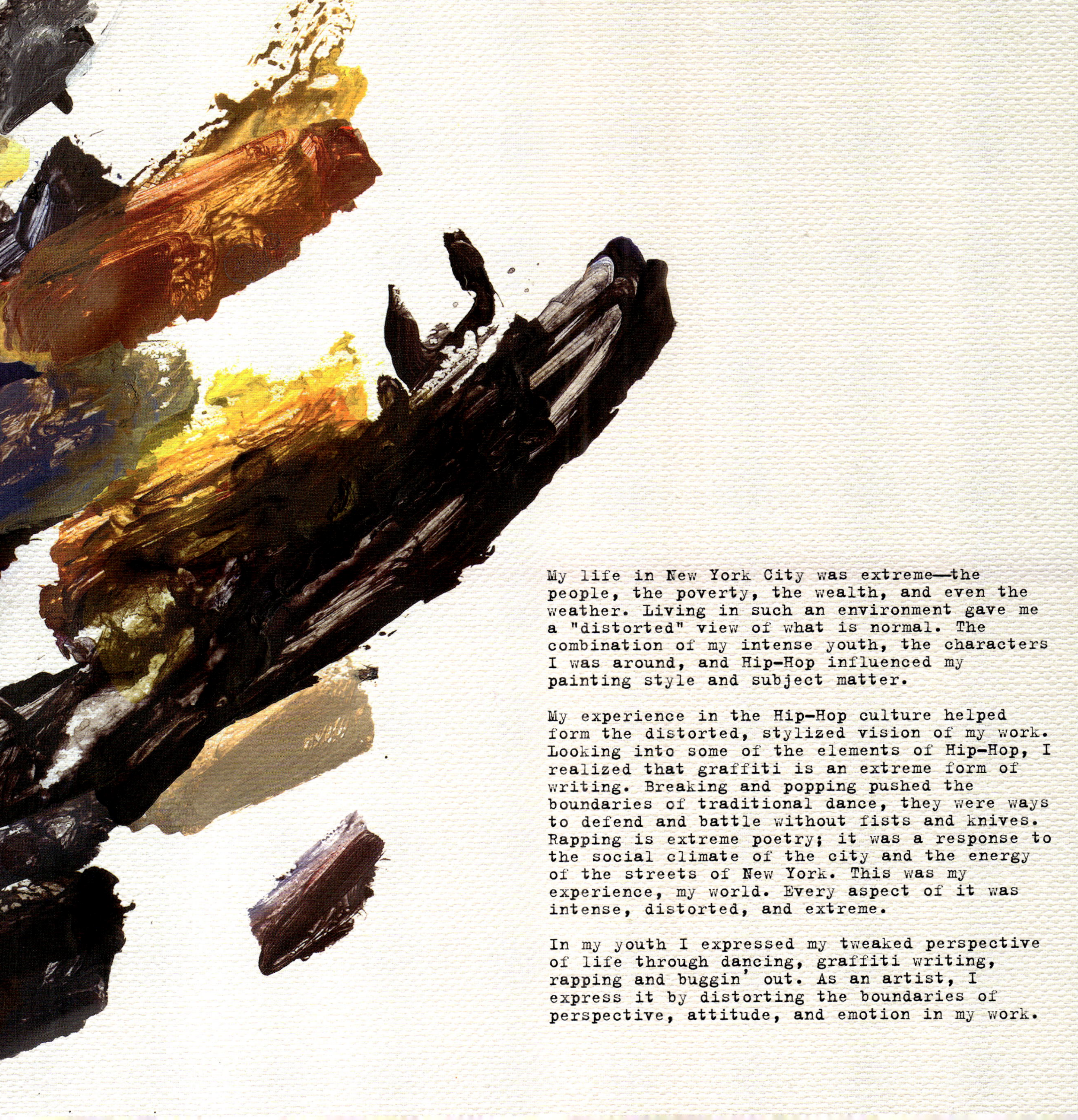

My life in New York City was extreme—the people, the poverty, the wealth, and even the weather. Living in such an environment gave me a "distorted" view of what is normal. The combination of my intense youth, the characters I was around, and Hip-Hop influenced my painting style and subject matter.

My experience in the Hip-Hop culture helped form the distorted, stylized vision of my work. Looking into some of the elements of Hip-Hop, I realized that graffiti is an extreme form of writing. Breaking and popping pushed the boundaries of traditional dance, they were ways to defend and battle without fists and knives. Rapping is extreme poetry; it was a response to the social climate of the city and the energy of the streets of New York. This was my experience, my world. Every aspect of it was intense, distorted, and extreme.

In my youth I expressed my tweaked perspective of life through dancing, graffiti writing, rapping and buggin' out. As an artist, I express it by distorting the boundaries of perspective, attitude, and emotion in my work.

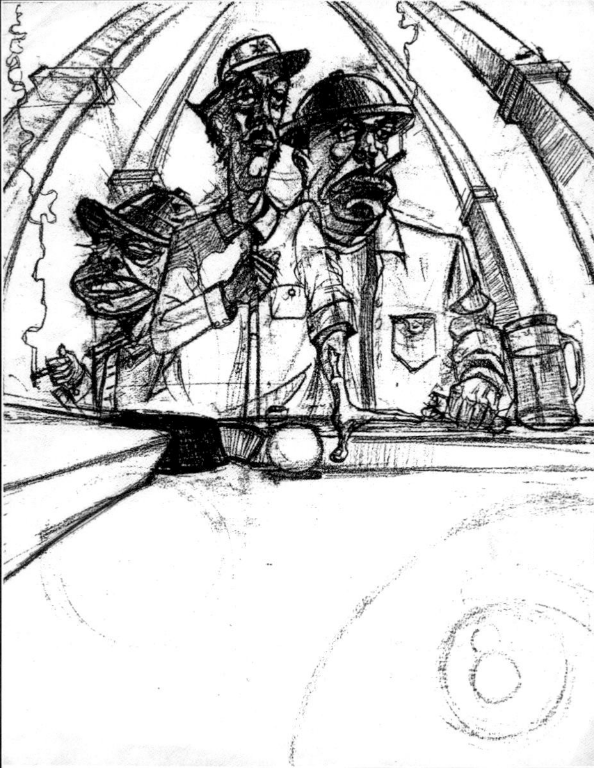

The Pool Hall was a pivotal pai
for me. I began working in full
(lights and darks) and full col
is also my first ever urban pai
It marked the very first time I
to recognize the direction I wa
go with my art.

With this piece I wanted to uti
skills that I learned at the Ar
College of Design. I studied wi
guru of perspective, Gary Meyer
taught me mad perspective skill
wanted to use this new found kn
in this painting and add my own
distorted view of the world.

In retrospect this piece is the
painting that shares strong sim
in style with my work today. Th
Hall marks the beginning of ref
on my experiences, using my pas
source of inspiration and my ar
education as an invaluable tool

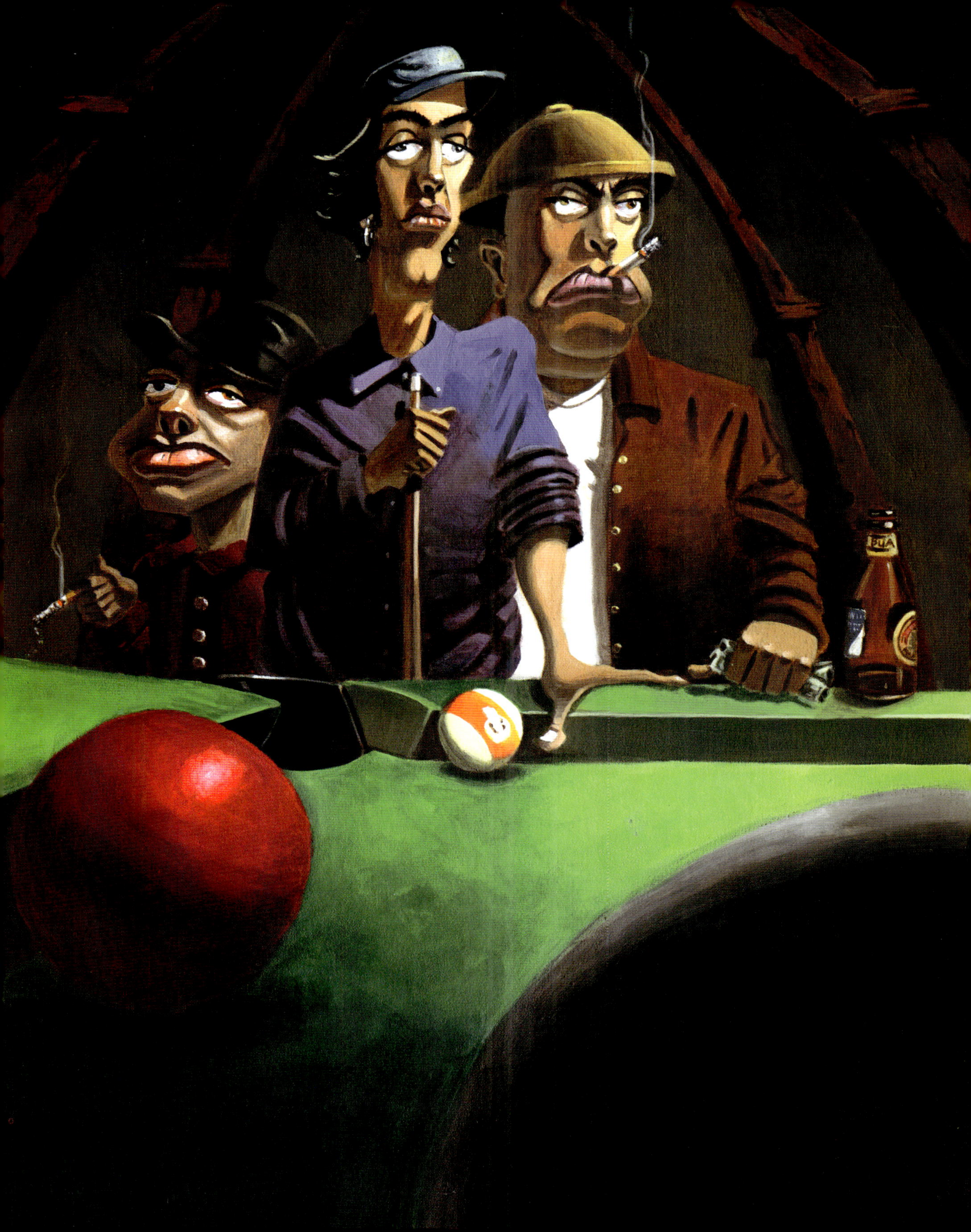

PIANO MAN

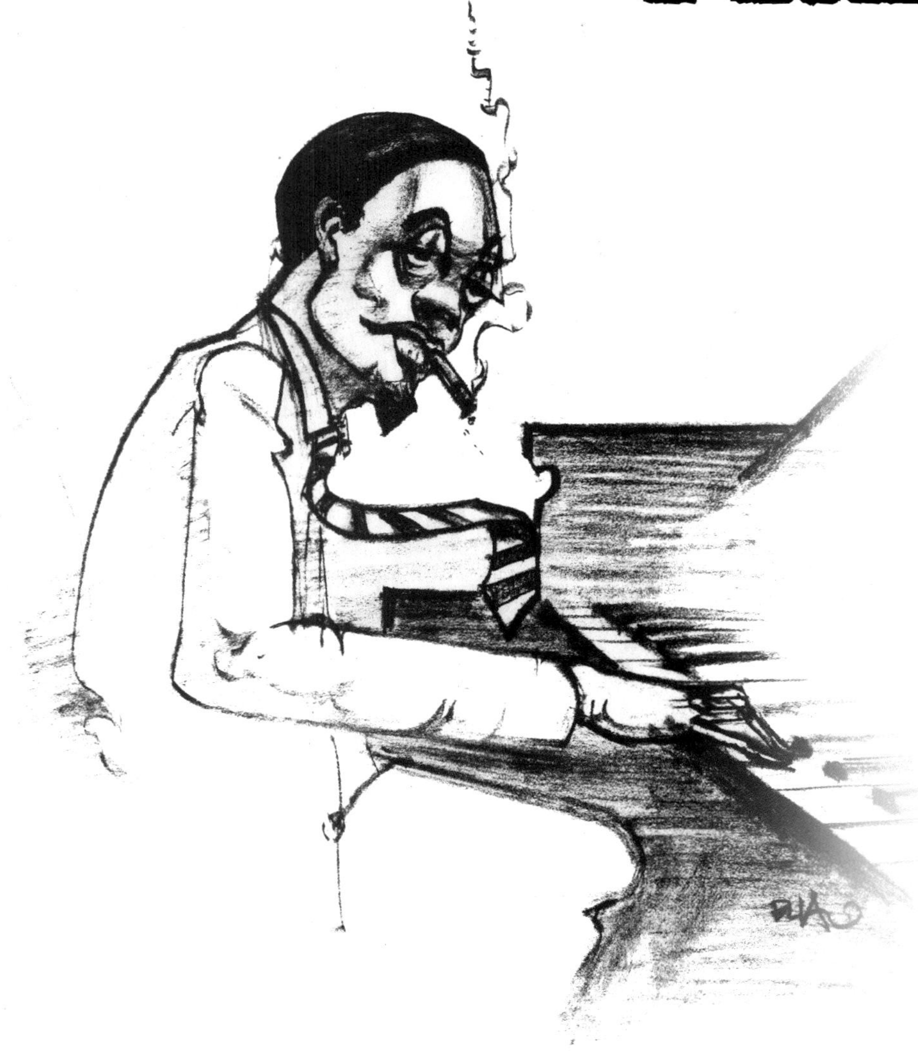

Piano Man came at a time when I was going through a very heavy jazz, marijuana, and double espresso phase. Picasso had a Rose Period, a Blue Period, and a Cubist Period. This was my Caffeinated Nocturnal Insomniac Period. In the span of three days I did "Three Home Skillets," "Midnight Solo," and "Piano Man."

While I was composing Piano Man, I started to recognize who I was and what my vision of art could be. I saw my style truly expressed on canvas. This was the type of painting that I wanted to do. This was gonna be my thing. I think my true style showed itself in Piano Man because I didn't plan anything. This character flowed out of my head on to the canvas. I painted it in one day.

It was purely emotional.

Even though this piece is technically not as sophisticated as other pieces, it still captures something raw and visceral. Its energy came from popping and the rhythms of graffiti. The stylized angularity of the piano, the tie, and particularly the jacket are the type of geometric shapes that I learned from the movements I made with my body when I was popping. The essence of graffiti also lends itself to this piece with its bold graphic outlines. However, I can only say this in hindsight. At the time, I didn't really know what I was doing—I was totally stoned.

Opposite:
Piano Man 1993
Acrylic on Canvas
48 in. x 48 in.

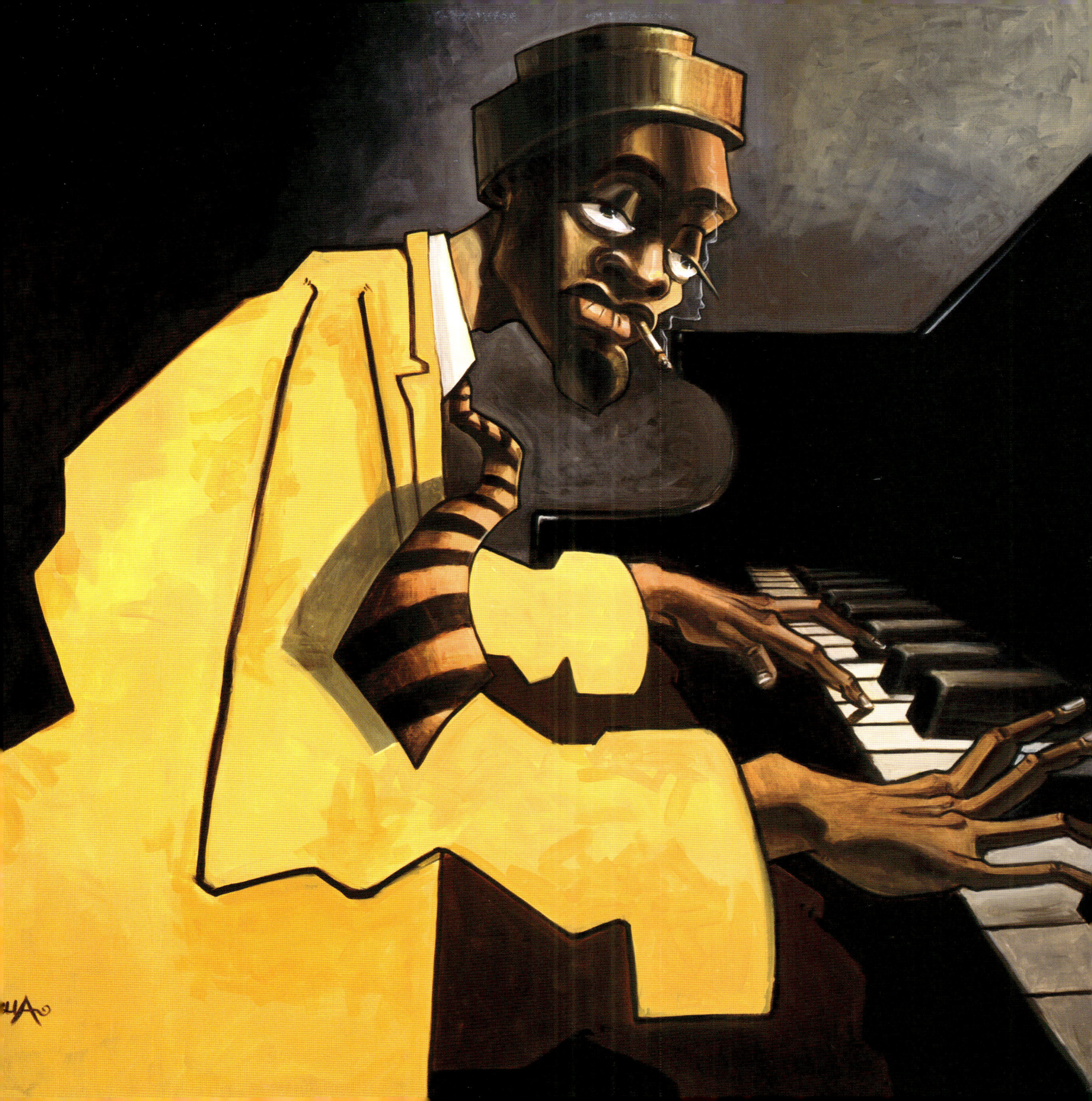

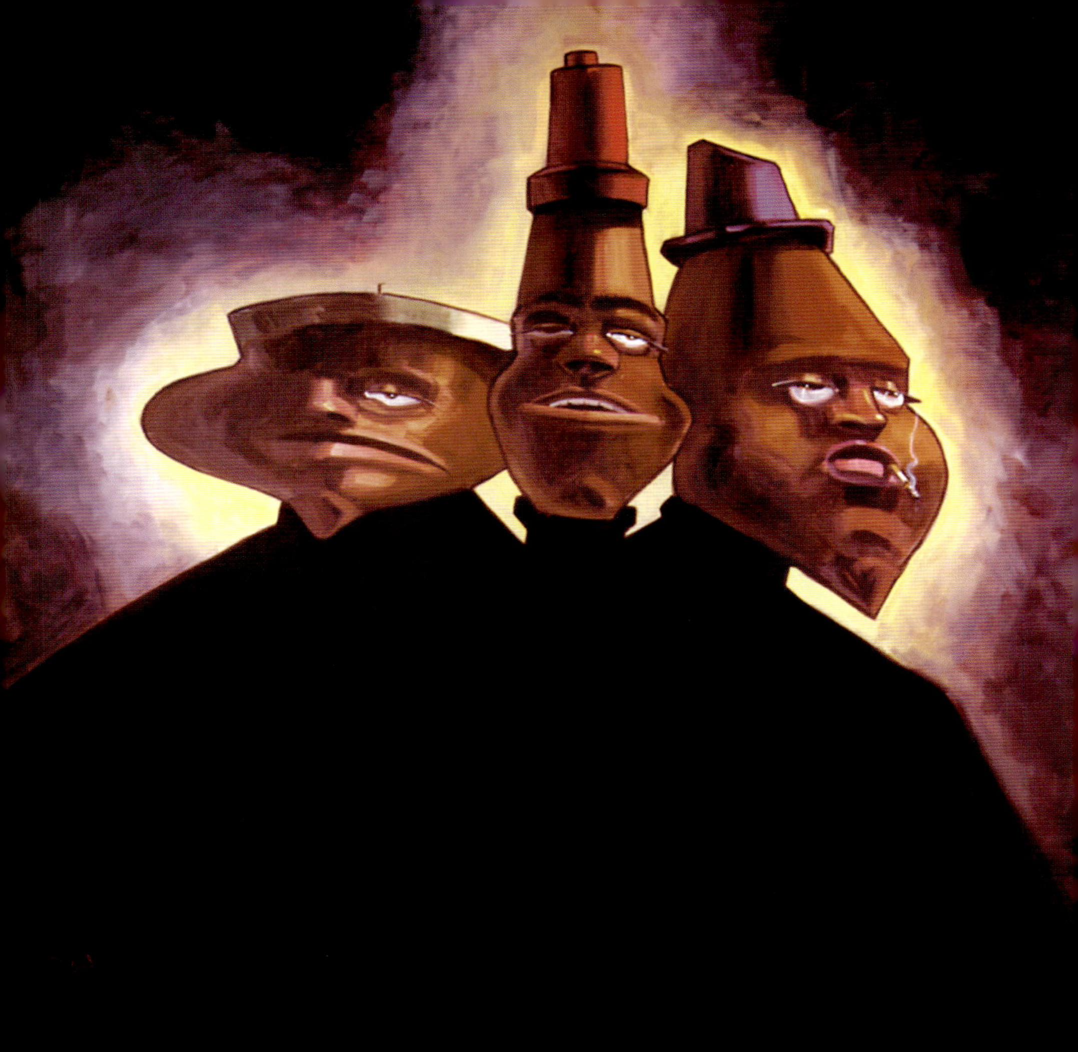

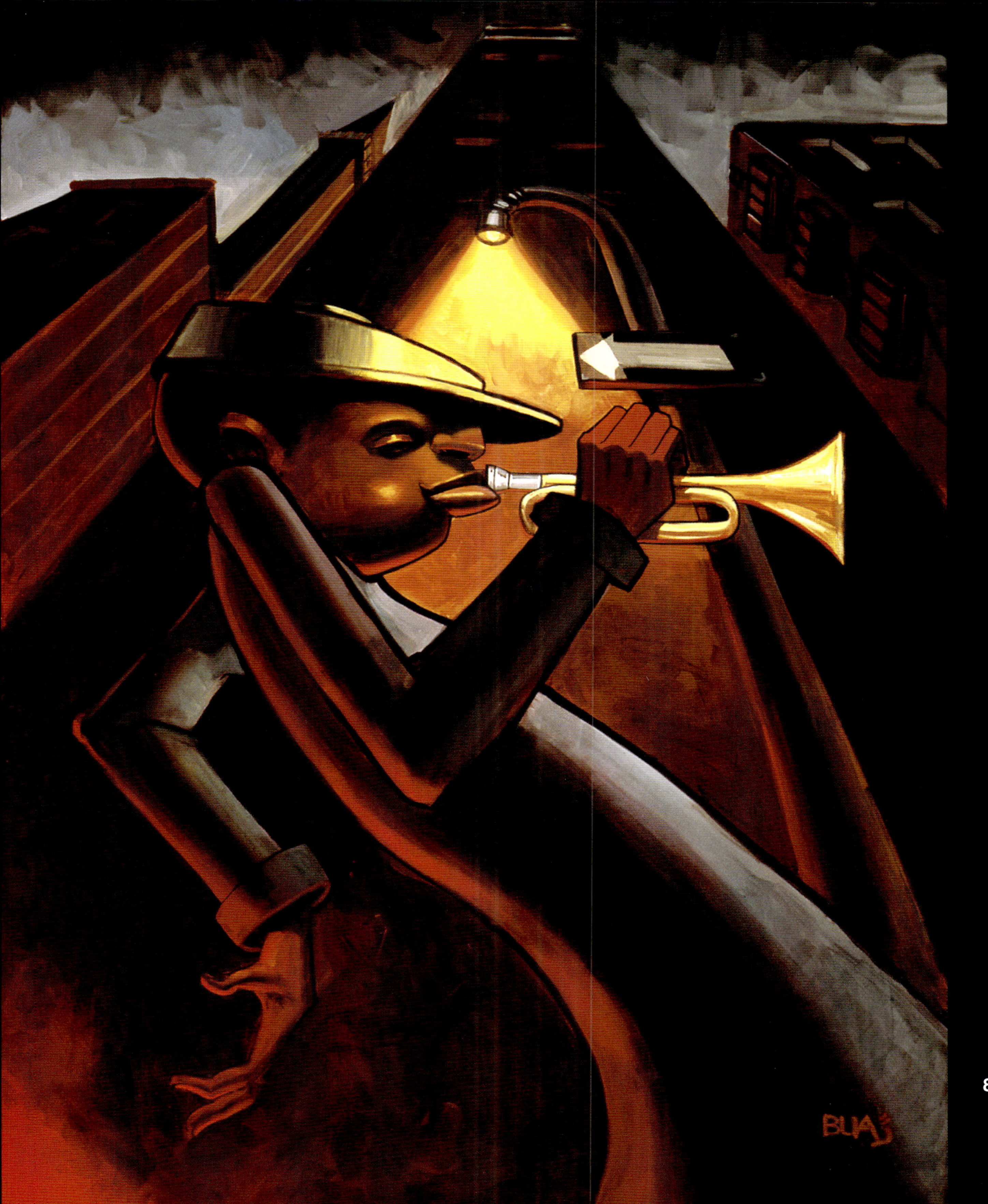

Jazz Trio

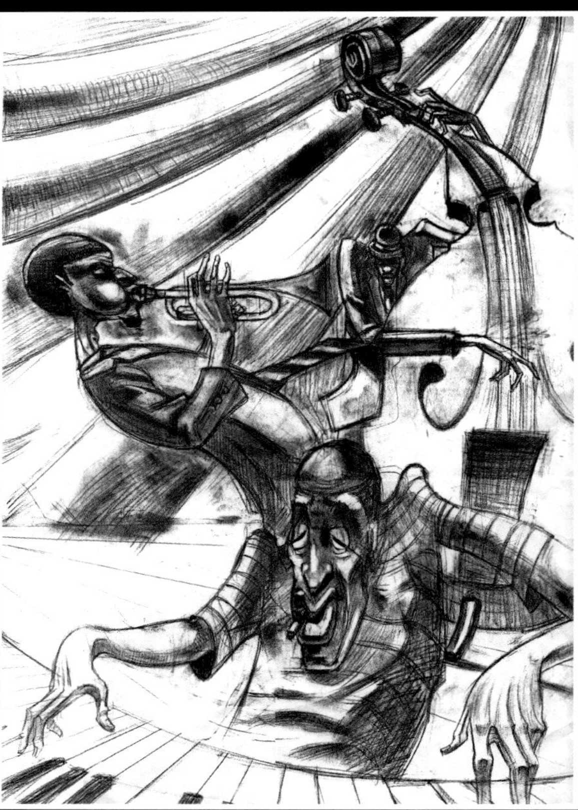

People ask me all the time why, being a B-Boy, I paint jazz so much. Why not? Jazz is cool. That's the best reason I have. The rhythm of jazz is akin to the rhythm of graffiti, breaking, and the rhythm of the streets.

The characters and their instruments in "Jazz Trio" have mad distortion. In this painting I really began pushing boundaries. All the elements composing this painting are pushed and pulled to mirror the rhythm of the music.

The piano player is extremely intent. There's nothing you can do to make him waiver when he's soloing. The piano keys seem pushed by the strong, determined musicality of his hands. He's hard, tough and very talented. He's the Tu Pac of jazz. The trumpet player is arching back almost as if he is blown by the power of his horn. He's lost in his music. The bass is beautiful and feminine, yet almost overpowering. It wraps around the bass player as he skillfully allows his hands to be led by the vibrations of her strings. The bass has a personality of her own. He has to give in to her and he's cool with that.

There is a harmony and an ebb and flow between the players and their instruments as if there has been a long-standing relationship. These cats have played together for years. They are one with their instruments and each other.

Opp

Jazz Trio

Acrylic on Illustration

19.5 in. x

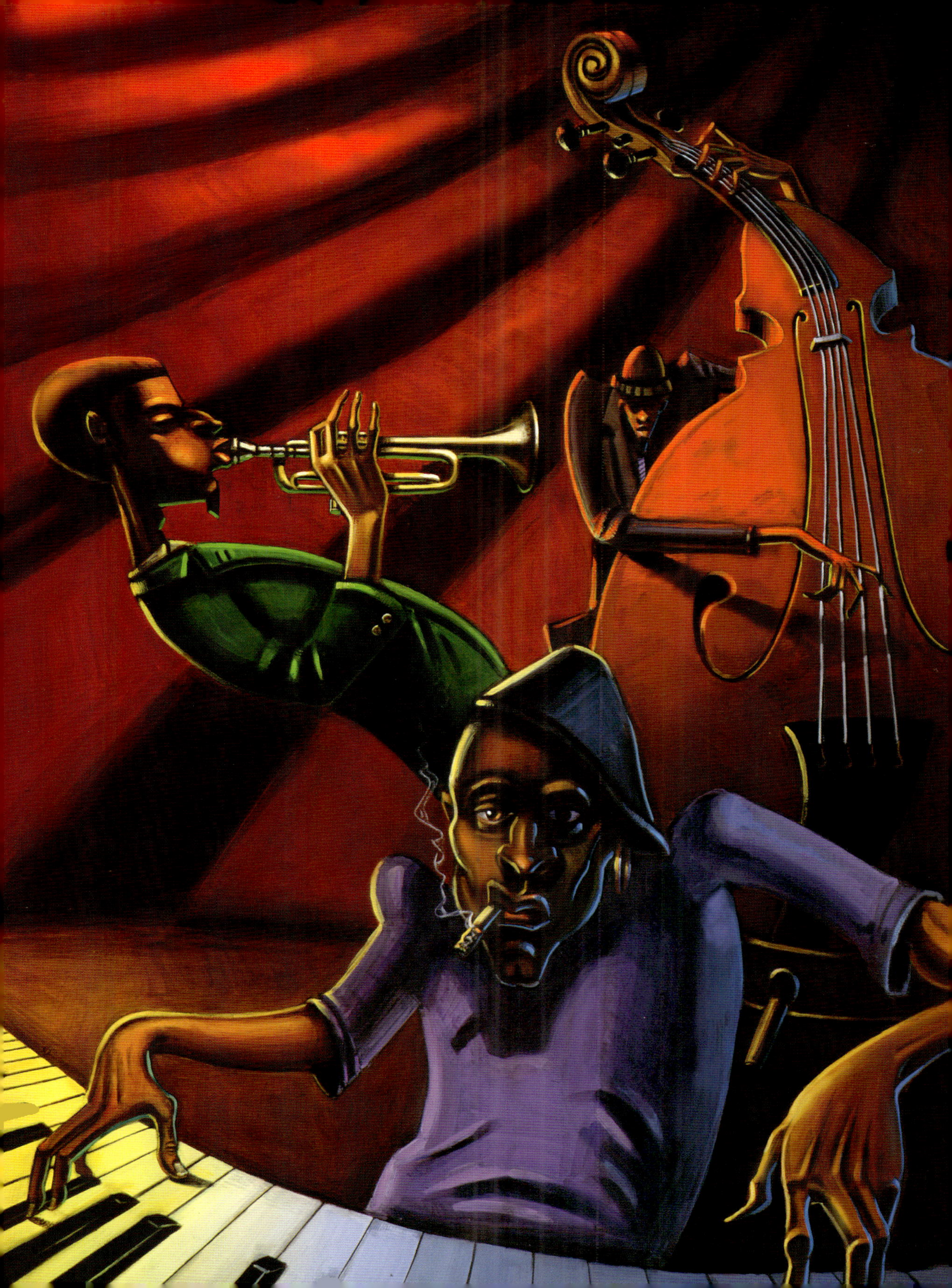

Sax Man

Sax Man is the Jimi Hendrix of the jazz hall.

This painting comes from a stony, stylized world in my mind where graf and jazz meld into one. The space where the abstract geometric shapes of graffiti and the free formed sounds of jazz are linked. To me, jazz and Hip-Hop culture share similar roots; both were born from the streets and are powerful movements of freedom of expression.

Opposite:
Sax Man 1994
Acrylic on Canvas
48 in. x 48 in.

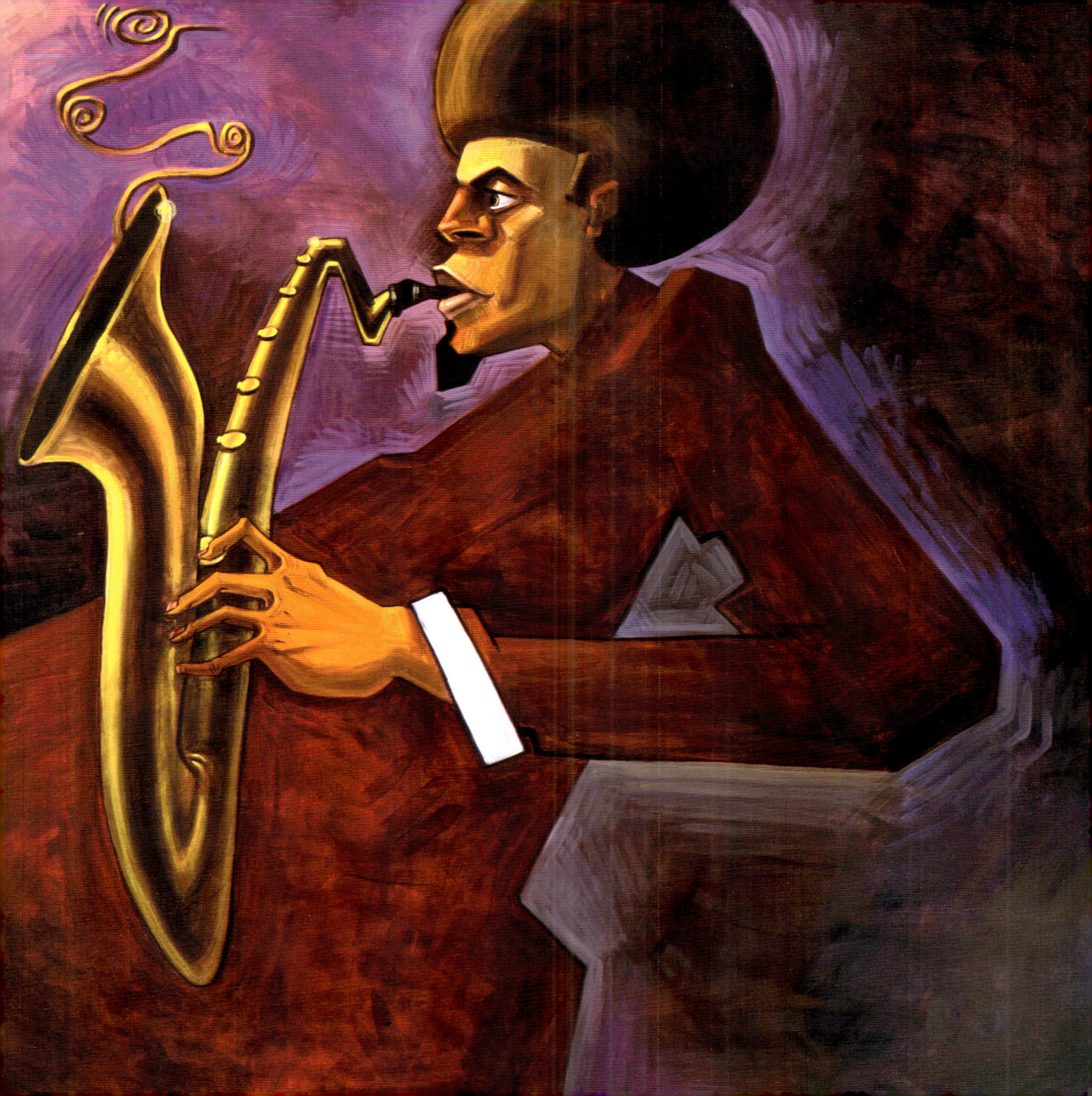

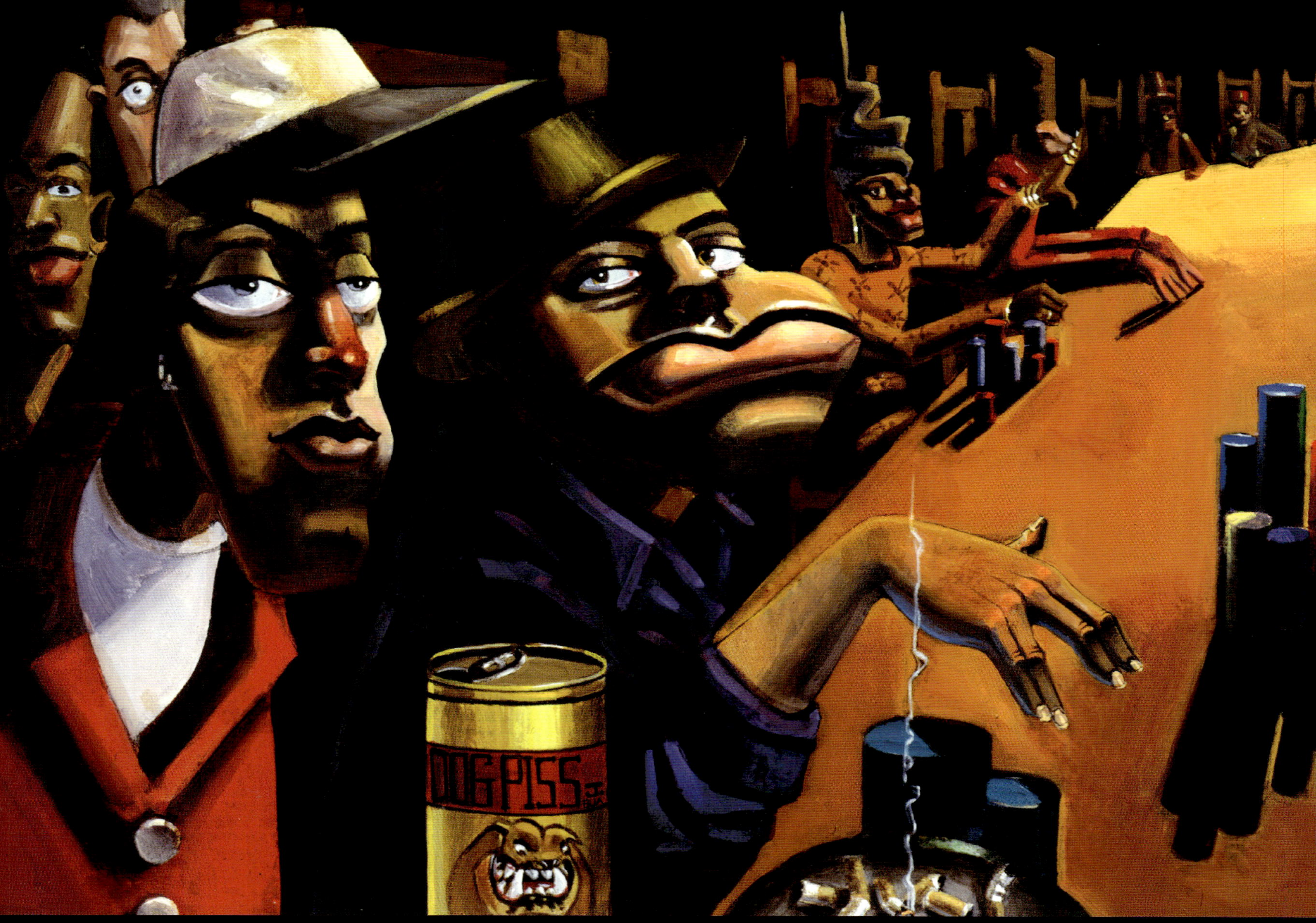

Poker Game

I first did this piece for a skateboard company to be reproduced on the underside of skateboards in the early 1990s. It was a time when I was having fun in my life and on the canvas. These characters are reminiscent of all the bugged out kids I grew up with in New York City. It's like an urban *Alice in Wonderland*; more like "BUA in Underland" with the Dog Piss Beer, Horse of Course Cigarettes, and my personal hero, Rembrandt, as the King.

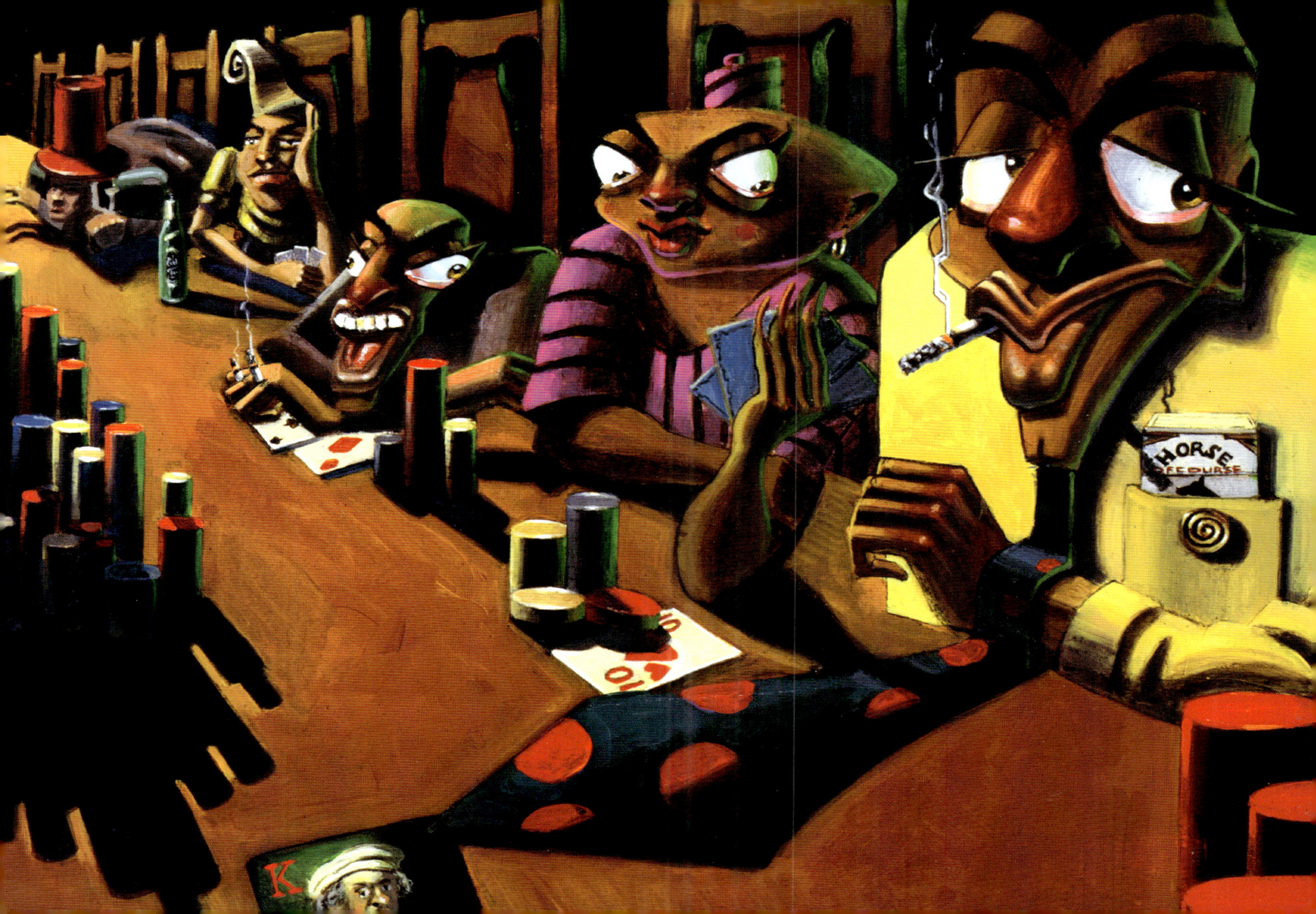
HORSE

Rising

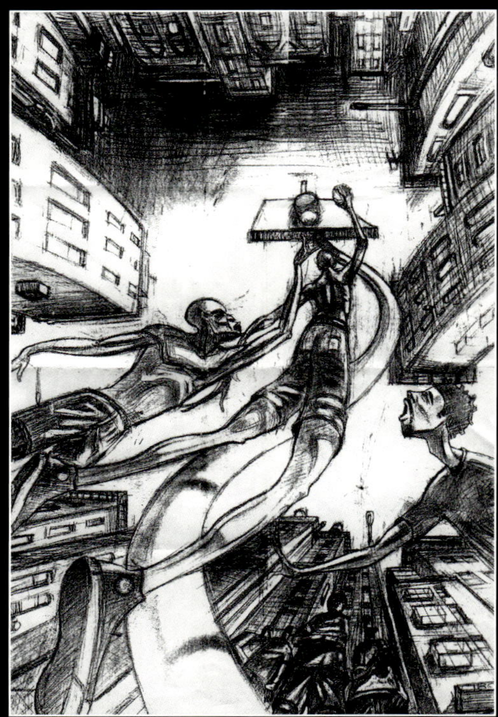

I love basketball. When I was young I would either go down to Riverside Park to watch and play with the ballers or trek downtown to West 4th Street to check out the semi-pro heads. They were serious ballers but often spent as much time arguing a call as they did playing.

The illest ballers were from the projects. That is what this painting is all about. "Rising" was painted from an ant's point of view or a "knocked-down-on-your-ass" perspective. It shows the game as a metaphor. Surrounded by the seemingly insurmountable concrete walls, the baller tries to rise above the stigma of the projects while players struggle to block him and onlookers sneer. There are so many obstacles: the torn net, the deceitful basket, and the player-hating friends. They play as if each possession will determine their fate. To them, there's only one shot.

Oppo
Rising
Acrylic on Illustration B
21 in. x 28.

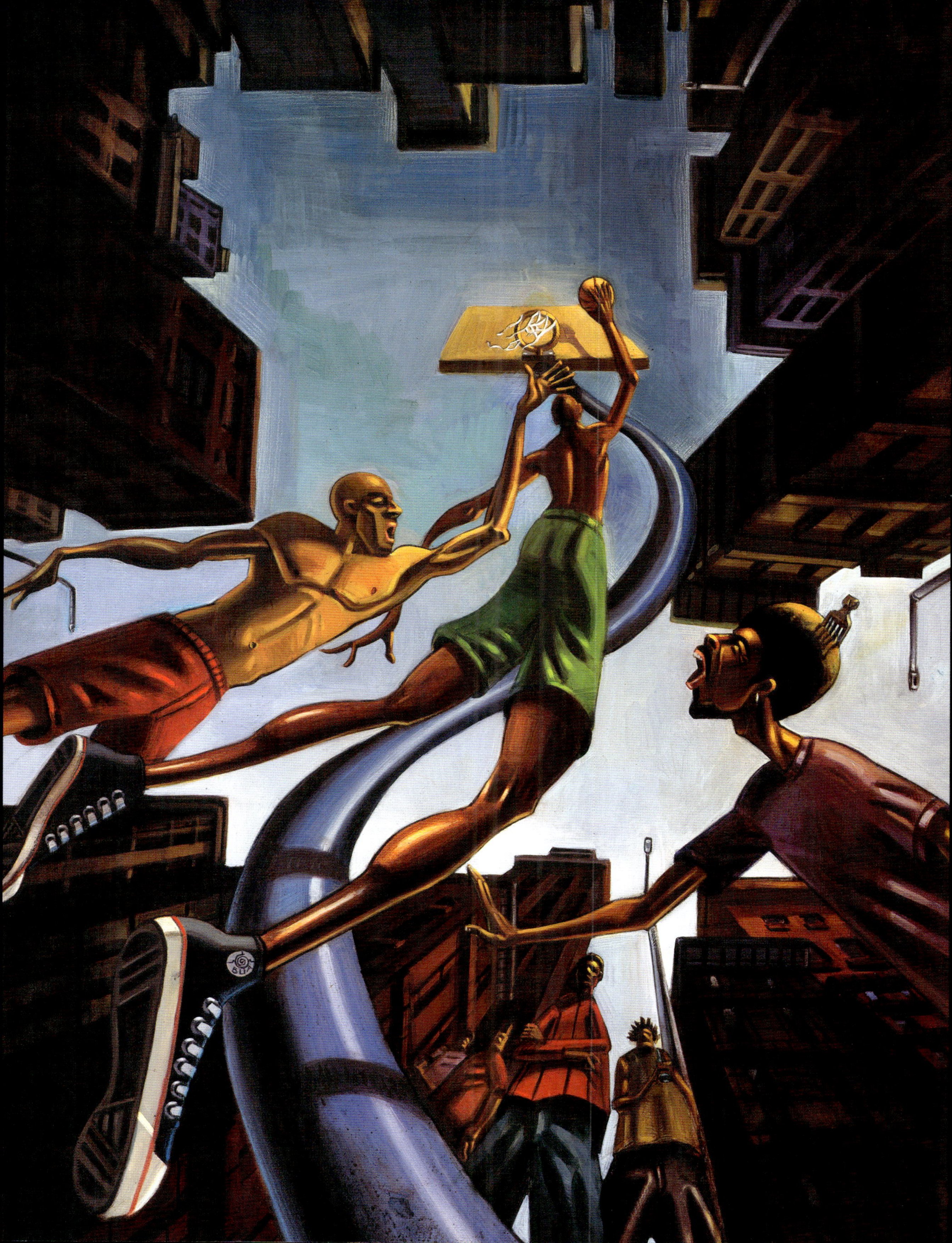

Behind the Eight Ball

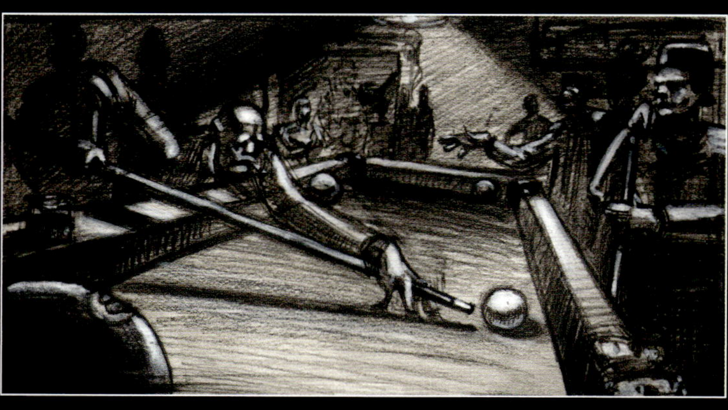

As a kid, I gravitated toward the underground spots in NYC, whether it was Marty Reisman's ping-pong parlor on 96th Street or the Guys and Dolls Pool Hall on 79th and Broadway. It was an adult world.

I took the risk to sneak in these joints to observe the games and listen to the tales. As a kid, I felt like I didn't belong. I was on the outside looking in. This was the old, old school generation. The working class that survived NYC through all of the hard times. To me, these were NYC relics. They were just as much a part of New York as the Brooklyn Bridge or the Empire State Building.

Behind the Eight Ball 1996
Acrylic on Illustration Board
28.5 in. x 20.5 in.

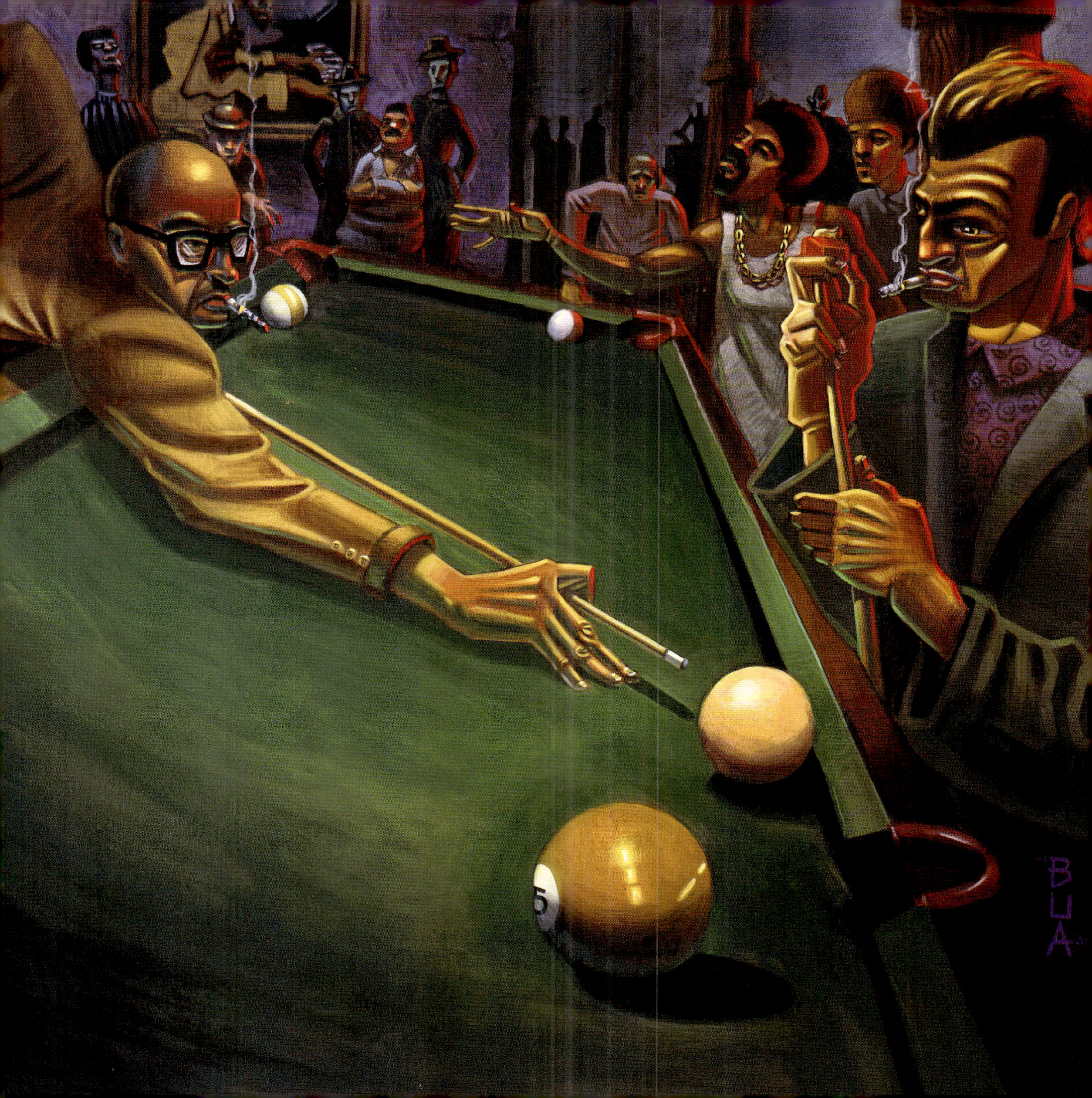
BUA

Four of a Kind

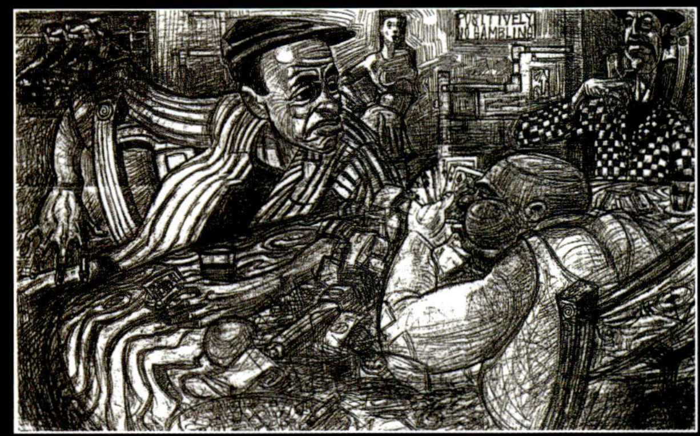

Poker is a familiar game to me. My grandpa and his friends would sit around, talk about old times, banter about politics, and gamble. I love the dynamics and expressions of people playing poker. There are so many layers to "the game." These guys have known each other for a long time. This is their life. Their competitive spirit is echoed by the George Bellows painting in the background, "Stag at Sharky's" (1909), one of my favorite paintings of all time.

Four of a Kind 1995
Acrylic on Illustration Board
28 in. x 18.5 in.

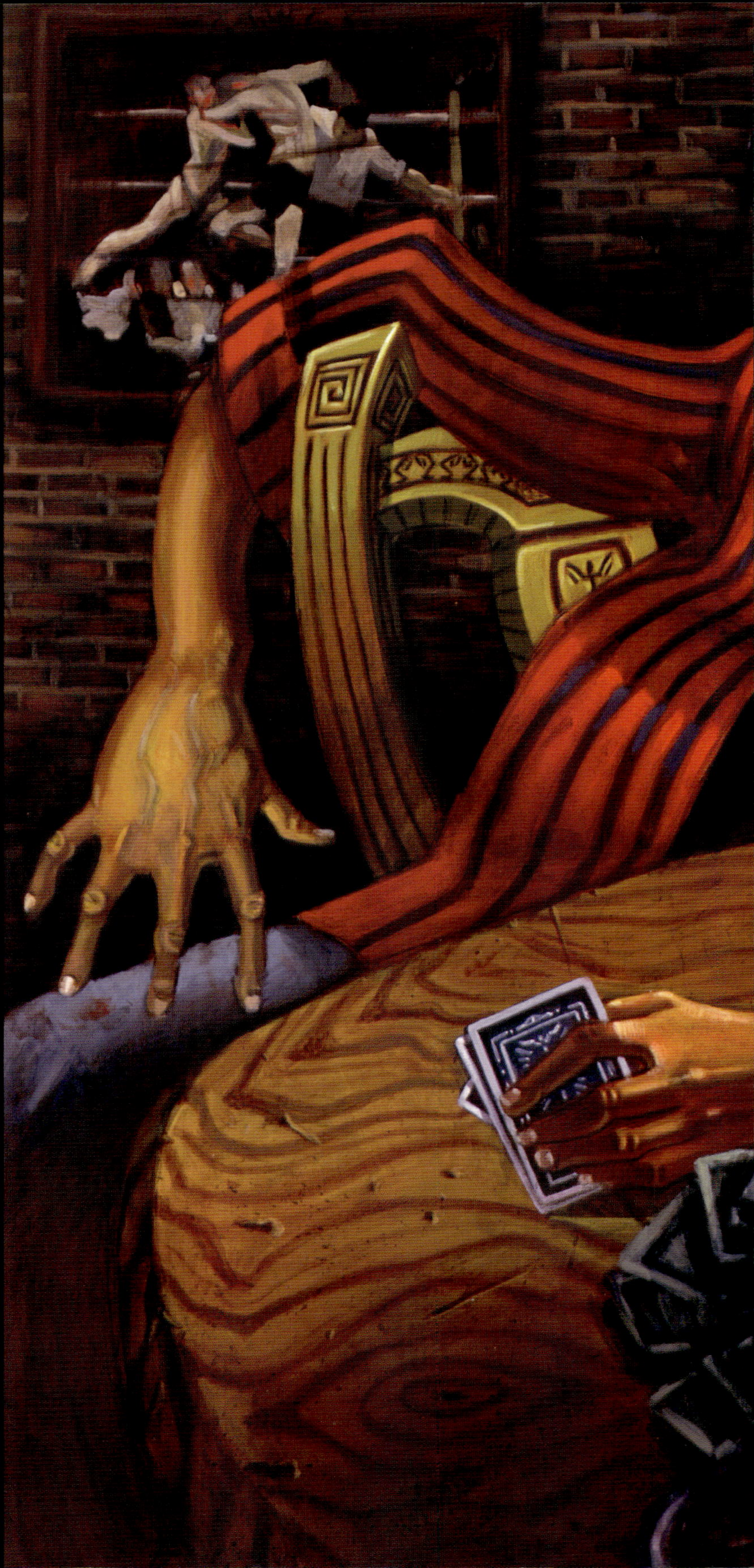

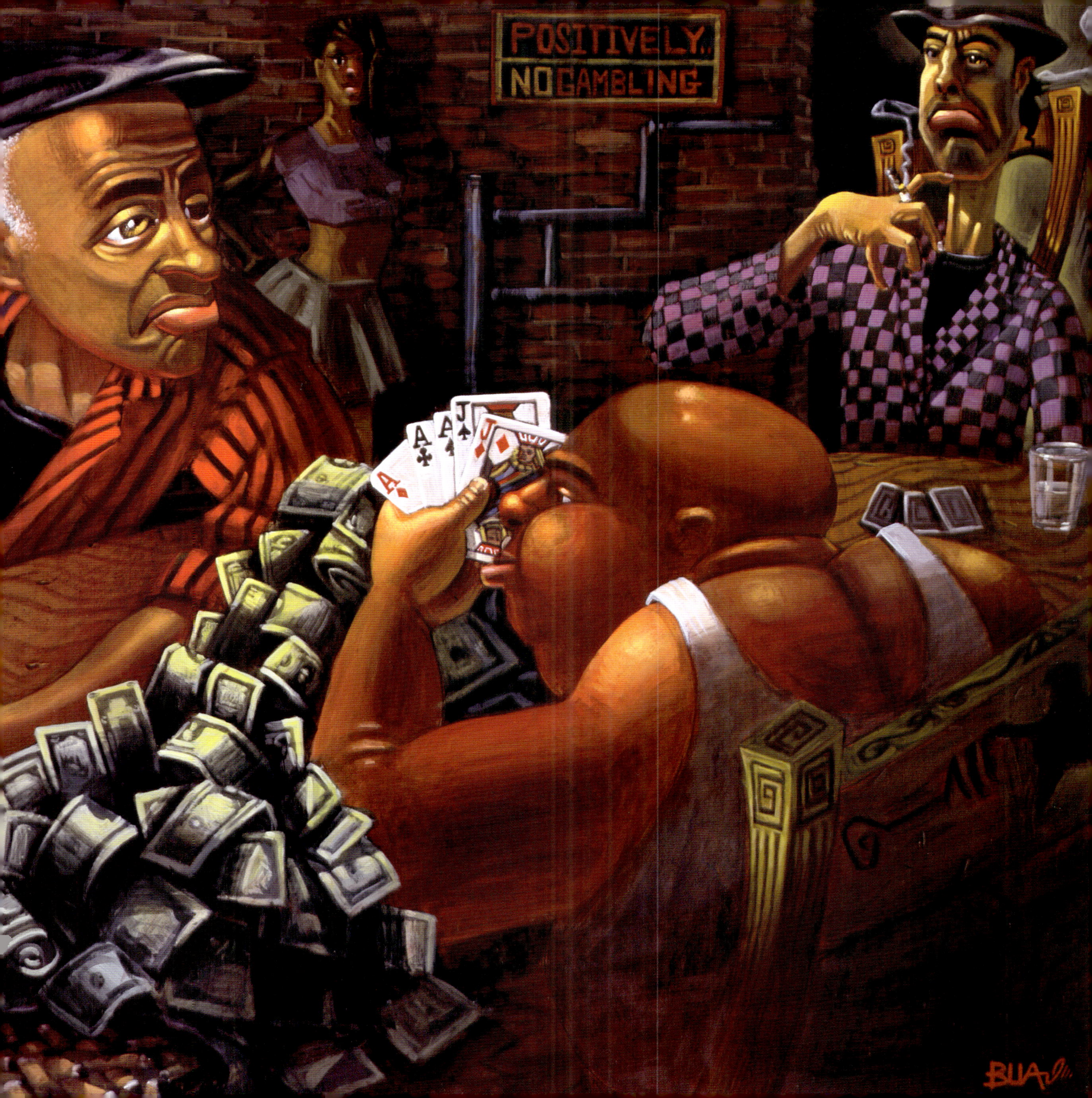
POSITIVELY
NO GAMBLING

These characters have been waiting for Santa for twenty years. Santa's dissed them by never showing up. Now it's payback time.

Saint Nick's about to get vicked!

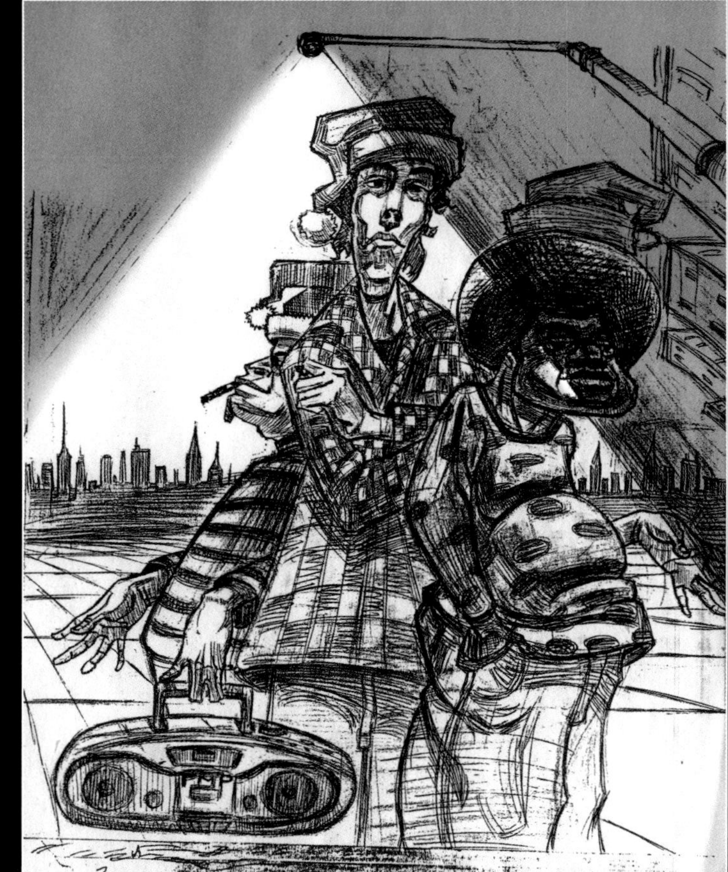

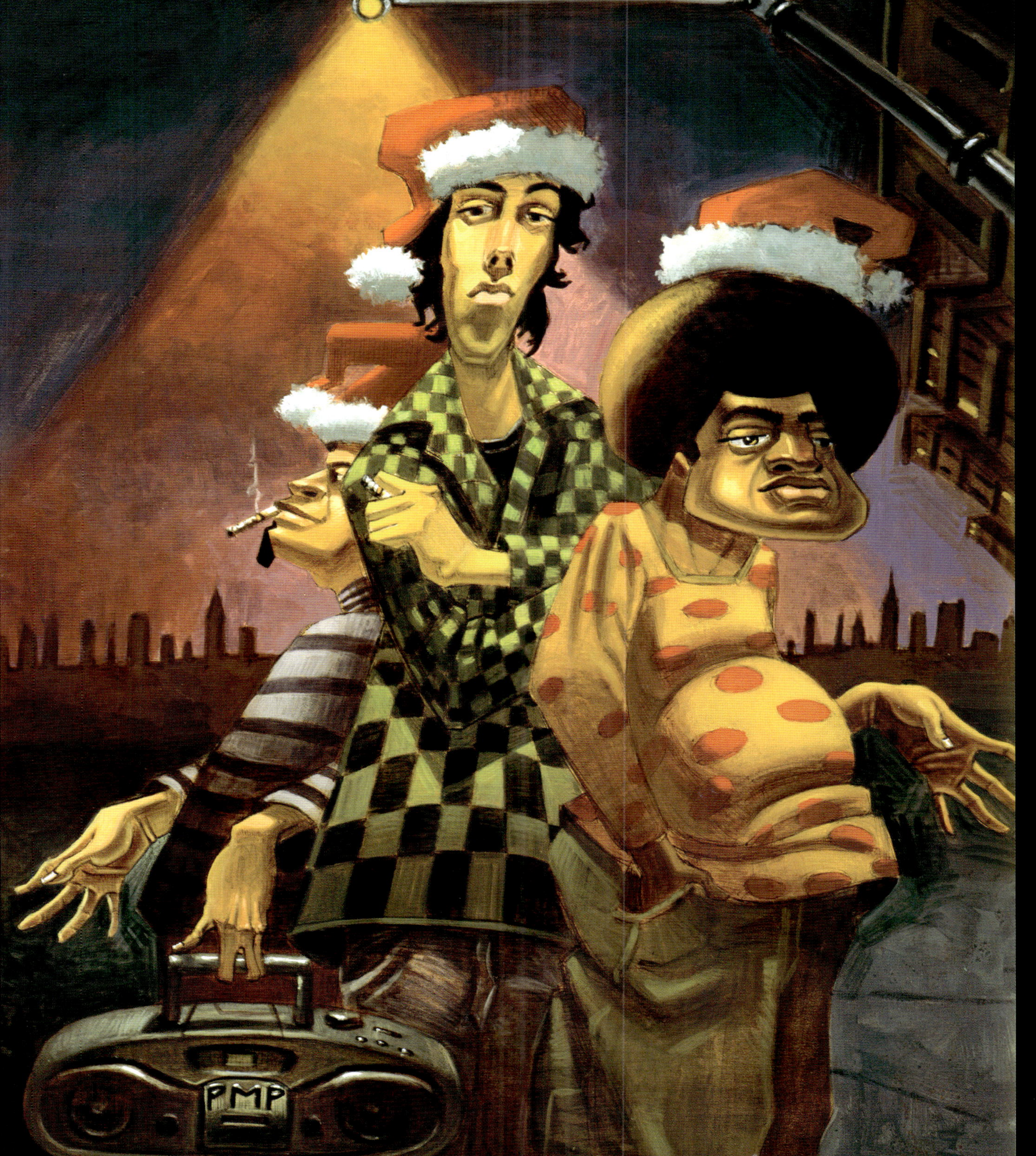
PMP

Jazz Quintet

These are just a couple of the compositional sketches that I did for "Jazz Quintet." A lot of thought and planning went into this painting.

The composition was intended to be two opposing S curves or a figure eight. The flow starts from the neck of the singer's mic, through her strong diagonal force, then through the strings of the bass. The neck of the bass pulls into a C curve to the drummer down through the sax, pulling a strong rhythm through the bassist's fingers. Completing the rhythm, we flow down the side of the piano, which completes the figure eight. There are a lot of other rhythms, verticals and diagonals that I was playing with for balance but that was my main compositional force.

There is a similar rhythm with the way the values read. First read are her gardenias. Then the edge of the bass, then the sax and the piano keys. I created these specific values so that the viewers' eyes would unconsciously travel in the direction I intended them to. Being an artist is like being a film director.

I actually like the muted colors of my color key better than the vibrant colors of my final painting. They gave me the feeling of being back in the era of jazz, like an old, washed out sepia toned photo. I feel like I might have lost the integrity and spontaneity of my color and value keys in my final piece, but the piece ended up with a glow that I wouldn't have been able to pull off had it been a muted painting.

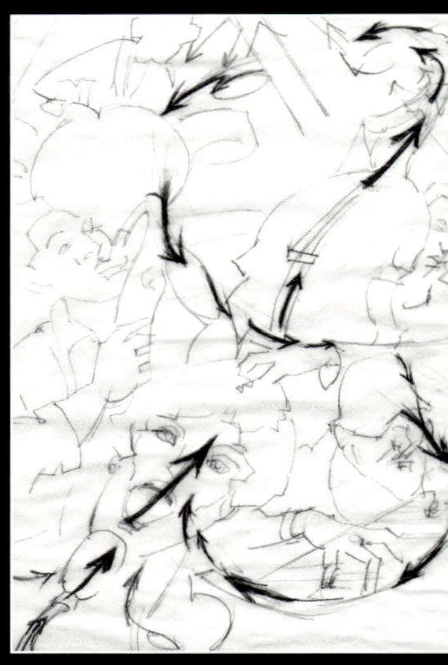

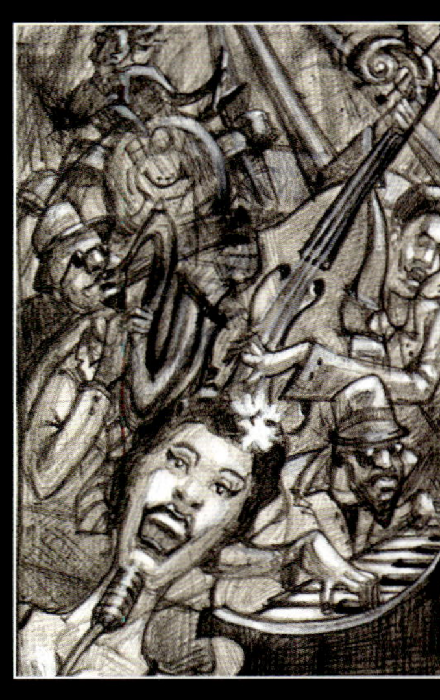

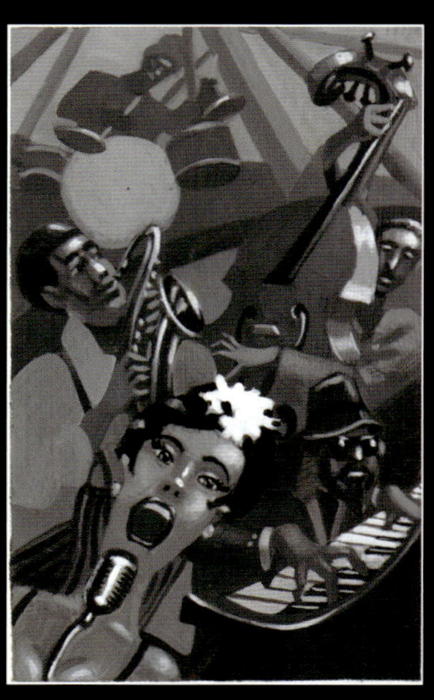

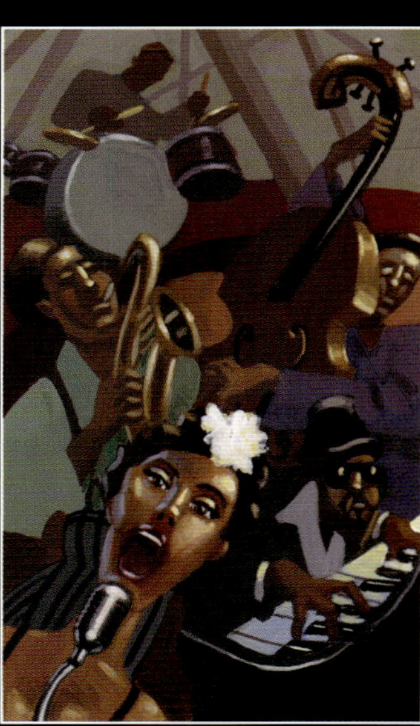

Opposite:
Jazz Quintet 1996
Acrylic on Illustration Board

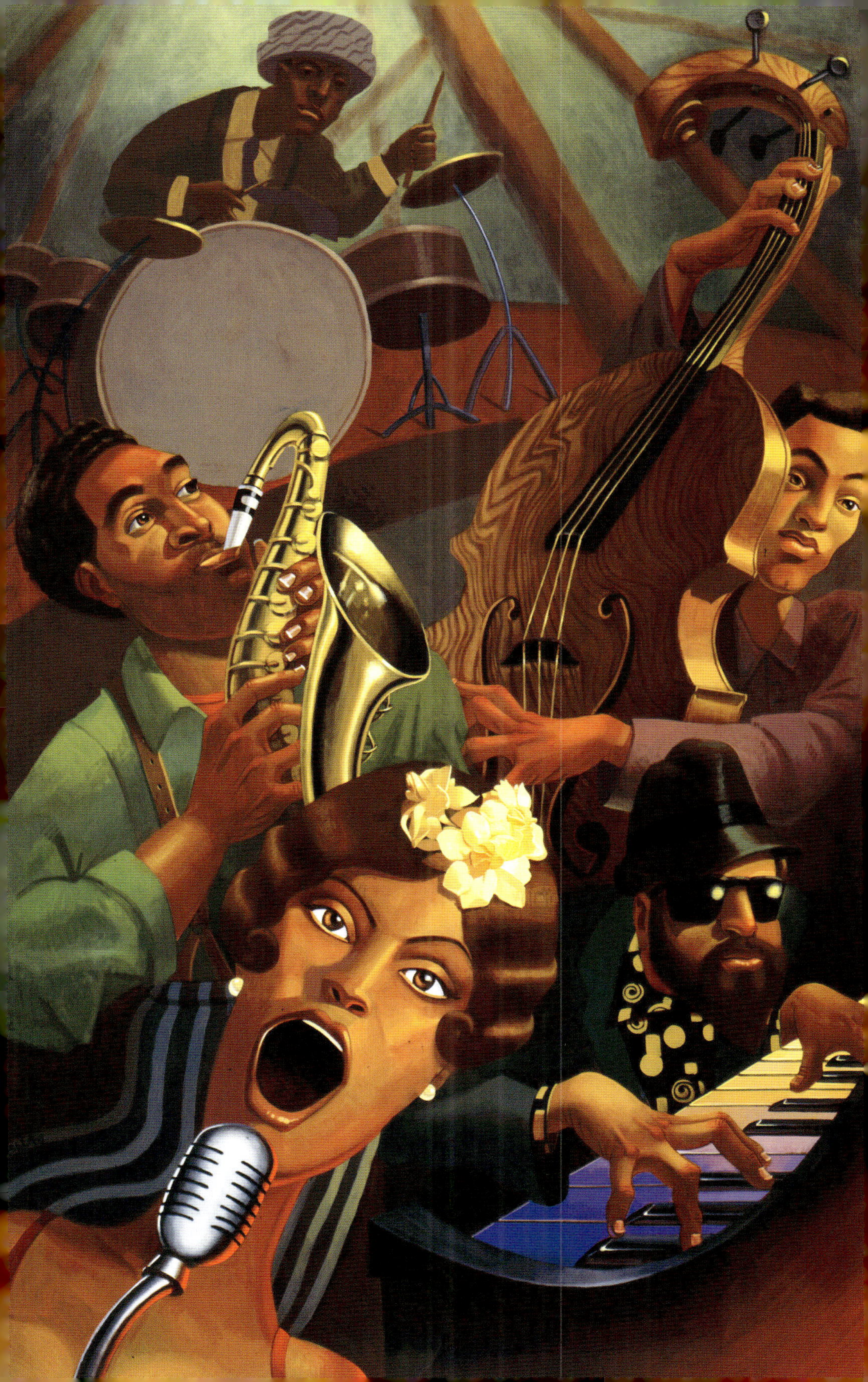

MONEY MAKIN' MANHATTAN

Subway

The subway is the quintessential melting pot of NYC. Different people from all walks of life, side by side. That is New York. The subway is the essence of the city. People's worlds that normally wouldn't mix—do; it is a New York petri dish.

Riding the subway back in the day was exciting and at times tense. The trains had such a complex dynamic. A homeless man clad in a potato sack would sit next to a wealthy, Upper East Side woman clutching her Donna Karan and Gucci shopping bags. The Hasidic Jewish boy studying the Torah would hold the same pole as the hoodlum from Brownsville who would be spitting RUN DMC lyrics about social inequalities. Where else would anyone be so close to a complete stranger? We shared the same space, which could be chill; but at times shit blew up, whether it was defending personal space or trying to avoid getting caught looking someone in the eye.

QUEENS

I had an experience once where I was on the 1 Train and this stick-up lookin' kid was mad doggin' me. Unconsciously, I looked right back at him and that was it: we locked eyes and like two pit bulls, refused to let go. When the train pulled into the station, he got out without breaking his gaze. He bum-rushed me, but the doors closed between us. He looked enraged and I felt angry. My eyes fastened and my brows furrowed deeper. He put his face up to my face, our eyes locked, separated only by the pane of glass. As the train pulled away he punched the window cracking the glass, my face still firmly pressed against it. Immovable with my stare, I couldn't back down. It was primal, but that's how it felt many times in the tunnels under New York.

On the real, the characters I saw on the train while growing up were some of the most inspiring, interesting people that I've ever seen in my life. When I had to take the long ride to Brooklyn, I really had a chance to study all of the unique characters. I overheard stories and conversations that I wouldn't normally hear. Riding the train when I was really young exposed me to so many different ways of living life, stimulating my mind and my creativity. In a weird way it educated and infused me with great stories and visuals that I would never forget.

It colored my imagination.

Jamaica Bay

Opposite:
Subway 1997
Acrylic on Illustration Board
12 in. x 16 in.

CROOKLYN

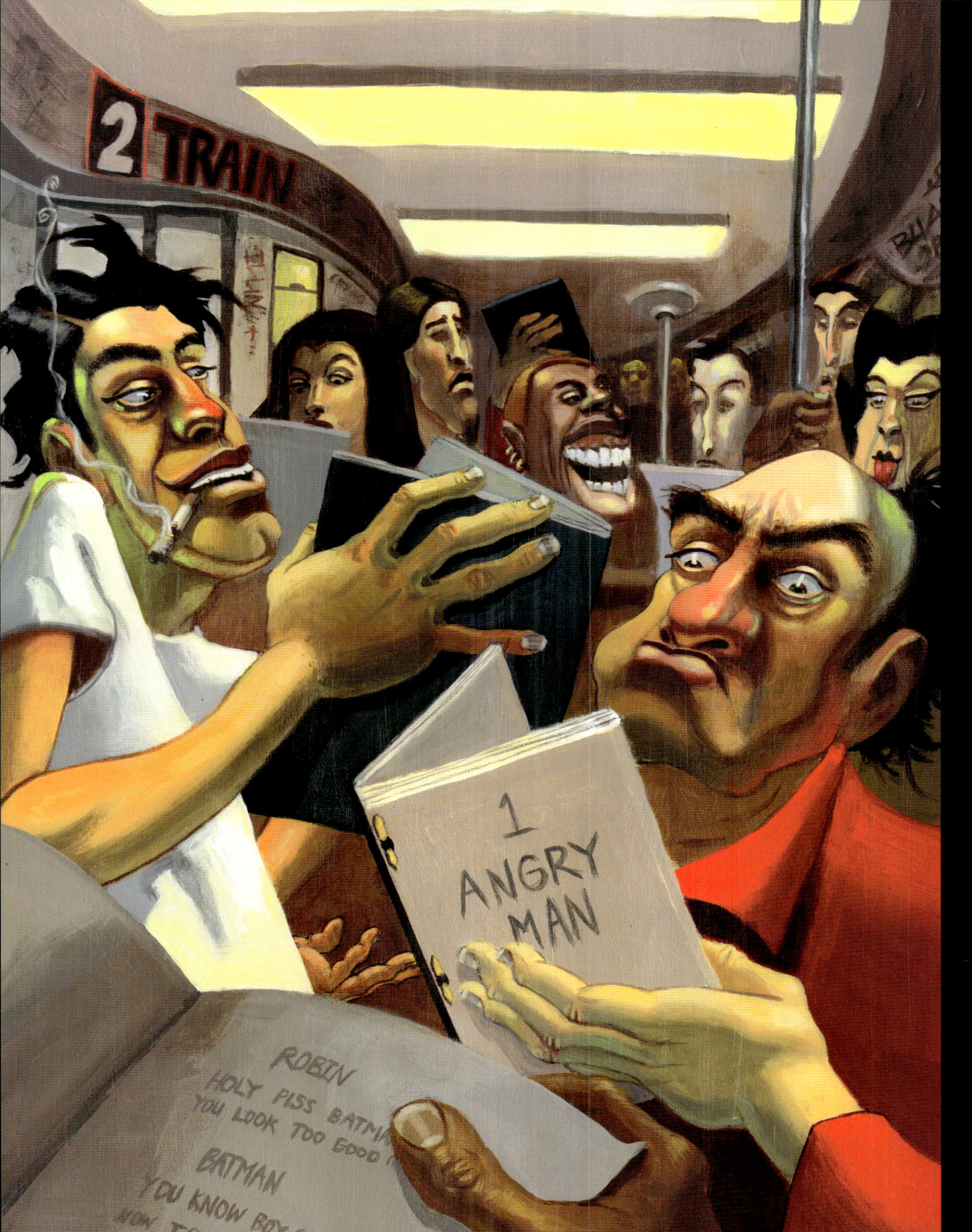

2 TRAIN
1 ANGRY MAN
ROBIN
HOLY PISS
YOU LOOK TOO GOOD
BATMAN
YOU KNOW BOY

GREEN $TREET

"Green Street" is life in the inner city. Enclosed in architectural concrete, there is no sky. No way out, yet these cats are content. This is what they live for—a ritualistic gathering of homies that have come to clear their heads of responsibility.

One of my goals for this piece was to take graffiti-like characters which are usually flat and graphic like Egyptian hieroglyphics, and bring them to life by painting them volumetrically.

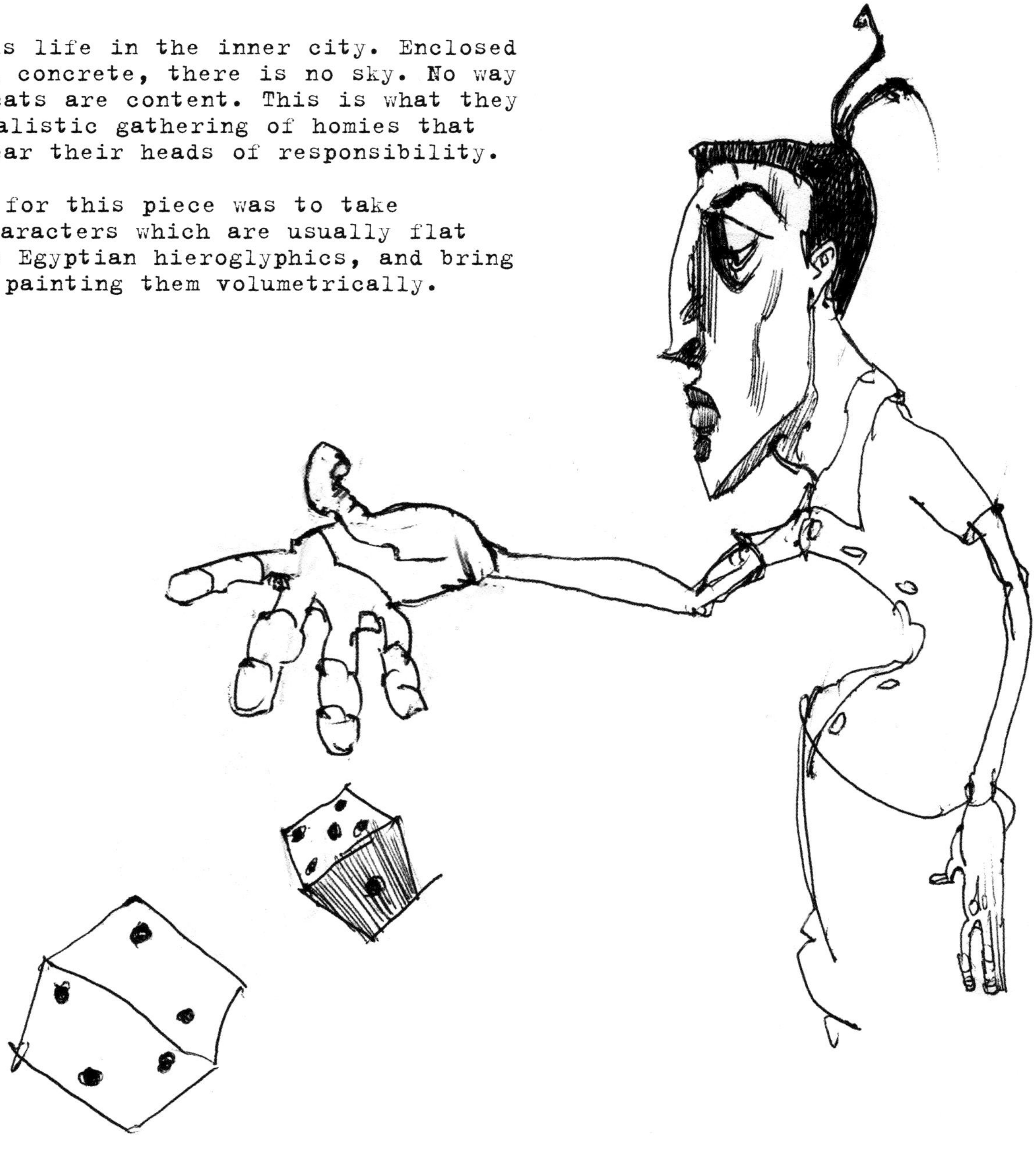

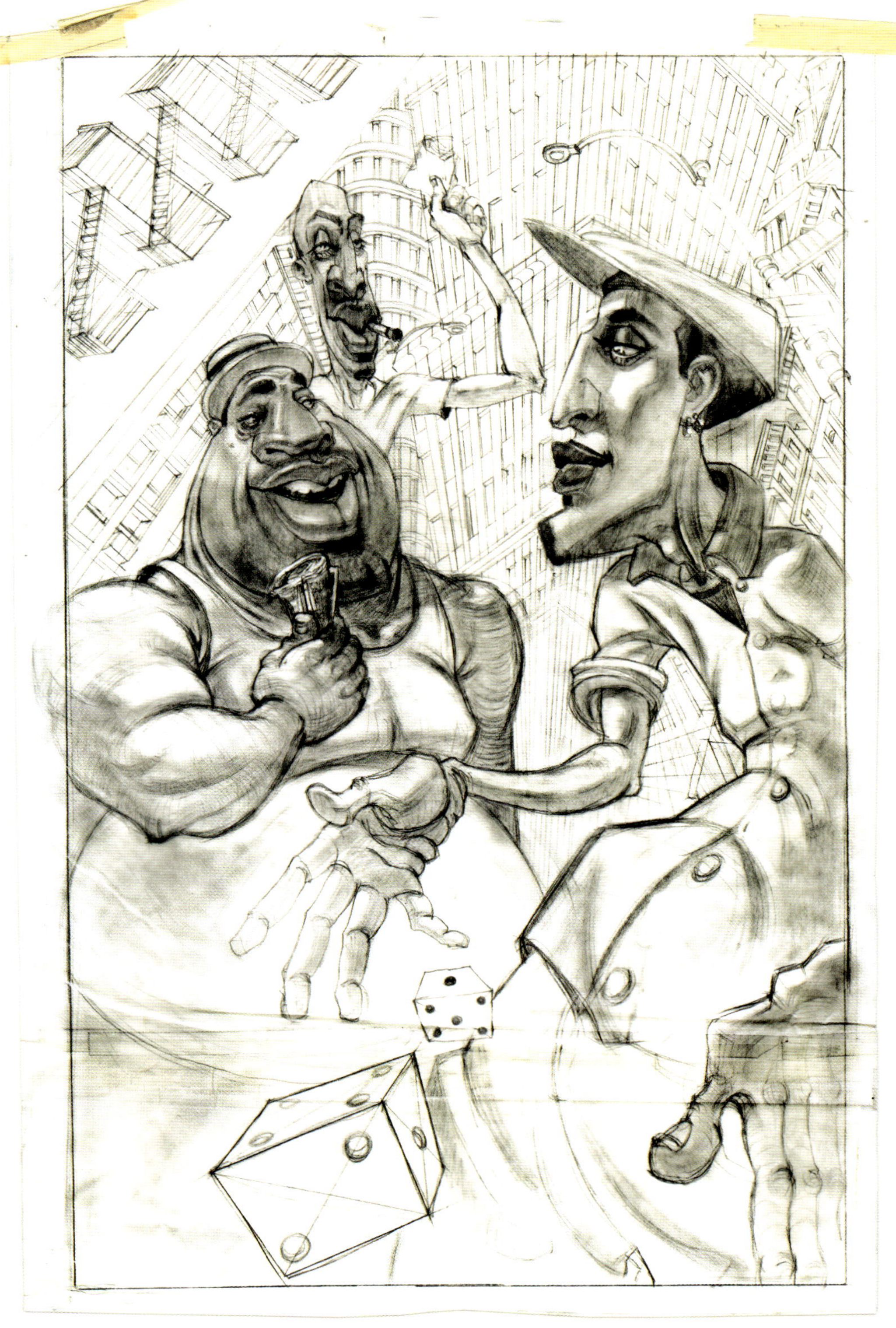

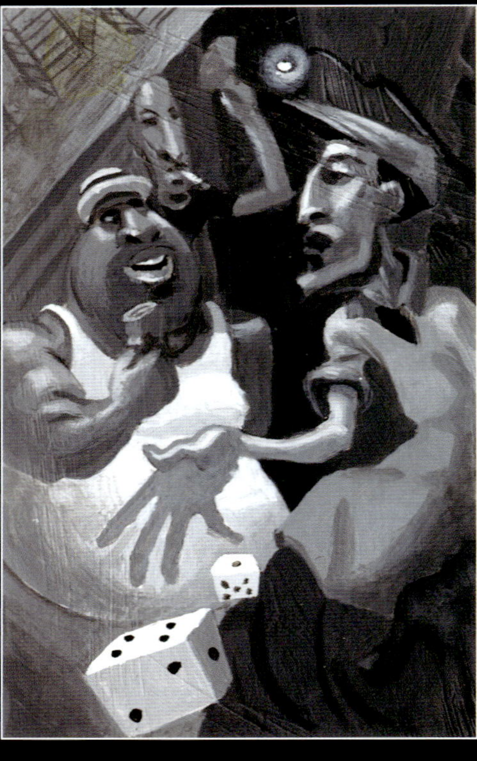

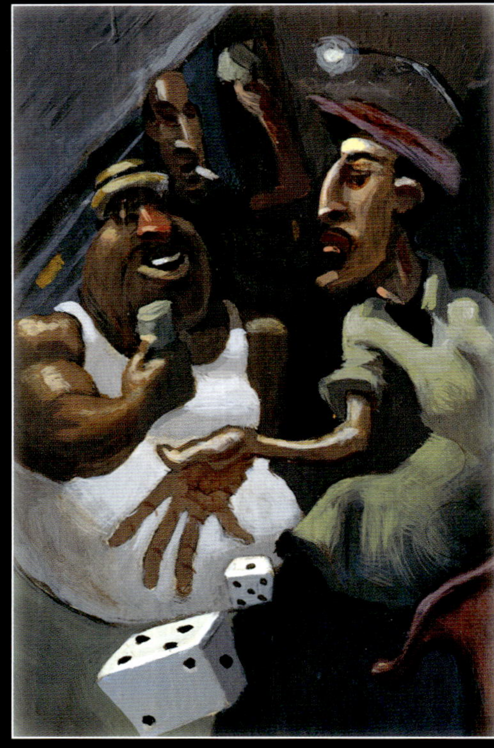

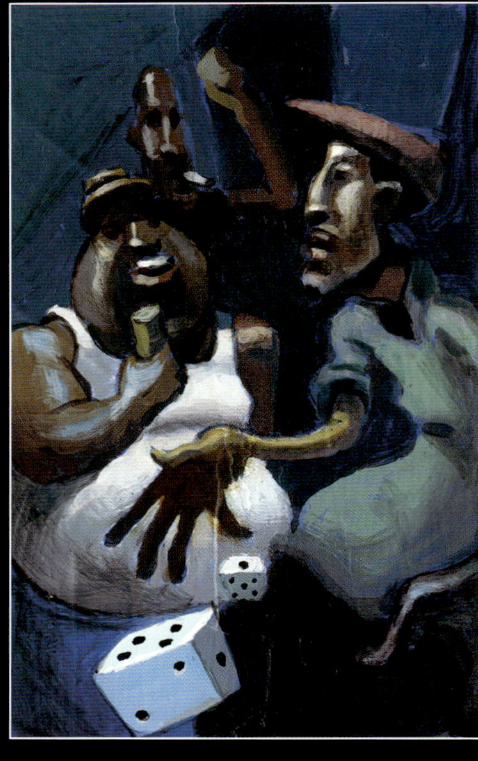

On Green Street the money ebbs and flows within the hood. Cash changes hands. Still, it stays in the same circle. It's the inner city version of Wall Street. But unlike those Suits who gamble with other people's money, on the street you make your own bets and deal with the consequences.

Green Street is a one way street. Some say it's the wrong way, but for some it's the only way.

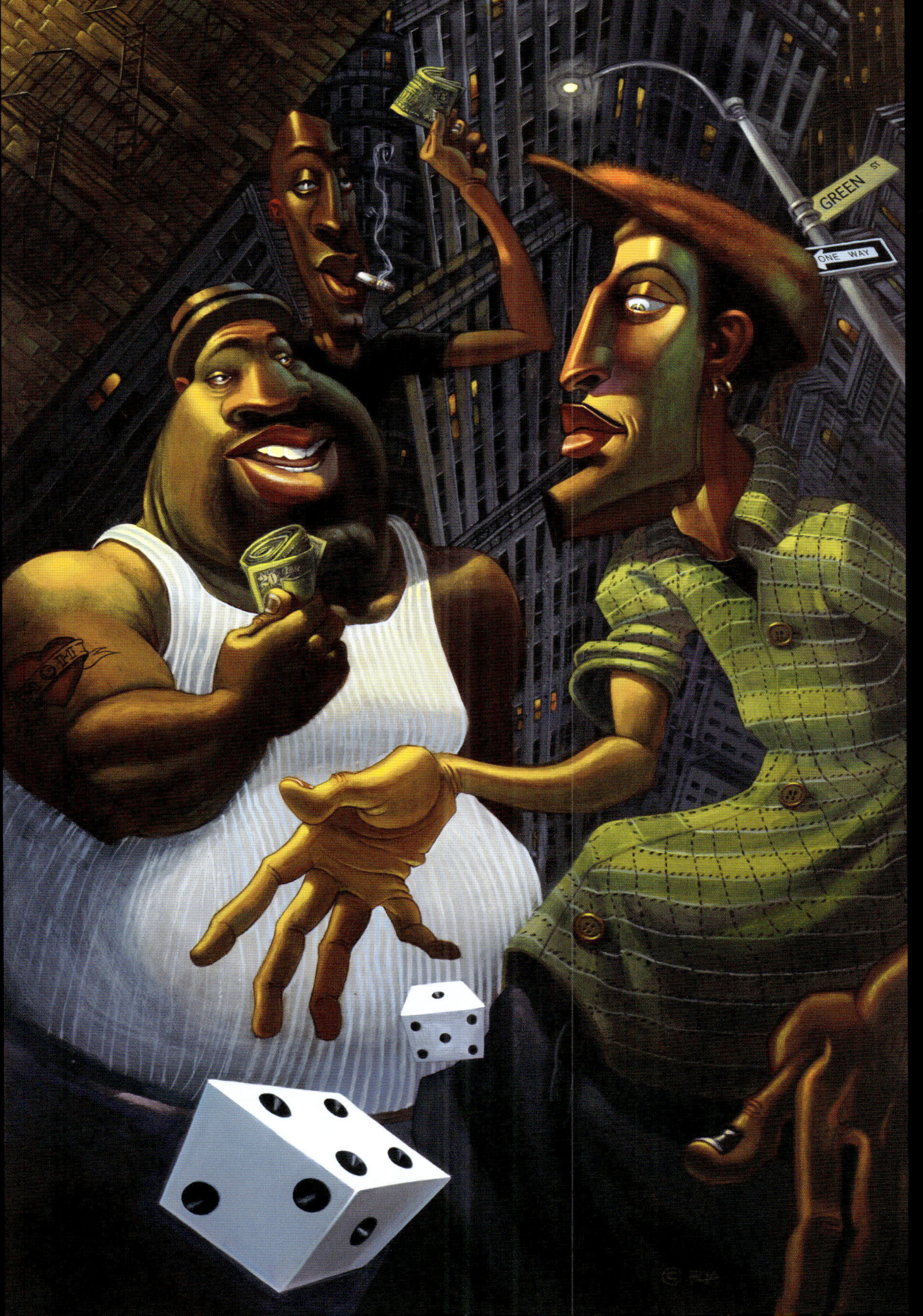
GREEN ST
ONE WAY

Piano Man II

Piano Man II is cool. He grew up listening to the tales told by old school jazz musicians like Piano Man. He takes pride in the masters, but he is humble and would never call himself a great musician; although everybody agrees that he is.

A true jazz lover, Piano Man II passes along the raw flavor of his jazz icons everywhere he goes. He pays respect to his piano by keeping his appearance elegant, sophisticated and refined. Women love him; there is something intangibly attractive about his essence. You just can't put your finger on it.

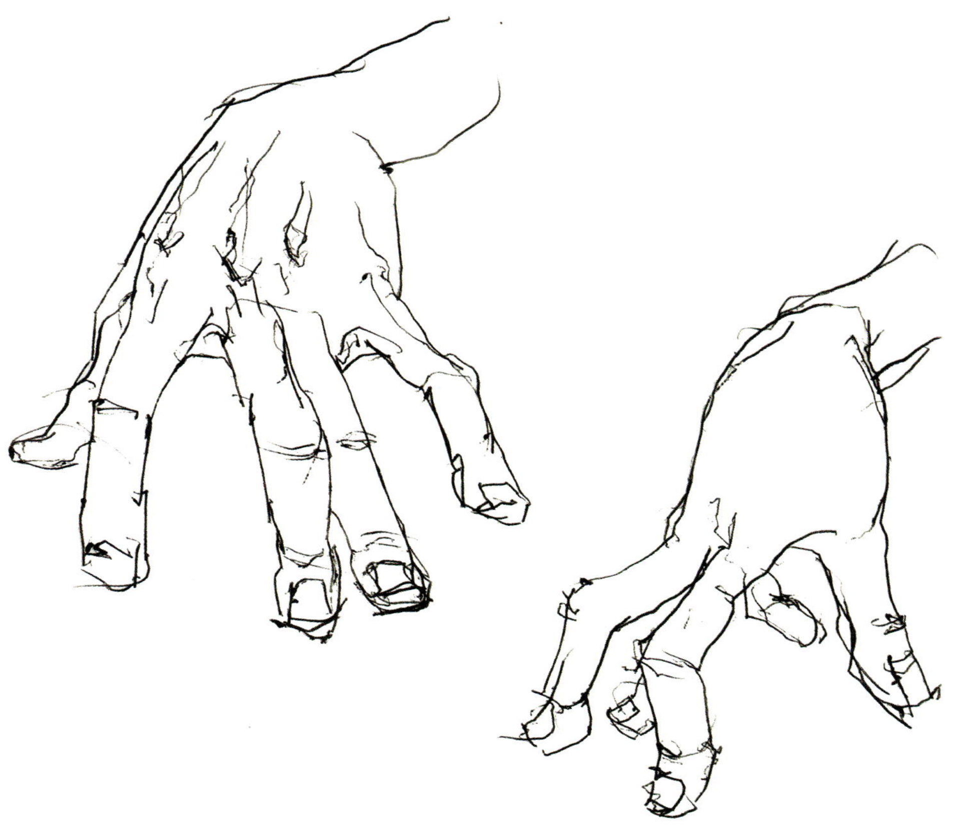

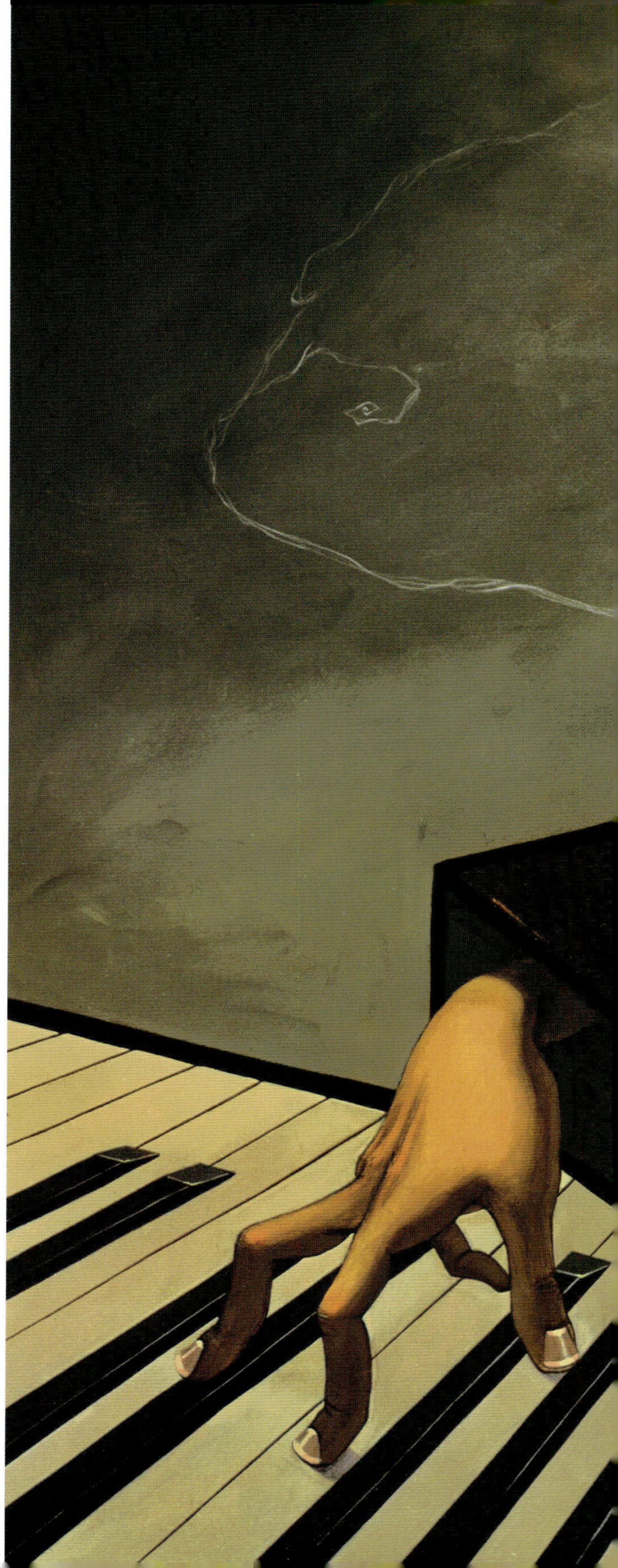

Piano Man II 1998
Acrylic on Canvas
48 in. x 36 in.

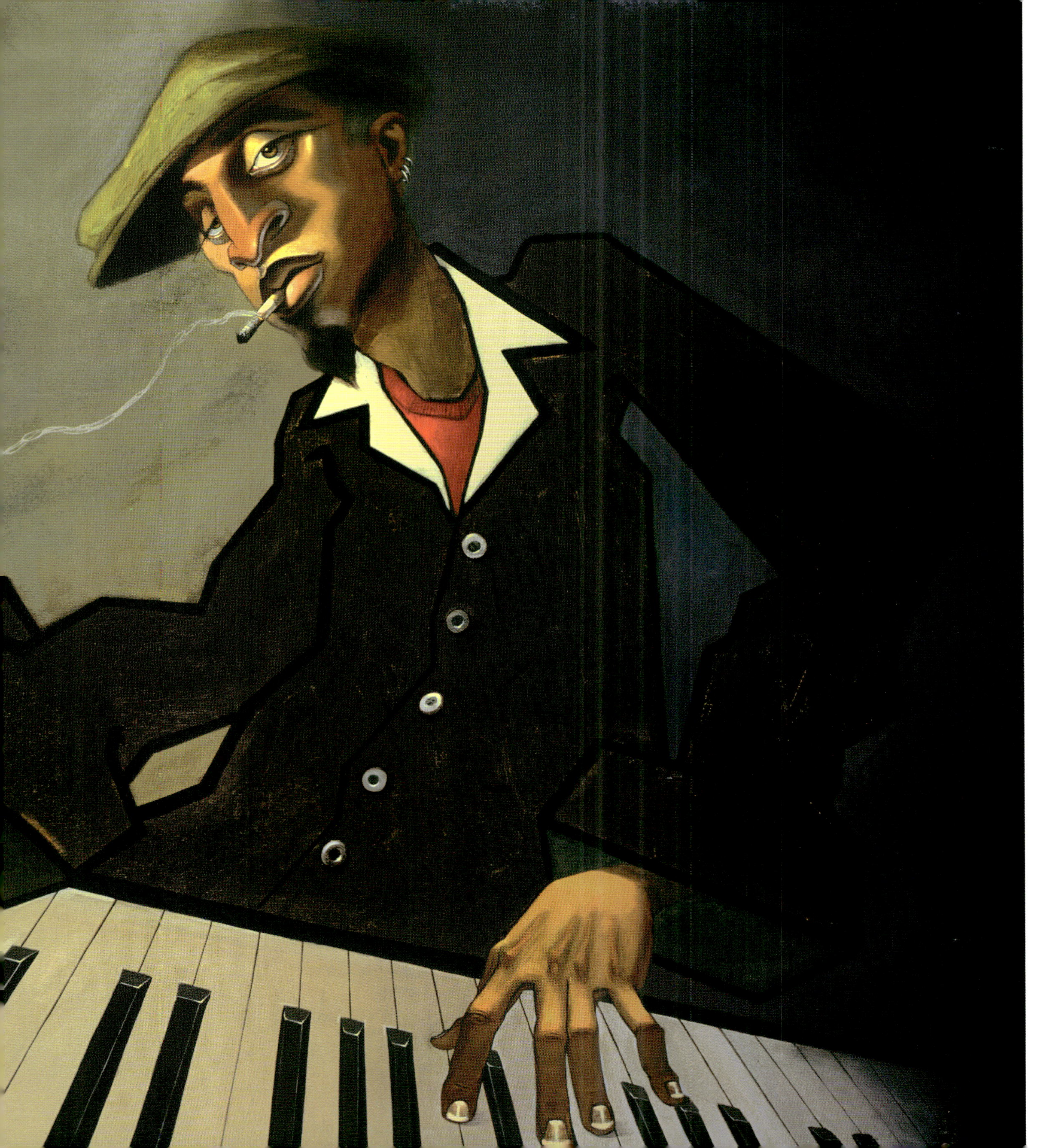

¿Como No?

¿Como Si? Como No.

This man is born from the loins of the inner city. Like the character, this piece flowed. It only took me a couple of days to paint it. I felt it. Como No has no past, no future. He is the moment. He is part of every urban landscape. He's chill, he's suave, and the ladies love him.

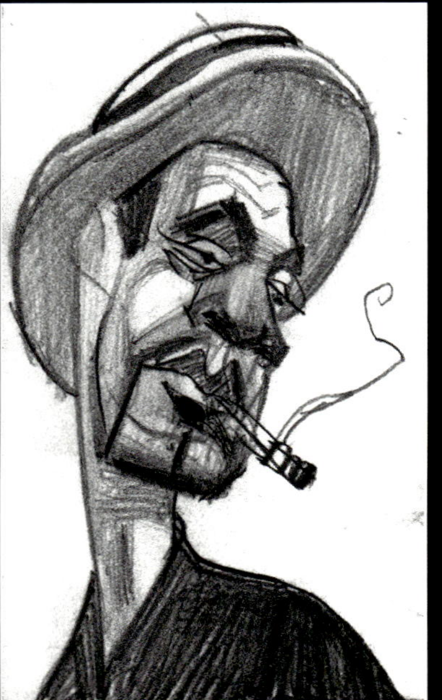

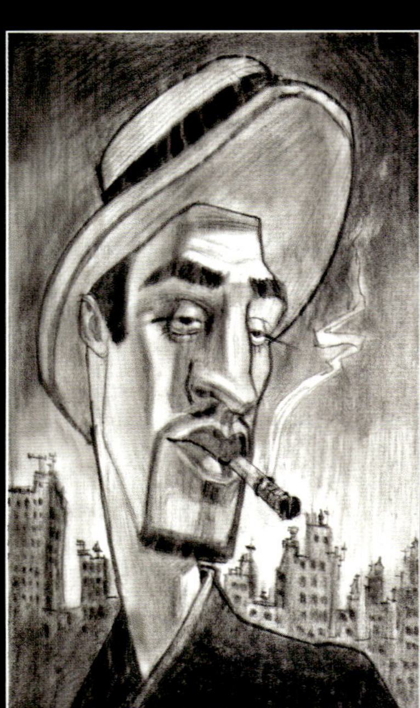

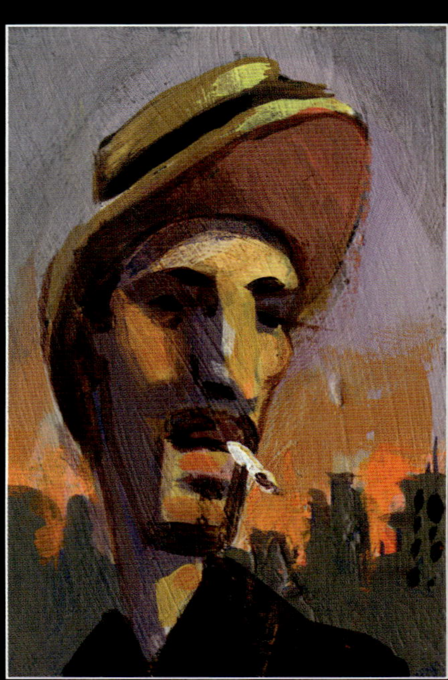

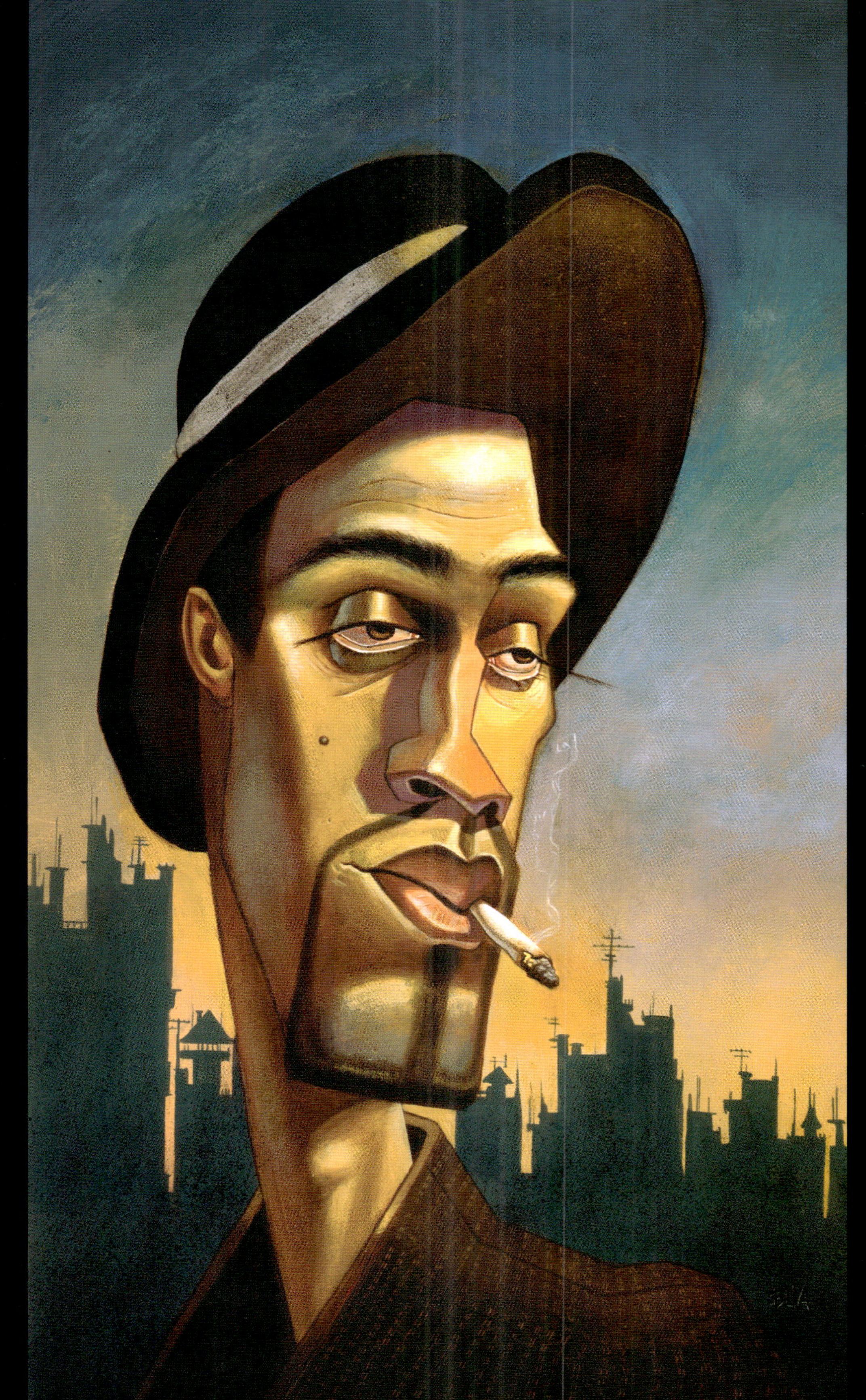

¿Como No? 1998
Acrylic on Illustration Board
17.25 in. x 26.5 in.

El Guitarrista

El Guitarrista plays his guitar out of love. He has no audience. He's not about fame or money. It's not even on his mind. Only music. He plays because he has to; music is his language.

If you listen, you can hear his music coming from the rooftops. He brings you into his world. Tranquillo.

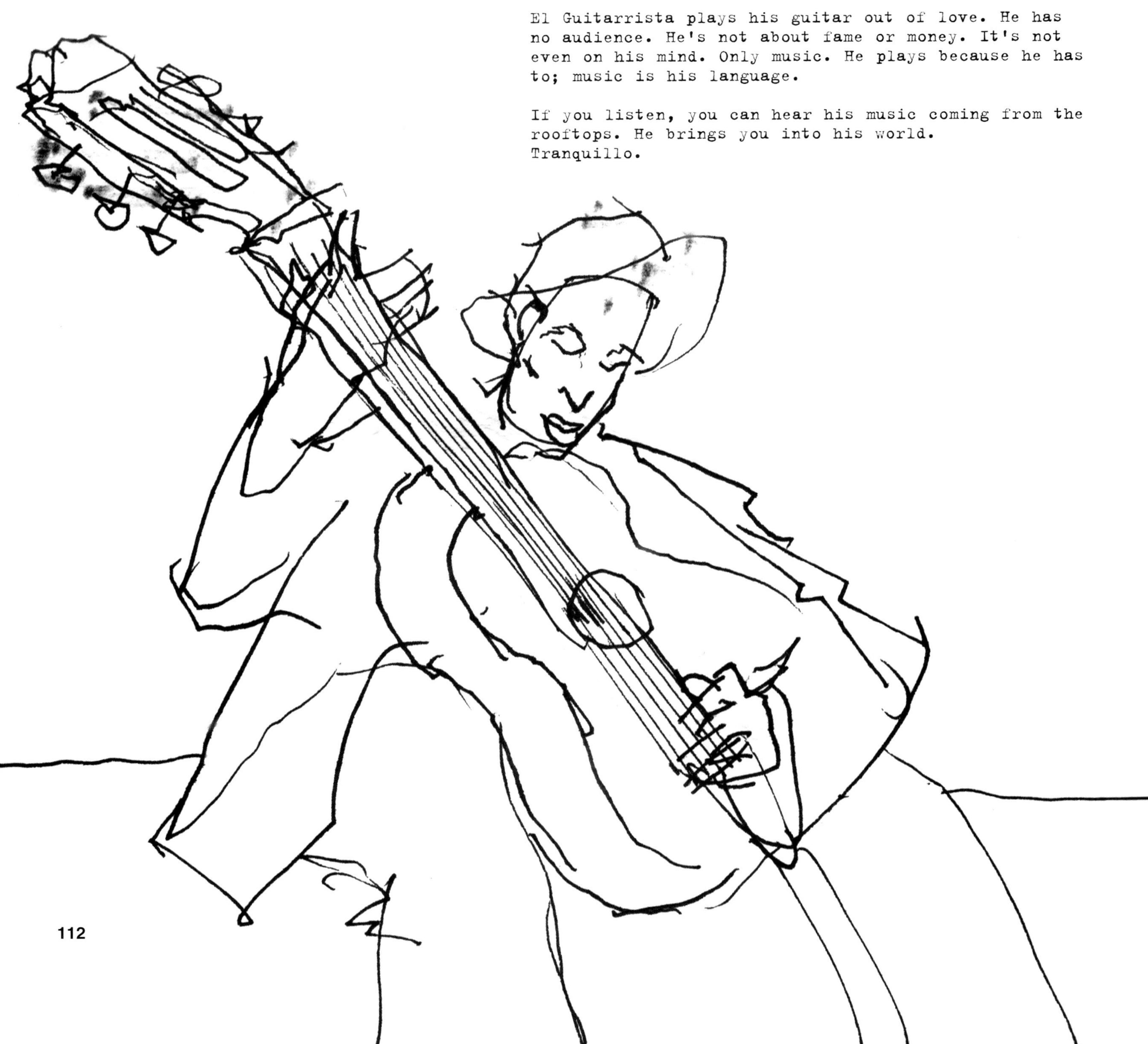

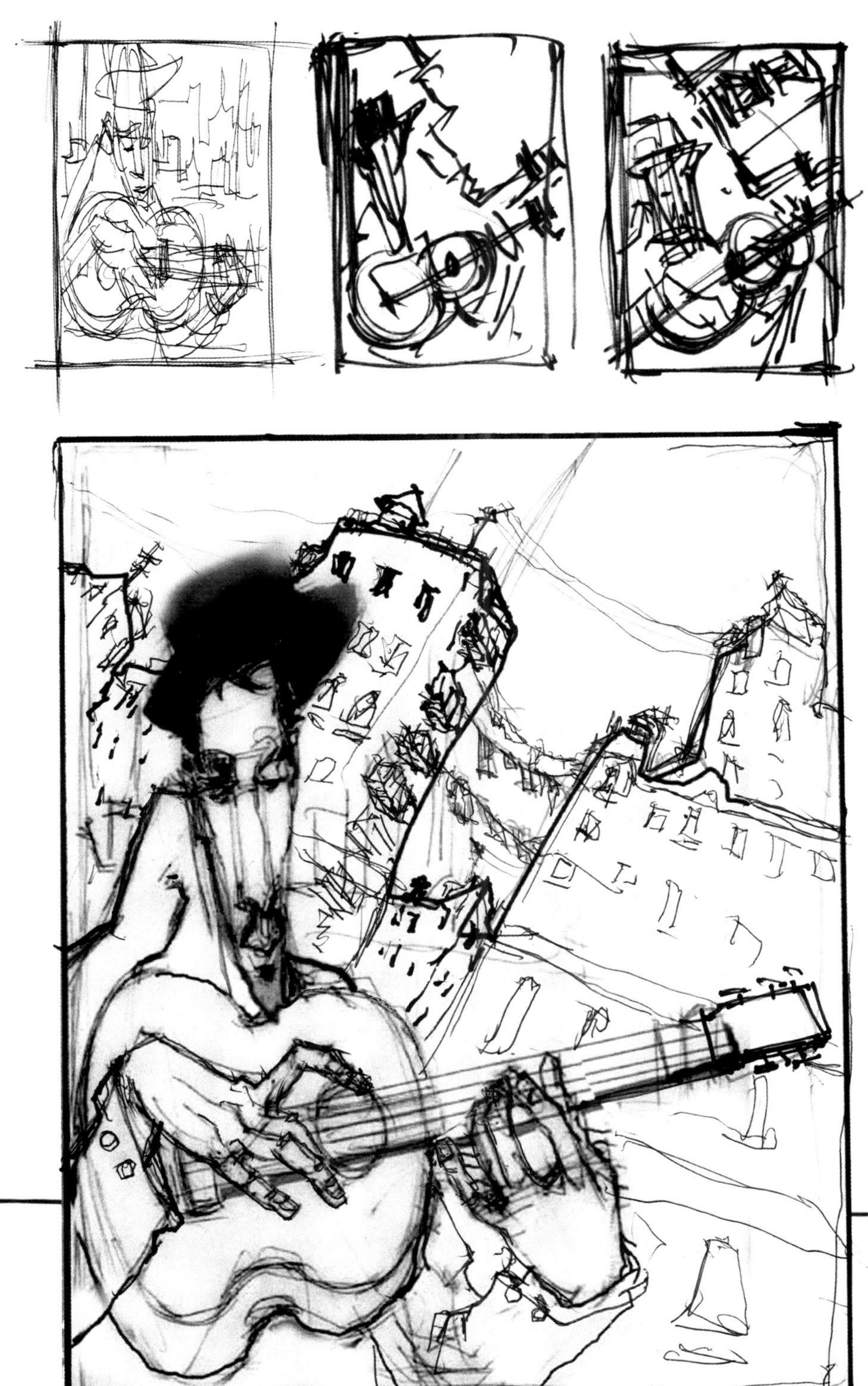

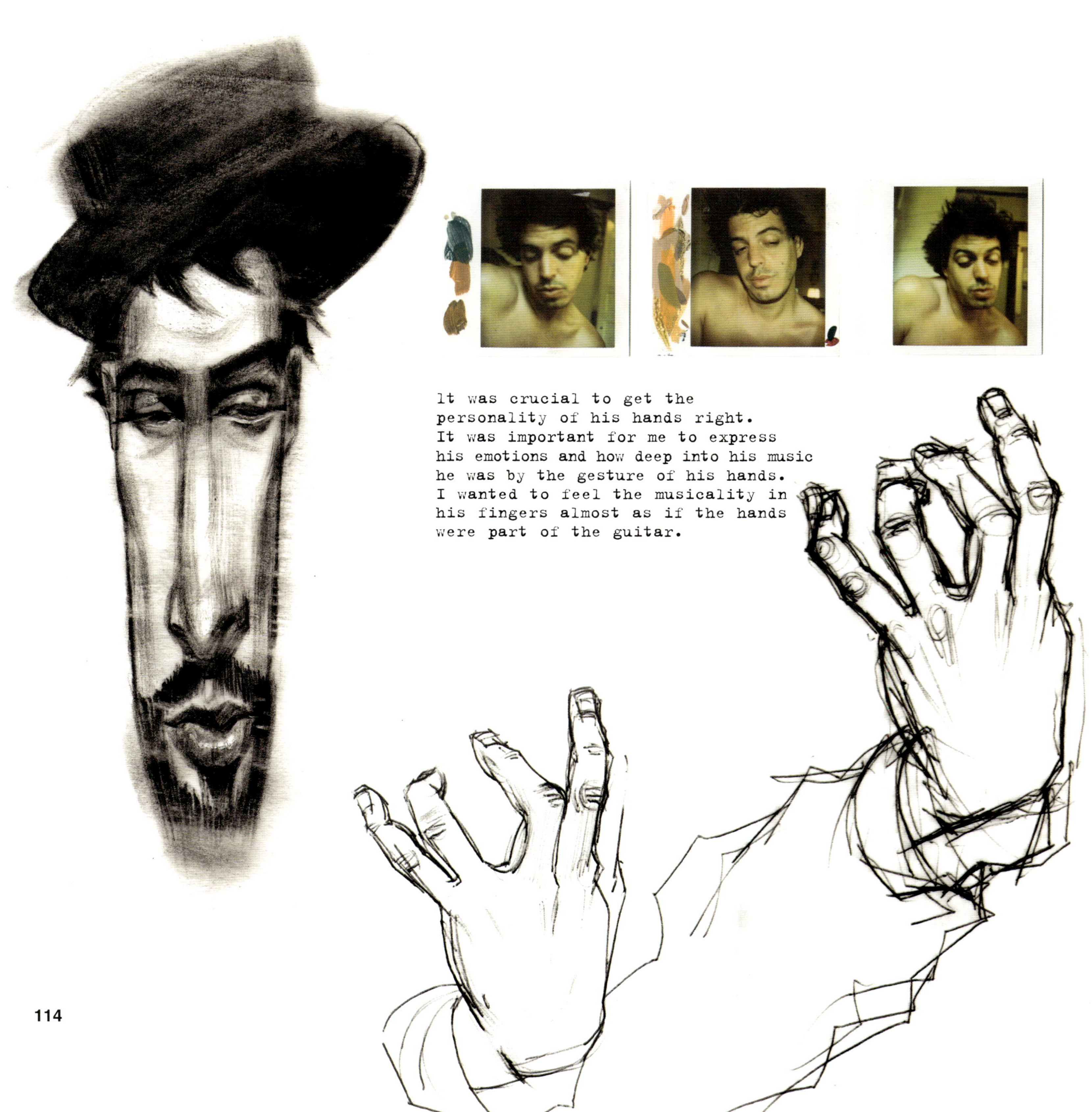

It was crucial to get the personality of his hands right. It was important for me to express his emotions and how deep into his music he was by the gesture of his hands. I wanted to feel the musicality in his fingers almost as if the hands were part of the guitar.

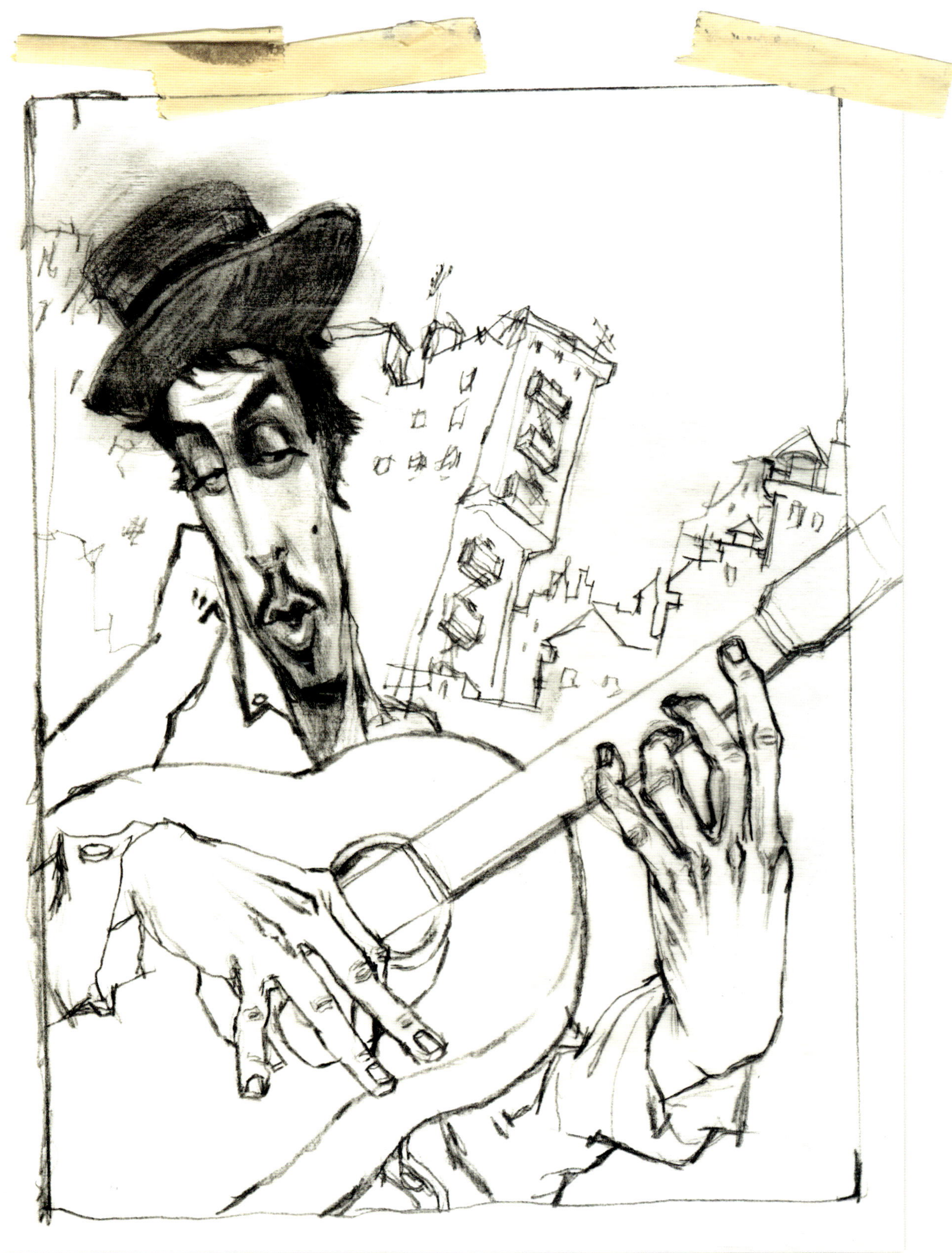

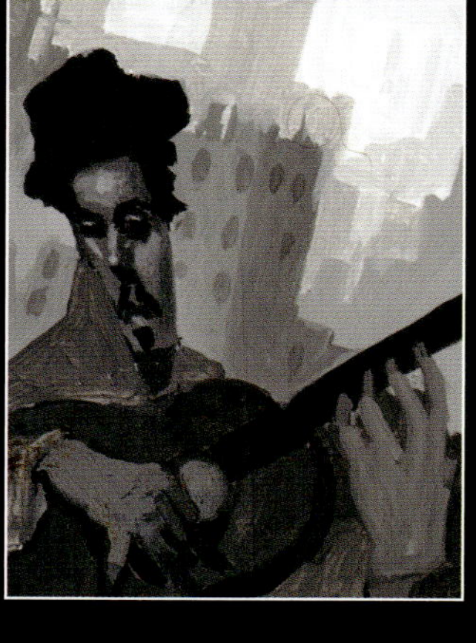
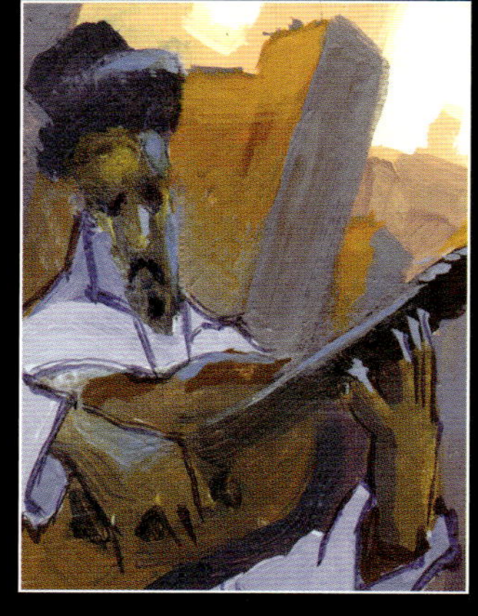
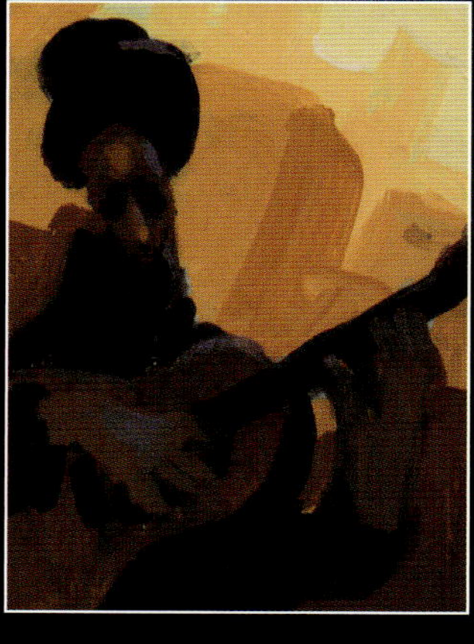
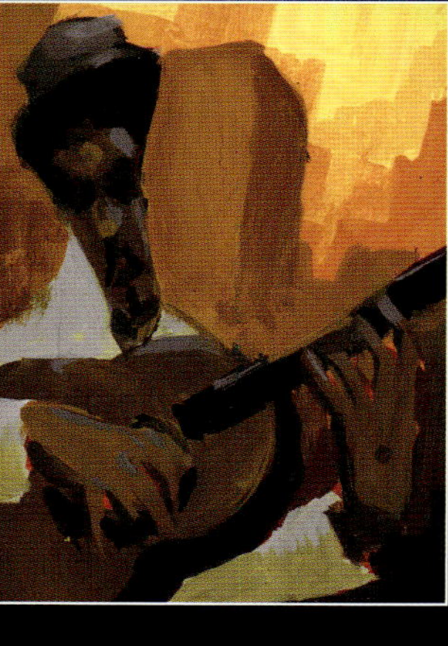

More color keys than usual were necessary for this painting because the color really conveyed the time of day and set the mood I wanted. If I nailed the feeling in my color keys, then I could avoid repainting on the actual painting later on.

Even though it was important to get the color key on point, the values were even more important. If you have the wrong value, you can be completely lost—even if you have the right color. With a good value key, the form, shapes, and perspective can still be articulated. You can squint your eyes and shapes hold together and make sense.

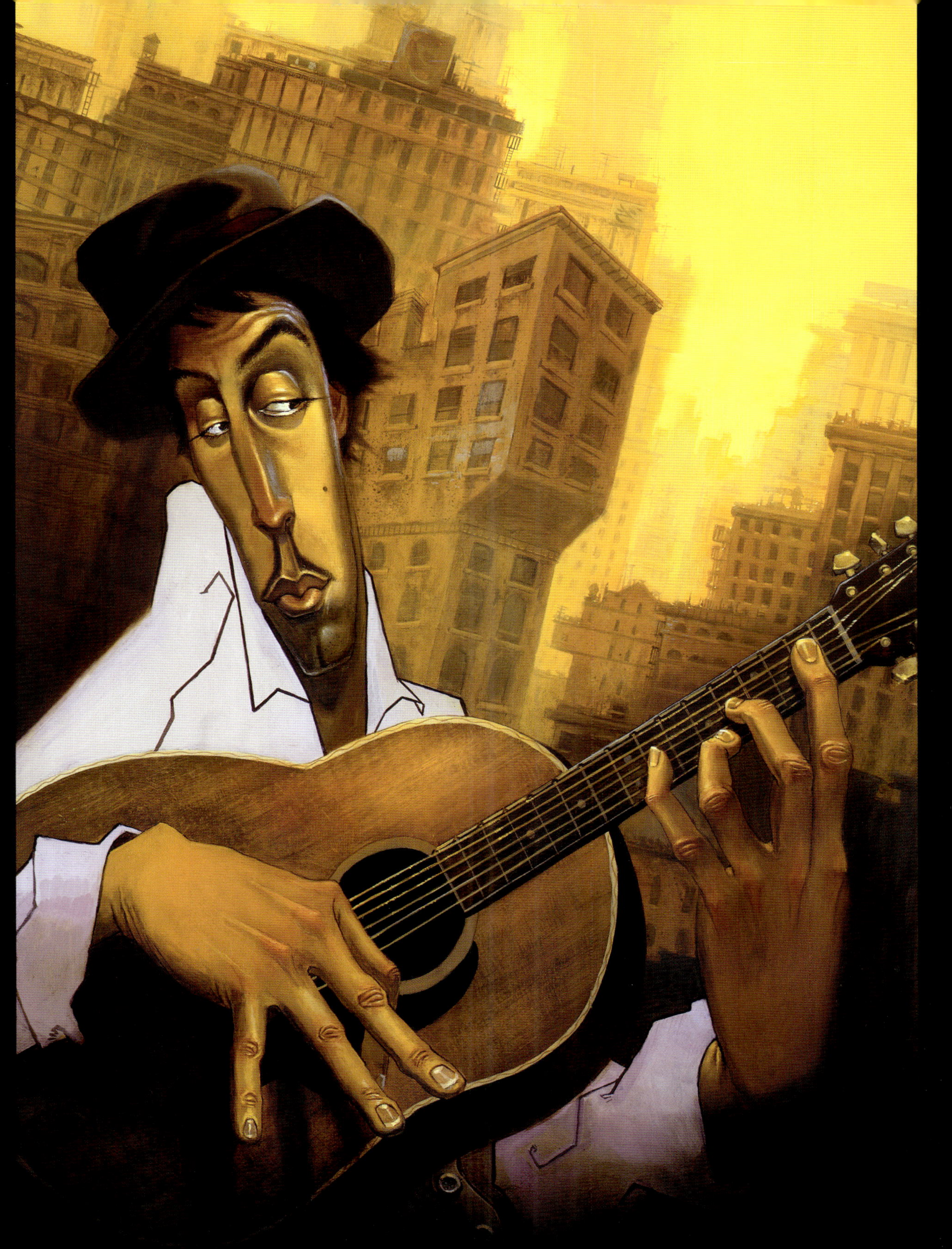

THE DJ

I wanted to paint a DJ for a long time. Some people said it wasn't a good idea because DJs were "too underground," but the DJ is an urban legend; controlling the break for the breaker to bust and the beats for the MC to rap to. The DJ is a hero of my generation.

One day sitting around, I sketched a DJ and I said, "This is something I have to do." This is that first sketch.

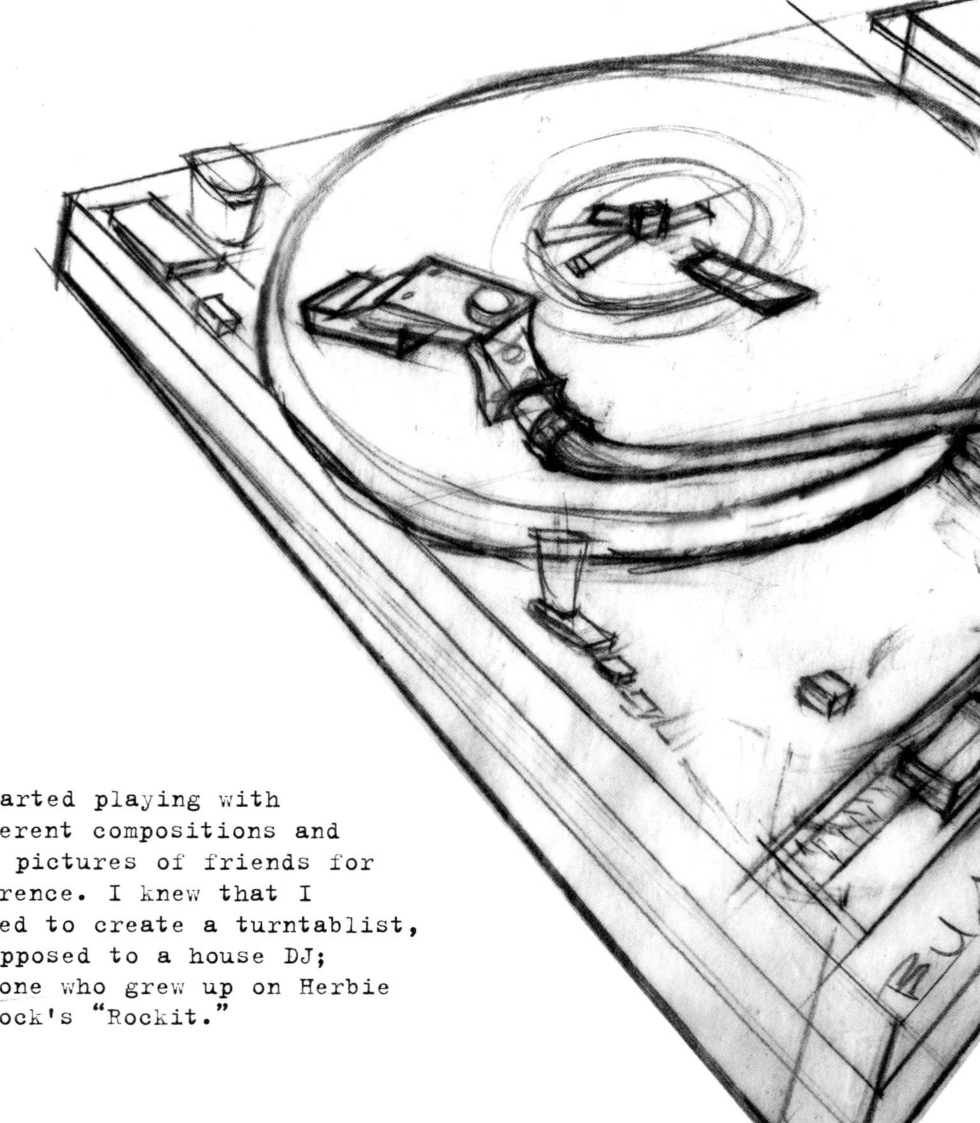

I started playing with different compositions and took pictures of friends for reference. I knew that I wanted to create a turntablist, as opposed to a house DJ; someone who grew up on Herbie Hancock's "Rockit."

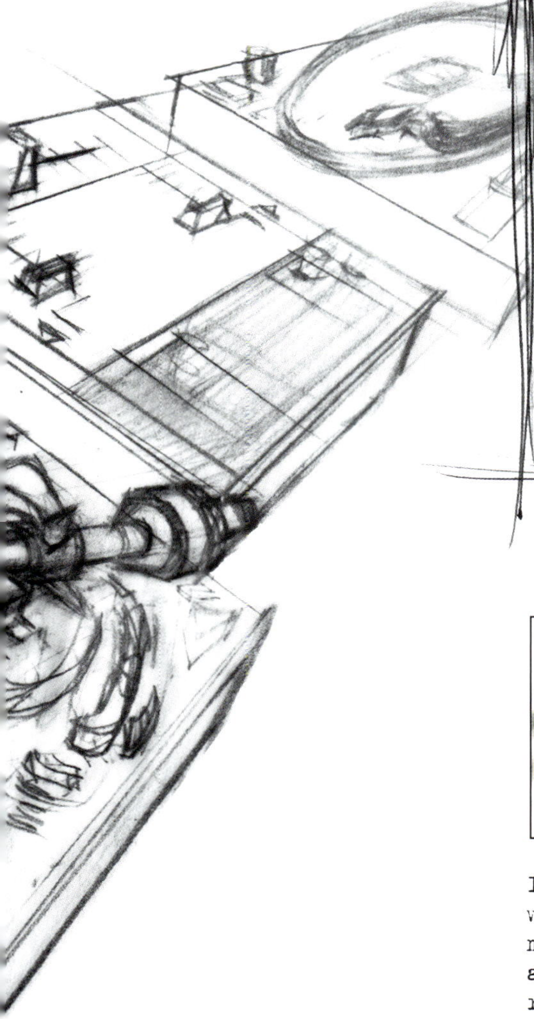

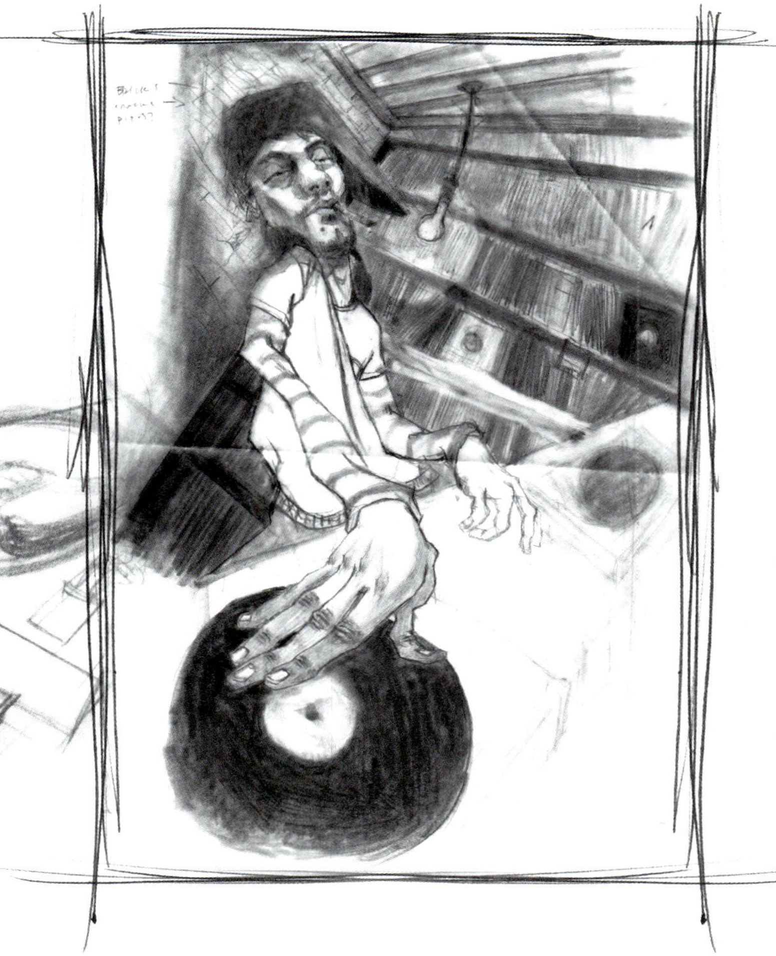

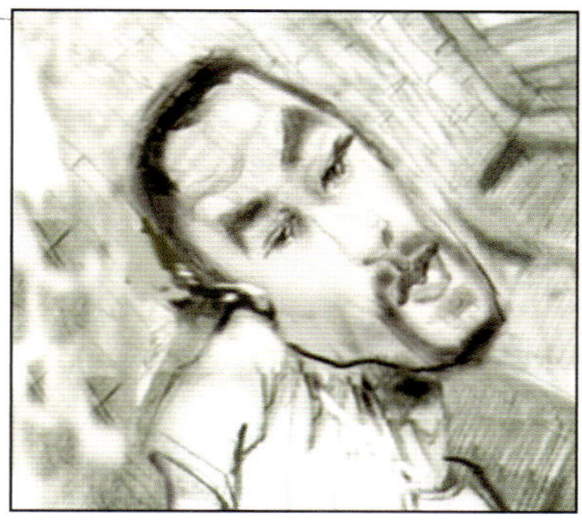

I wanted to put the DJ in a true environment, a place where he was surrounded by the tools of his trade, objects that would define him and all the things that make him who he is. All the "digging" he did created this towering wall of vinyl. He's in the zone with just a single light bulb, his turntables, and records.

With no one to impress, he spins alone.

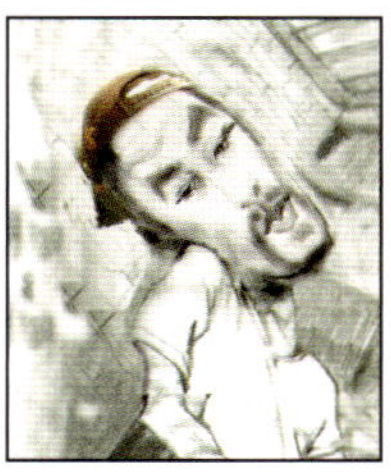

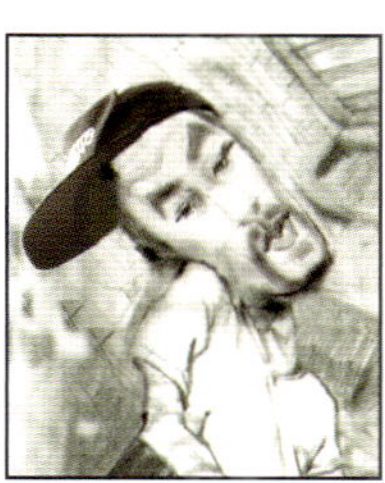

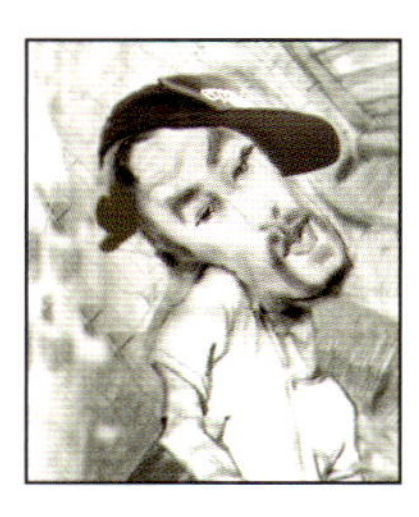

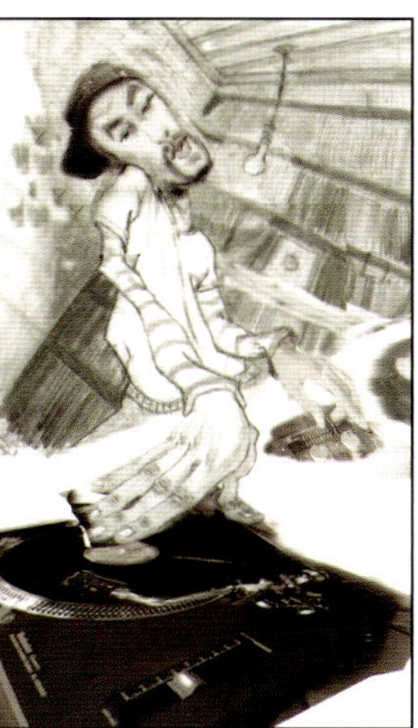

I realized during this piece that the DJ's hat was going to be very important as it says so much about his personality. I had to get the angle just right to convey his dedication and represent his cool, genuine, bona fide flava. A little to the left could be really dorky and too far back could be trying too hard. I had to have the hat in the perfect spot, so I messed around with it and I thought that this one, off at an angle, slightly to the side and back, was the coolest.

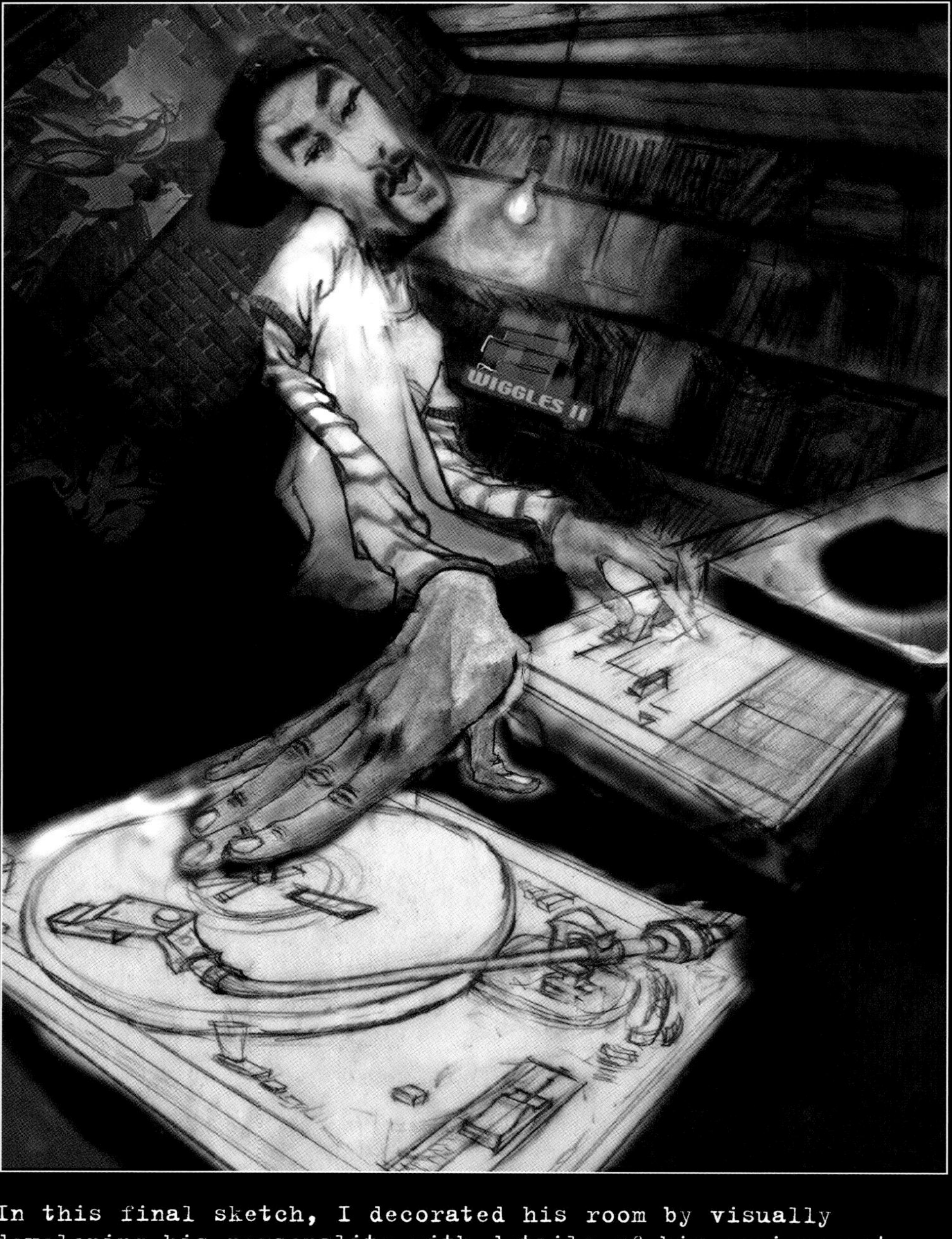

In this final sketch, I decorated his room by visually developing his personality with details of his environment. I got into his head to figure out what he would hang in his world. I envisioned him having a Mr. Wiggles II VHS tape on his shelf, a BUA basketball poster, and a graffiti piece on his wall...

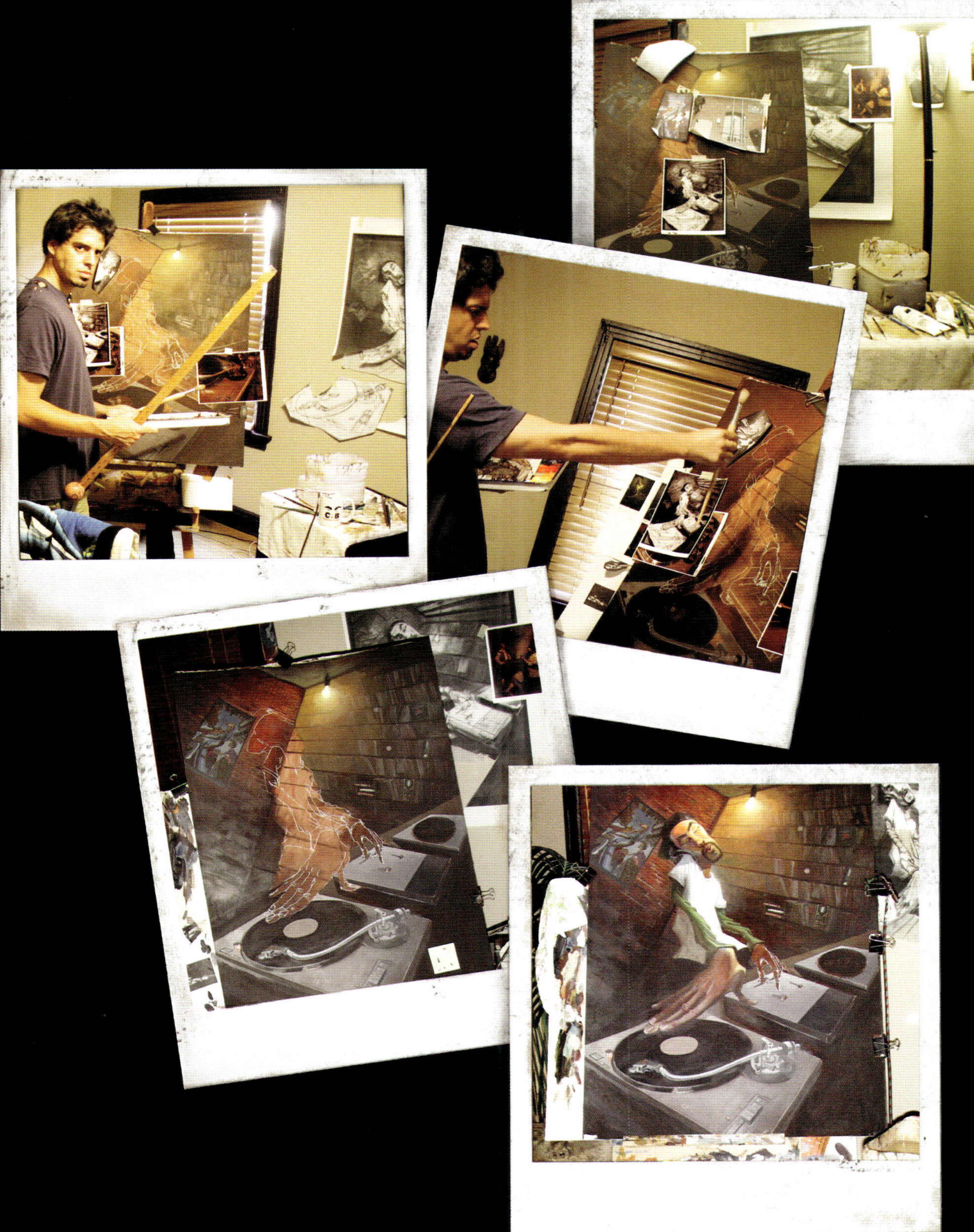

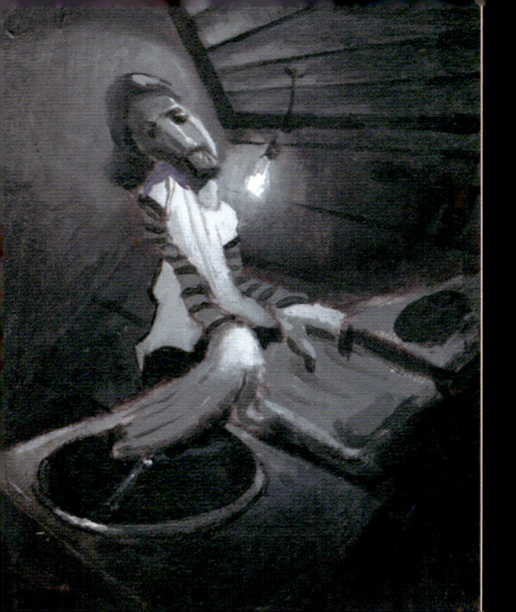
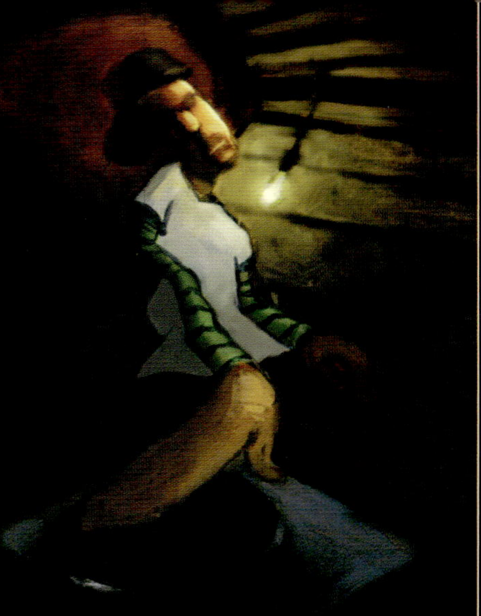
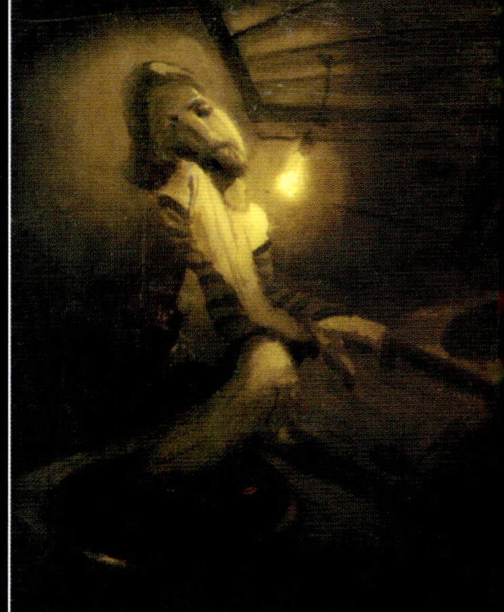

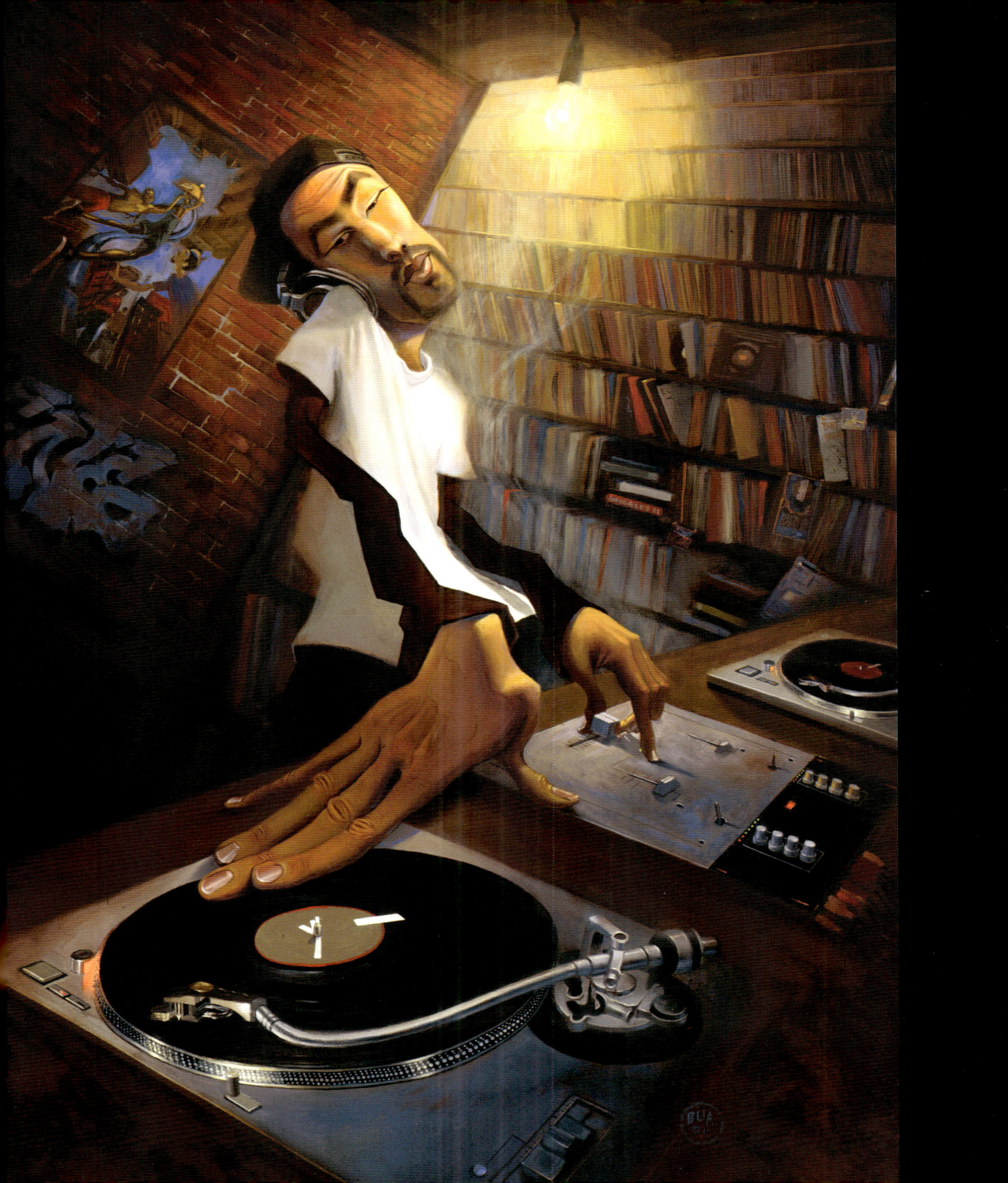

Opposite:
BUA 420 2002
Acrylic on Illustration Board
17 in. x 21.5 in.

BUA420

This is a nostalgic reflection of life back at the NYC train yards. Going out to write graffiti was exciting. This is a piece I felt strongly about getting out there. The writing on the train says, "Graf Is Art." I think there is a misconception about graffiti. Graffiti is an art; most think that it is not. I'm not talking about tagging. I'm talking about pieces, murals, letters. The art of lettering has been taught in schools around the world for centuries. Graffiti is at the very least a progression of the evolution of typography. At its best, it is a high art.

In my youth the trains were dirty, dark, and broken down. Graf gave the trains more character, more flavor. The yard was our gallery.

Some people in New York used to look forward to the next train pulling in so they could check out the latest works of art. But when the new "graffiti-proof" trains came in the early '90s it changed the whole dynamic for young artists. The trains became boring and sterile. It marked the end of a great artistic era led by freedom of expression, spontaneity, and individualism.

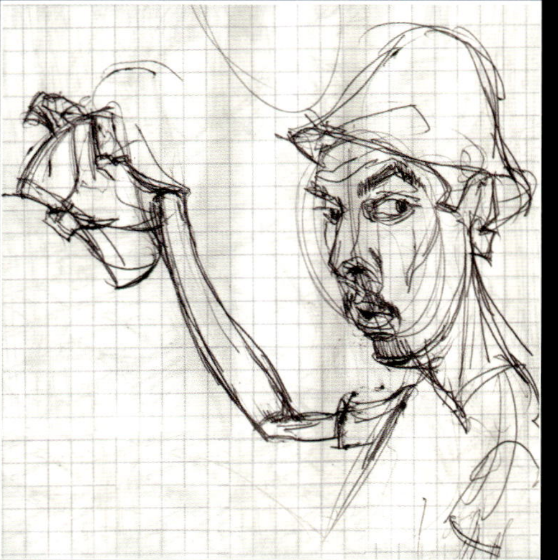

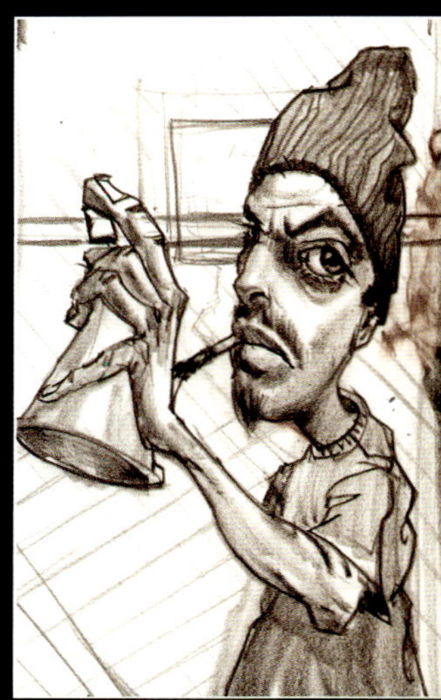

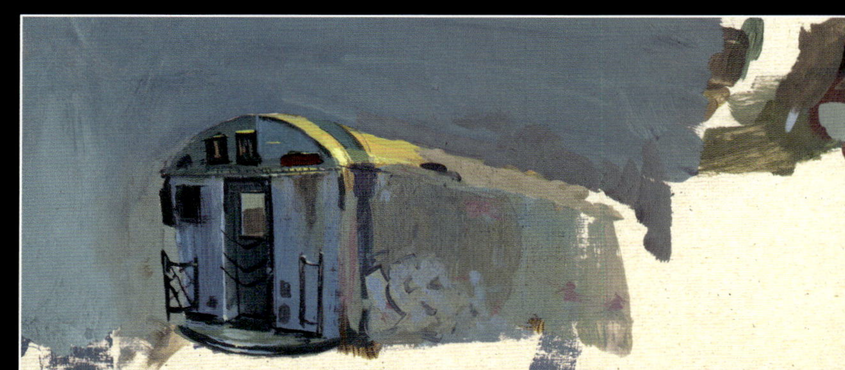

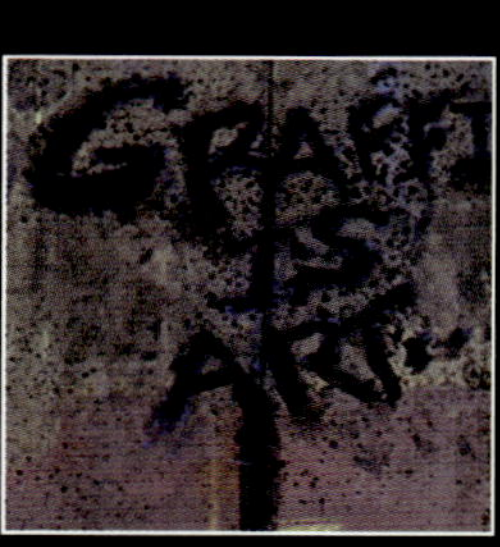

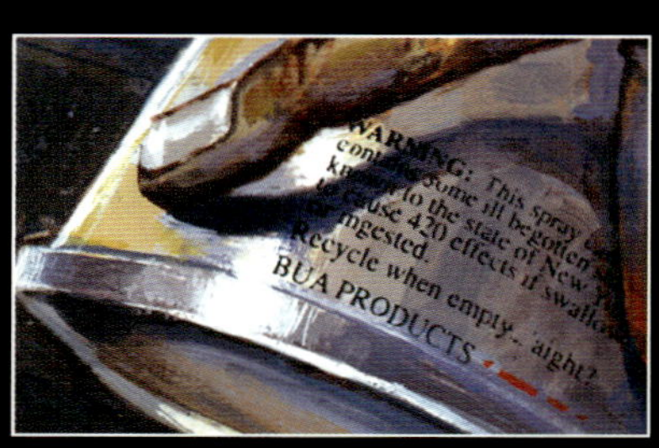

These giant steel worms traveling from tunnel to tunnel were huge canvasses for kids who had no platform for their creative expression; no place to draw and paint.

There was no funding for art in the inner cities. So young artists went to the streets, to the yards to be seen and to be recognized.

They wanted to express themselves because we as human beings have an inner need and desire to be creative. There is a whole generation of artists that were

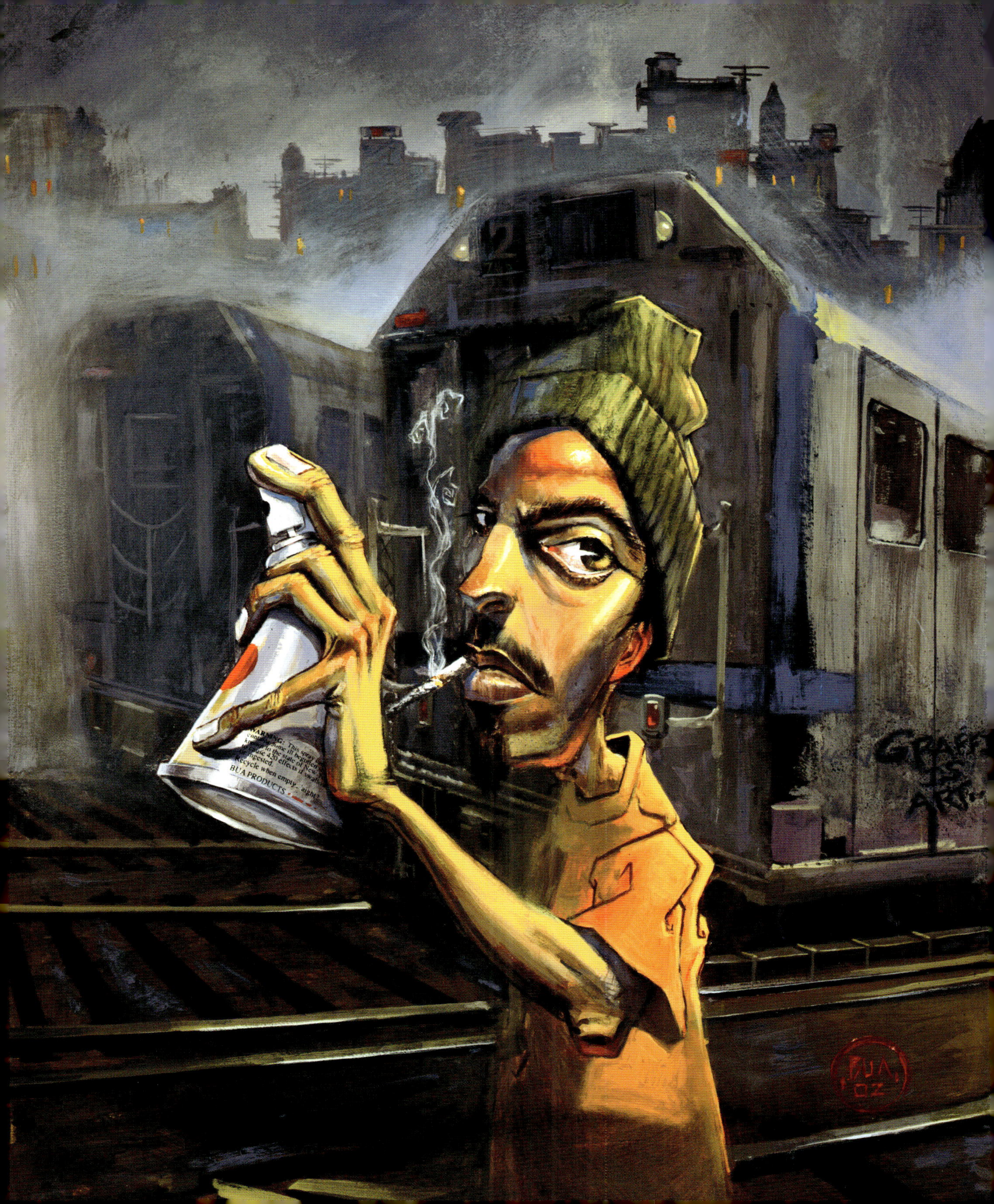
2
Recycle when empty
BUA PRODUCTS
GRAFF
IS
ART...
BUA
02

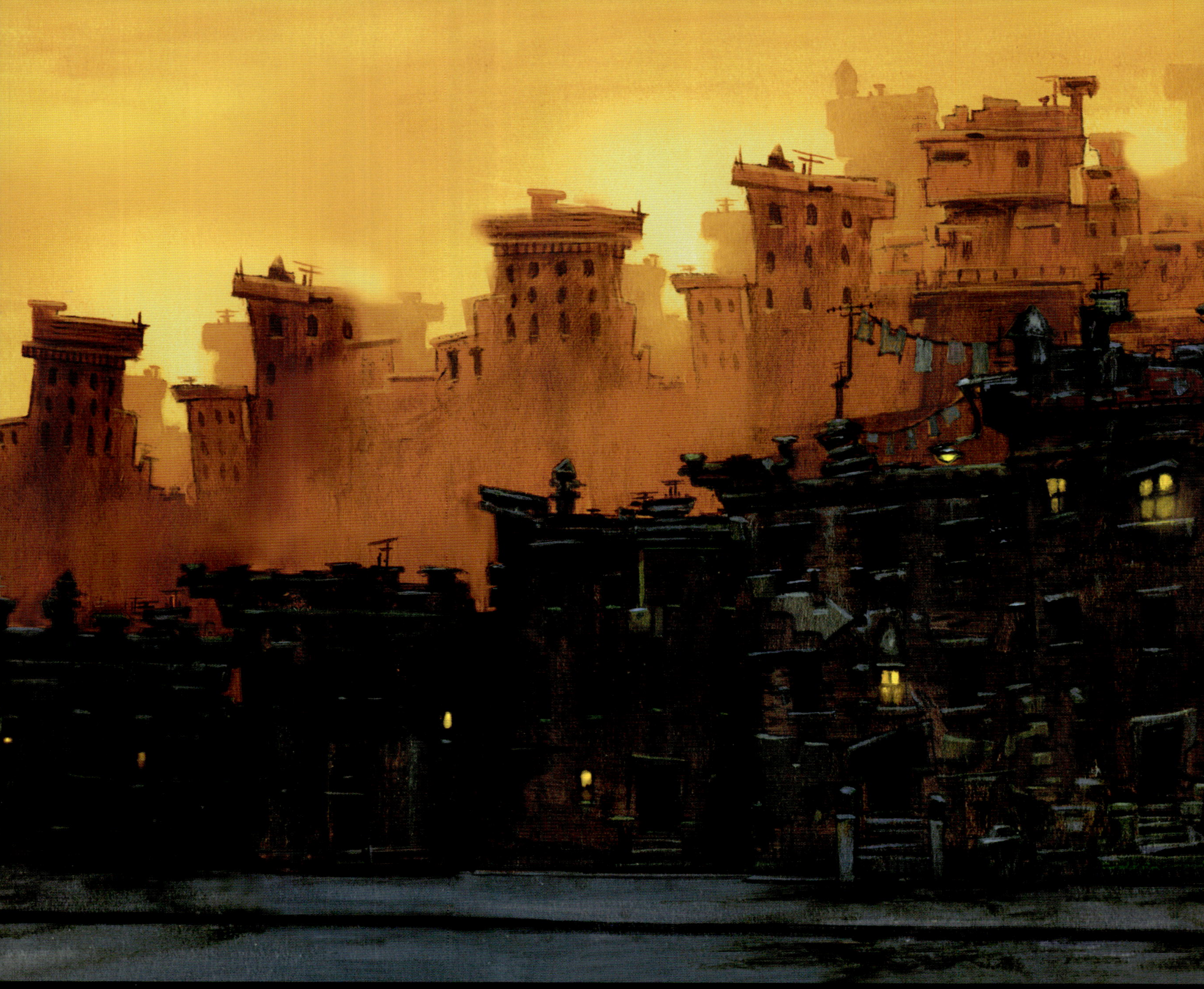

The Block

"The Block" is my perception of an urban landscape. Most landscapes are of nature: hills, valleys, trees...I wanted to do an architectural cityscape that represented my world, my surroundings. This is the block where my characters live.

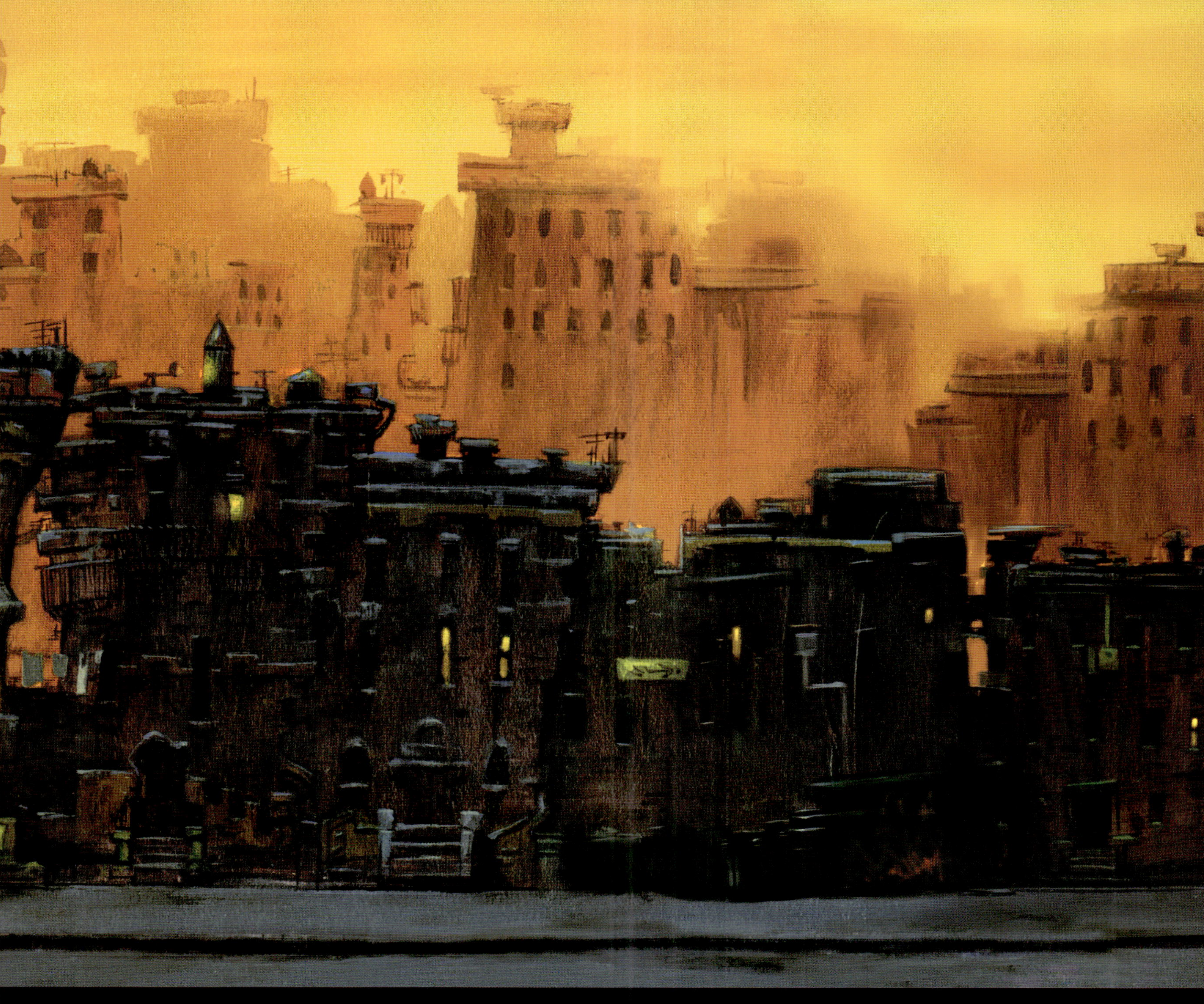

The Block 2003
Acrylic on Canvas
29.5 in. x 11.5 in.

Smokers

In the city we can be so disconnected from nature that we don't even notice that there are no plants, no trees, and no room to breathe. We've become removed from life, from our true gut instinct. There's something ironic about the connection between man and the man-made city. We've made so much "progress," yet in doing this, we've created an unnatural, toxic environment.

In this painting, the world is polluted, toxic, and forgotten almost like a modern day T. S. Eliott's "Wasteland." This piece represents the darkness of the city. The guy smokes as the smoke stacks spew; his eyes are glazed with malaise. Like the graffiti on the wall, The Smoker blends in with his environment. He has become a part of it. His back is turned as if unaware of the factory and his hands are crossed passively behind him.

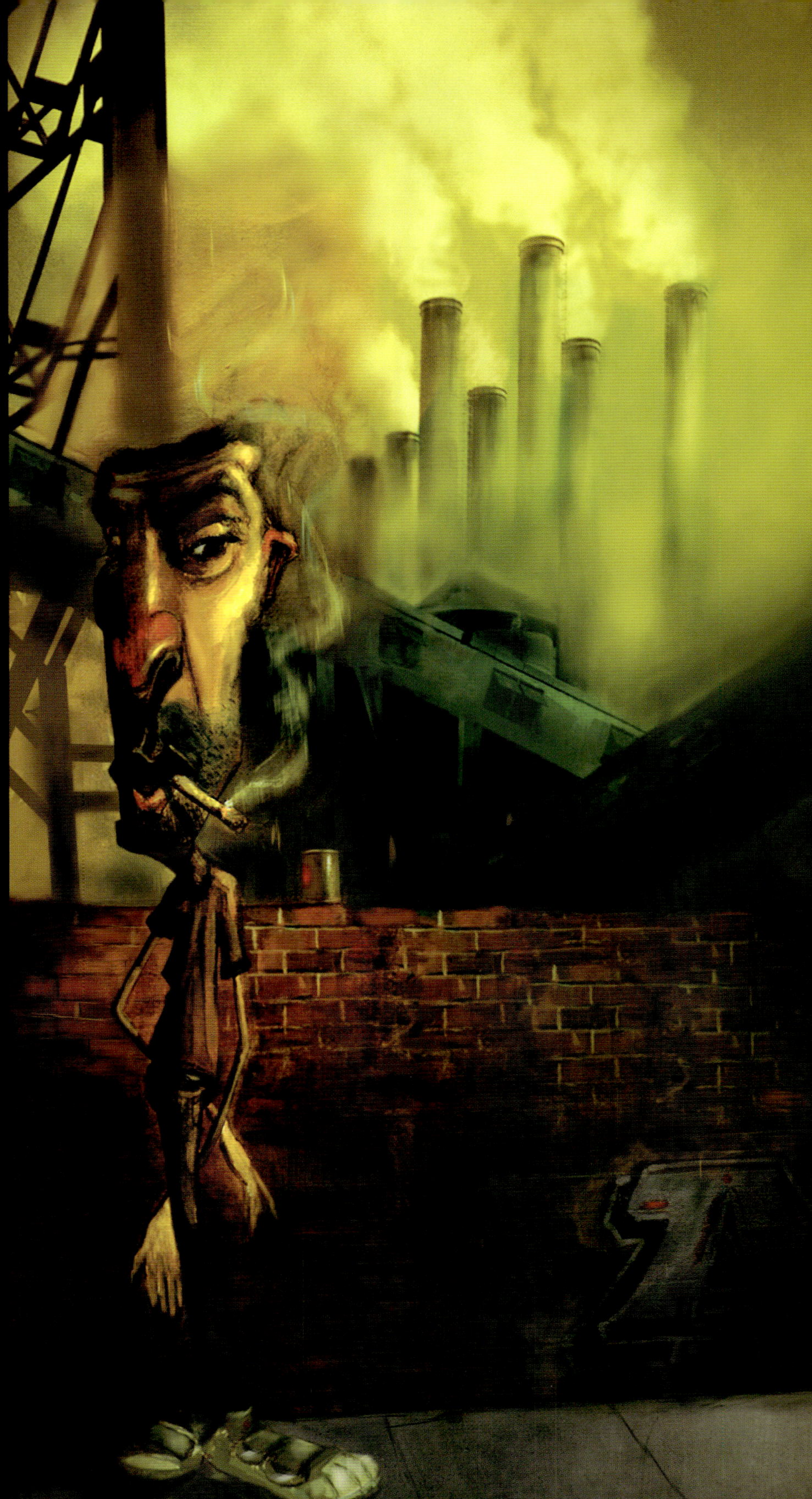

Smokers 2002
Acrylic on Canvas
9 in. x 17.5 in.

Somethin's Going On

New York City is so diversified yet separated. You could be on the right side of the street one second, and the next you might find yourself on the wrong side with no friends.

Anyone who has walked in a sketchy area in the 'hood late at night can relate to the paranoid need to watch your back. I grew up with the awareness that there could be something about to go down. These emotions make you alert, make you tap into your primal instincts. That's the mode this sketcher's in.

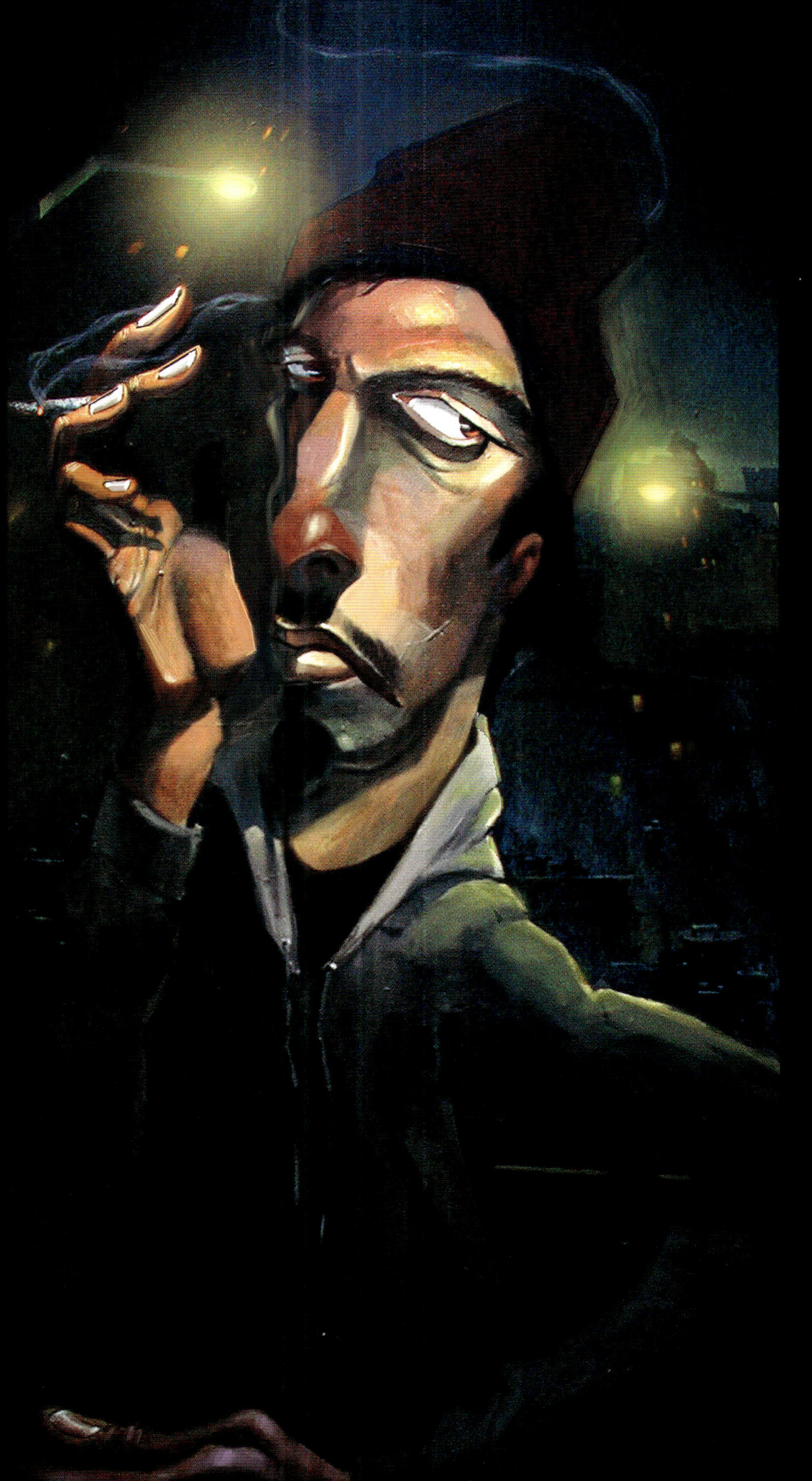

Somethin's Going On 2003
Acrylic on Canvas
24 in. x 48 in.

THE MC

Front and center the MC spits the rhymes that, like Big Daddy Kane says, "co-rock a party 'til the a.m....and captivate the whole crowd majority." In the beginning the MC worked in harmony with the DJ and the B-Boy. The DJ provided the beats, the MC the rhymes, and the B-Boy, the dance. The MC soon took center stage.

The MC is known as the "Microphone Checker," the "Mic Controller," "Mista Cool," and the one who "Moves the Crowd," but the original meaning is the "Master of Ceremonies."

This piece is my Hip-Hop version of Art Nouveau. The design of The MC was inspired by the graphicness of the Art Nouveau movement which stylistically captures the undulating, flowing, organic rhythms of nature. In "The MC," I wanted to capture the tribal, urban rhythms of nature. There is an angular, funky flow in the lines of the mic wire and the MC's clothes are rhythmically similar to the words, music, passion, and dance of Hip-Hop.

Incoroporating the graphic title into the piece was an opportunity to give the MC his original old school crown, which embodies his power to move a crowd with his lyrics. He has the potential not only to entertain but also to change the world by teaching his unique philosophies and wisdoms to the people.

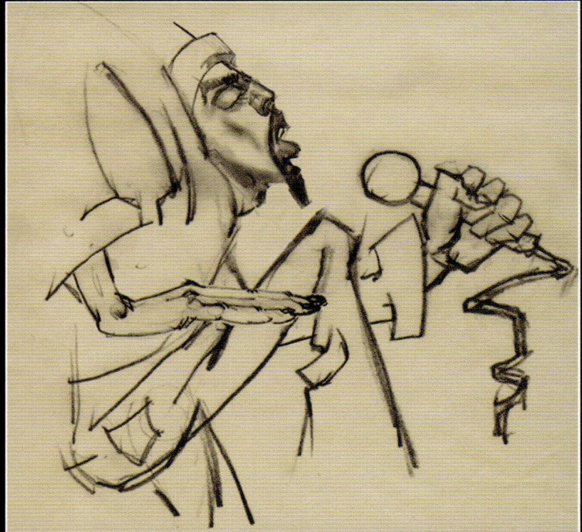

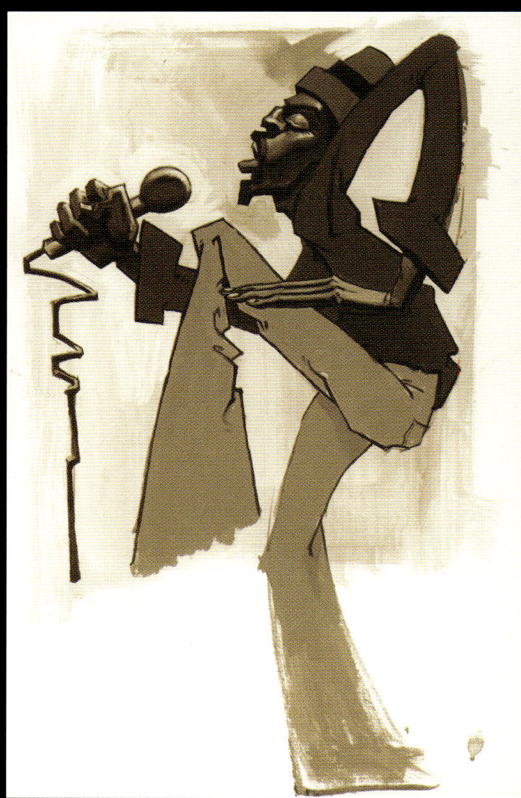

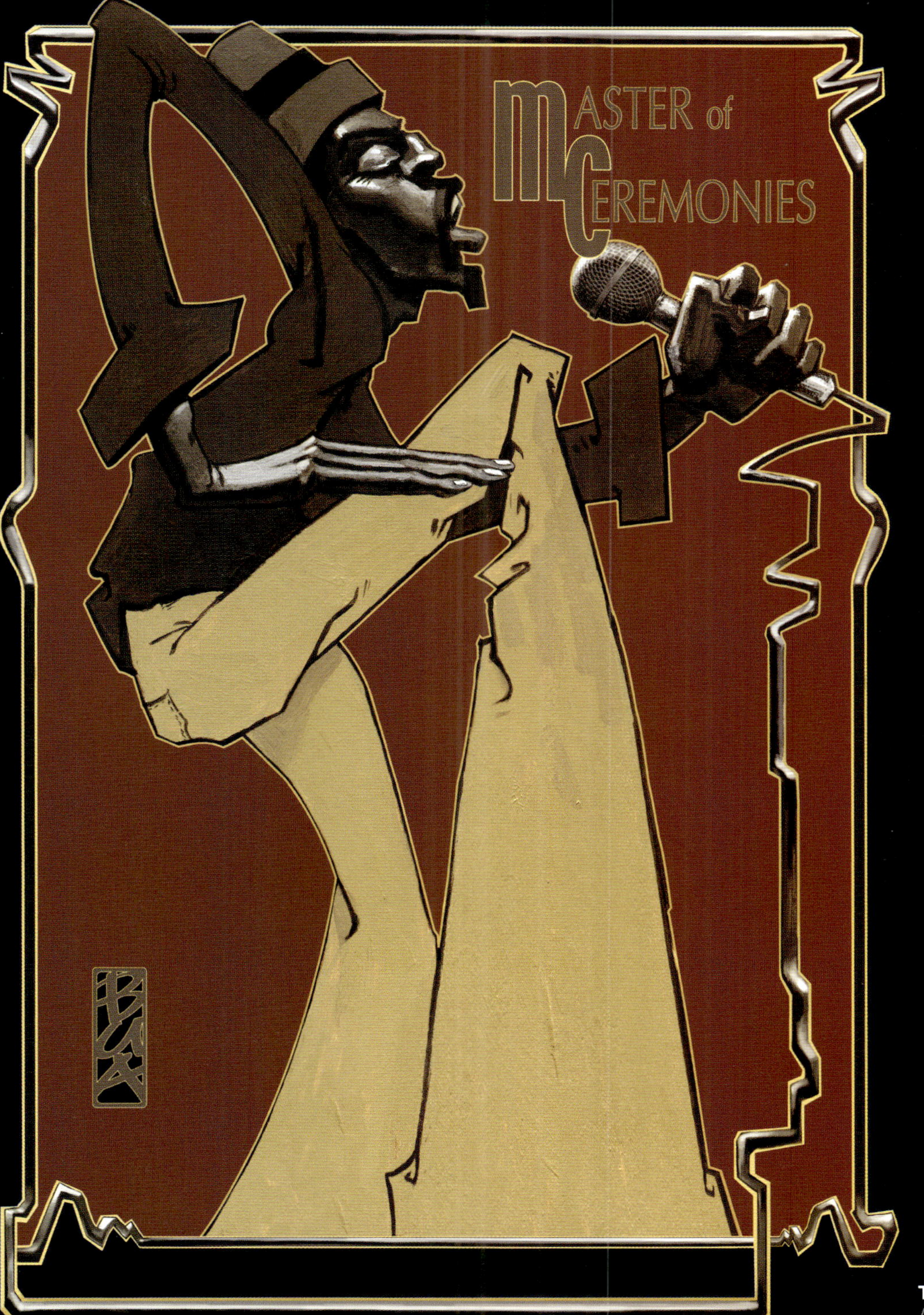

The MC
Acrylic o

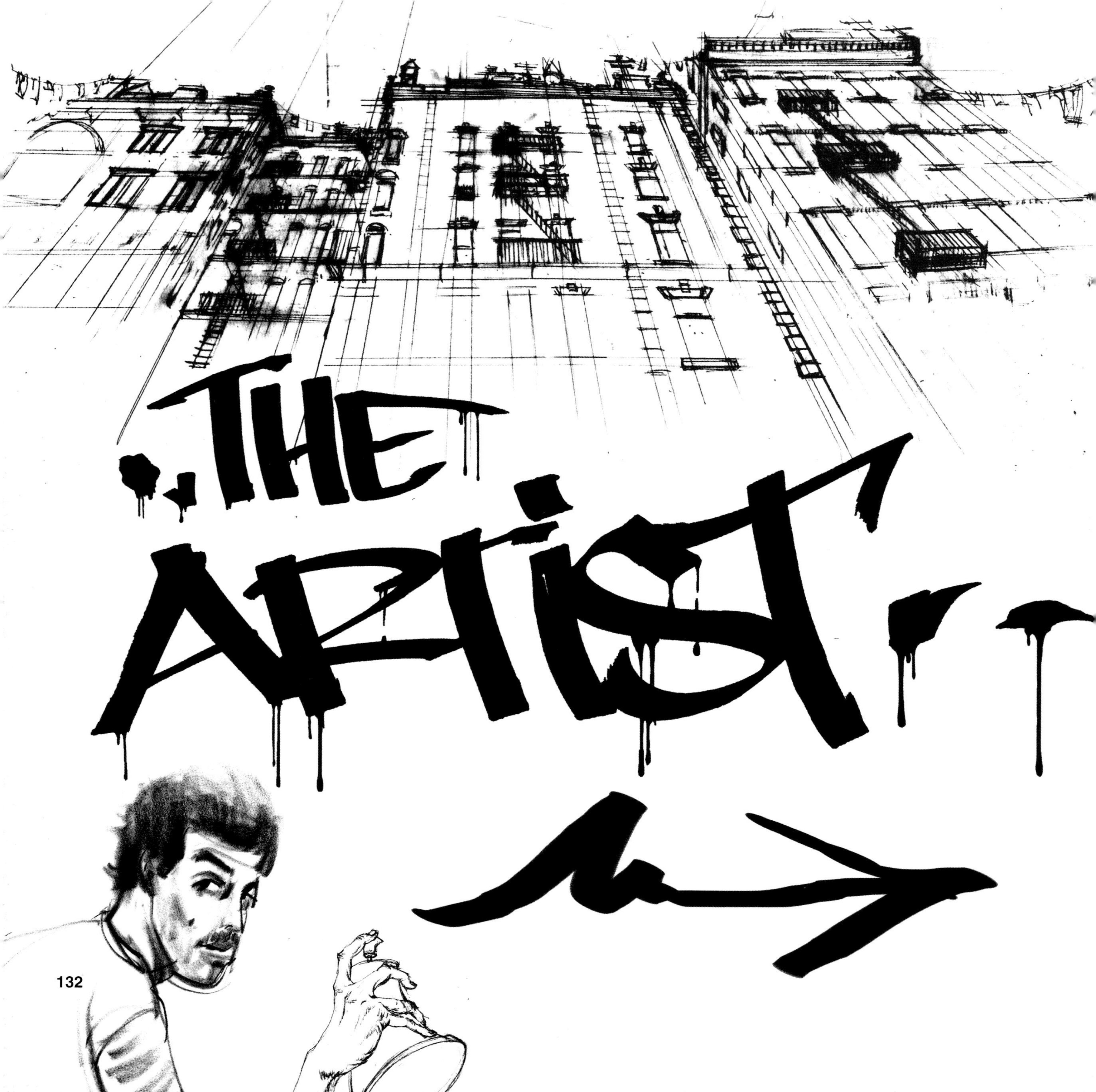
THE
ARTIST

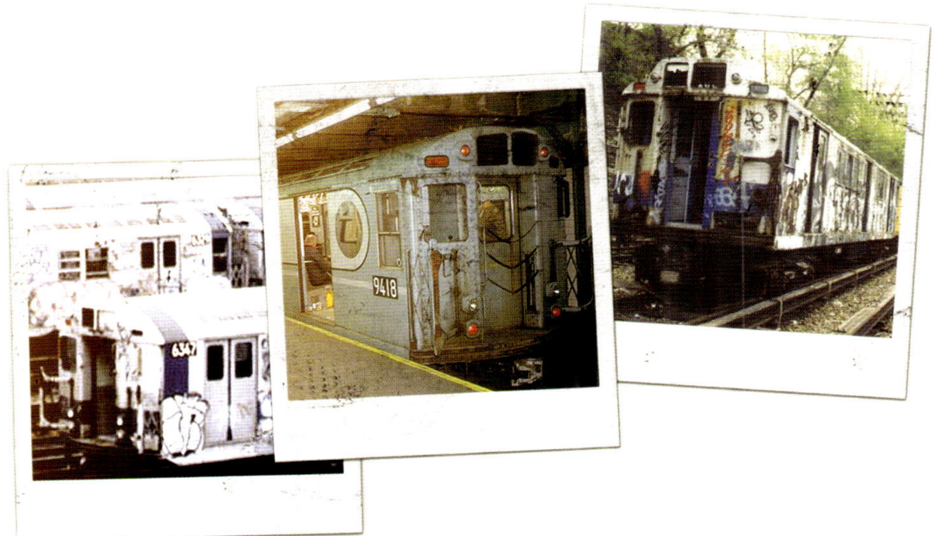

I wasn't a regular in the 1 and 2 Line yards but my friends were. I went to the yards and the tunnels from time to time and observed the passion these artists had. Equipped with their spray cans, I saw their need to create, to be artistic, and to share their voice with the rest of the city. They gave a unique flavor to the urban landscape. Whether it was LEE's pieces on the 2 and 5 trains or the handball courts that Bill Blast rocked at Rocksteady Park, the city was alive with the energy of art from the streets.

I entitled my painting "The Artist" to challenge the notion that graffiti writers can't be artists. Anyone who associates graffiti with only negativity is overlooking the underlying sociopolitical complexities of this art form.

The difference between a "tagger" and a graffiti artist is hard to explain. Both can be defined as someone that gets their name out there as a mechanism, i.e.: to take back public space from corporations, see their name up for the fame of it like a ghetto marquis, mark their territory, or make a social or political statement. The negativity arises when a person without permission writes his or her name on someone's private property. This insults all who write graffiti as an art. It is disrespectful and an injustice to the entire community if the victim's personal property or business is economically or otherwise damaged.

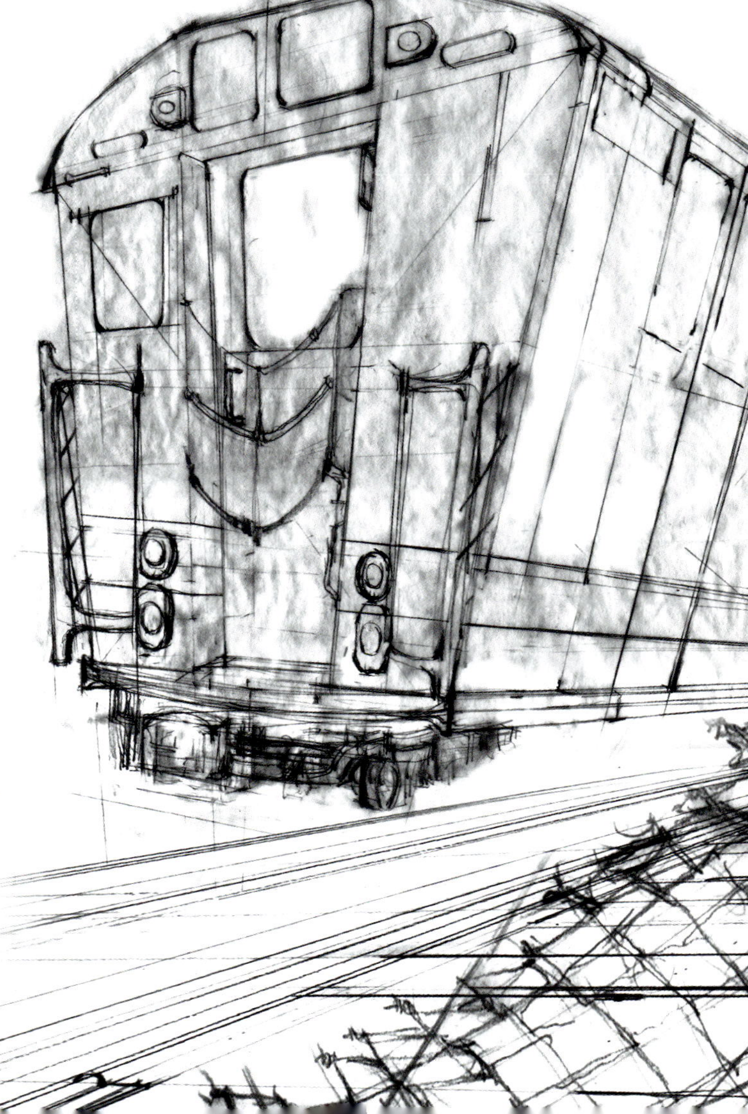

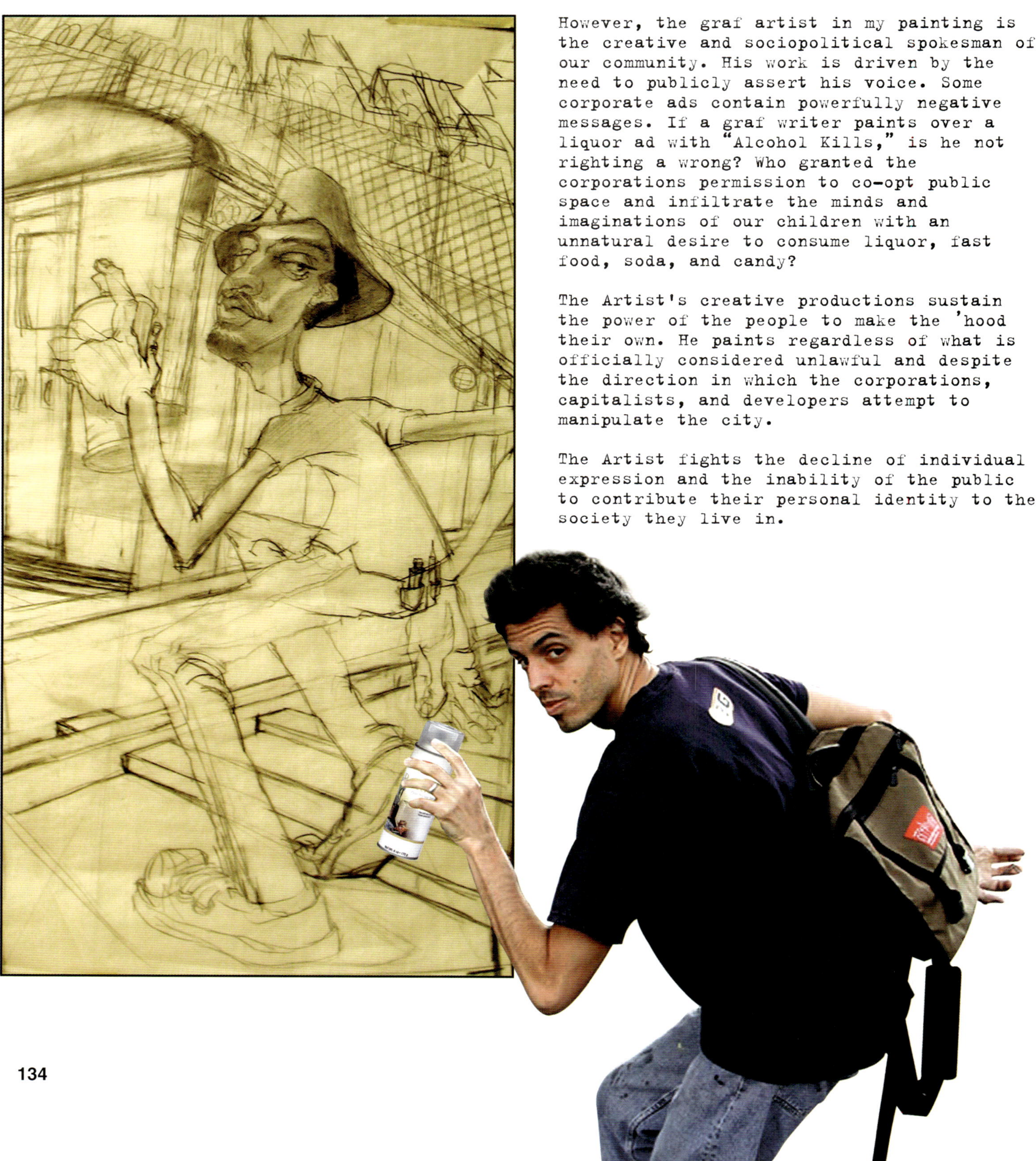

However, the graf artist in my painting is the creative and sociopolitical spokesman of our community. His work is driven by the need to publicly assert his voice. Some corporate ads contain powerfully negative messages. If a graf writer paints over a liquor ad with "Alcohol Kills," is he not righting a wrong? Who granted the corporations permission to co-opt public space and infiltrate the minds and imaginations of our children with an unnatural desire to consume liquor, fast food, soda, and candy?

The Artist's creative productions sustain the power of the people to make the 'hood their own. He paints regardless of what is officially considered unlawful and despite the direction in which the corporations, capitalists, and developers attempt to manipulate the city.

The Artist fights the decline of individual expression and the inability of the public to contribute their personal identity to the society they live in.

Commercial advertising and postings have become the norm, replacing colorful handwritten, hand-painted signs that enrich space, like those in San Francisco's Mission District. We allow public space to be homogenized. Step into the streets almost anywhere and you are likely to be overwhelmed by advertisements that are more concerned with making a quick, hard dollar than with the well being of any individual. This is especially true with the working class and the poor who are advertising targets for liquor, cigarettes, and companies that make cheap and unhealthy fast food.

Ironically, while city officials strictly enforce their anti-graffiti campaigns, they allow environmental and health discrimination. The money expended on anti-graffiti campaigns would be better spent on grass roots facilities like Precita Eyes Murals in the Mission District of San Francisco that offers a place of artistic expression, historical mural tours, and classes that teach art and its history in the neighborhood.

All of this defined my motivation to create "The Artist." This painting is of an old school graf writer who has broken the law by cutting open the fence and is consciously risking his life to paint a mural. Like the great Mexican muralist Diego Rivera and his sociopolitical art, the graf artist has a need to get his art out on the trains and a message out to the people. Even if his message makes no specific political statement, his actions do because of the fact that he has broken the laws that society has imposed on him. His artwork creates an atmosphere where it is visually apparent that the city both belongs to and is conceptualized by the people who live, work, and imagine there.

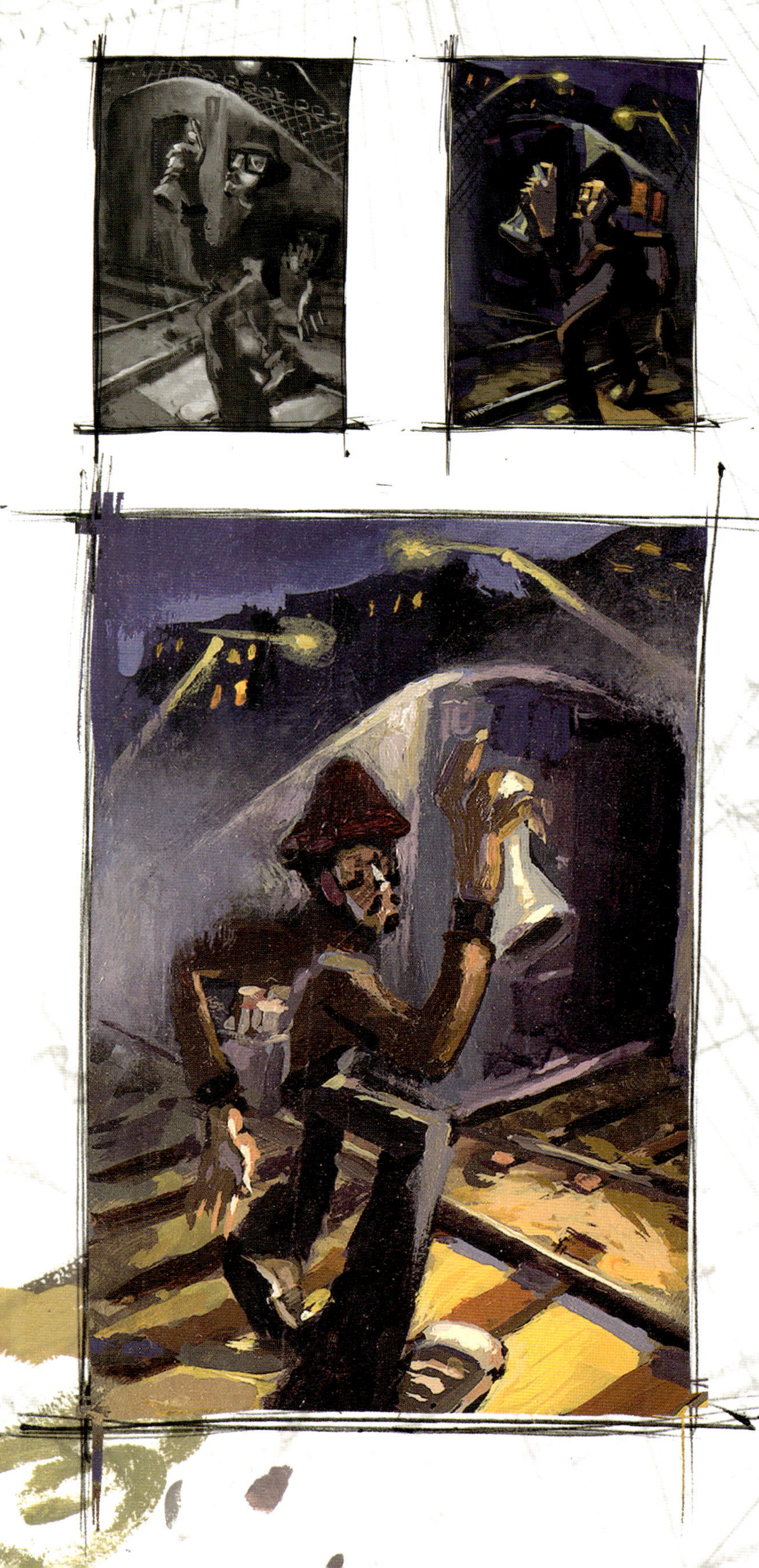

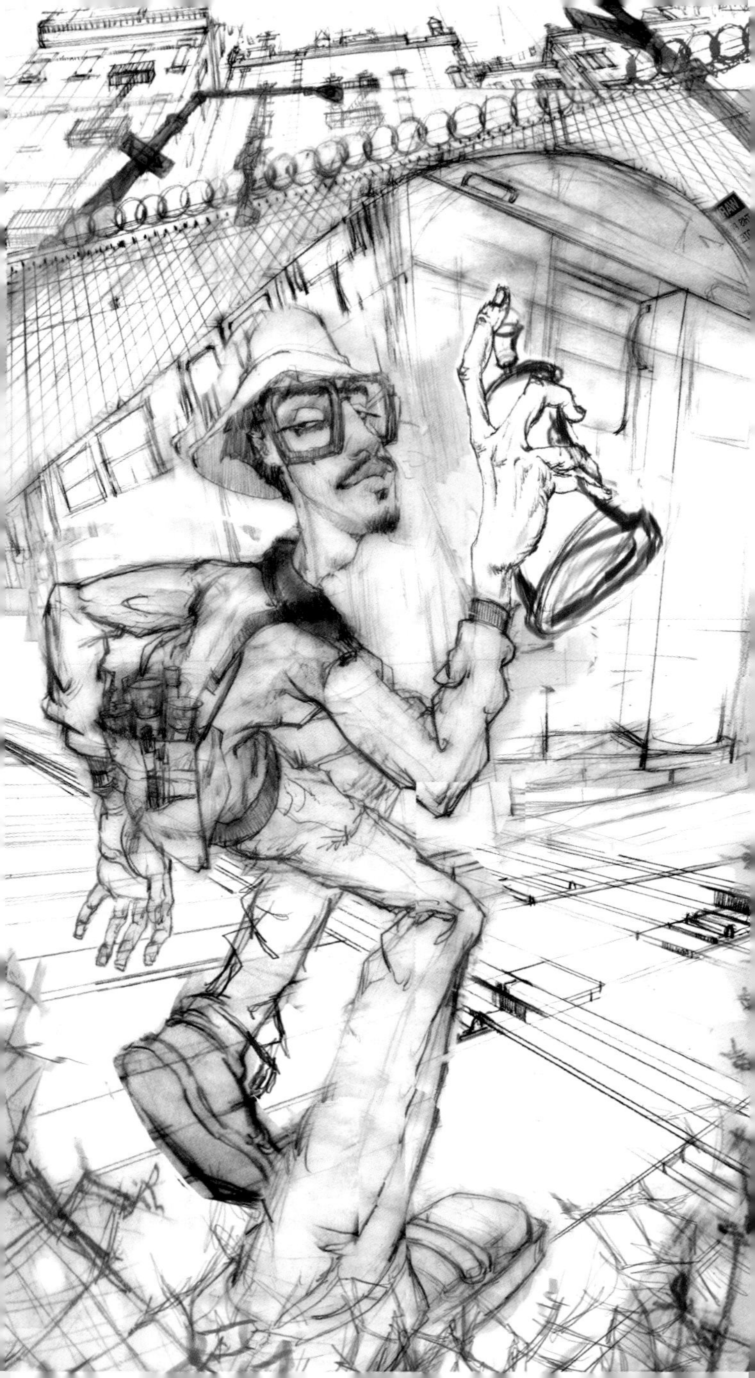

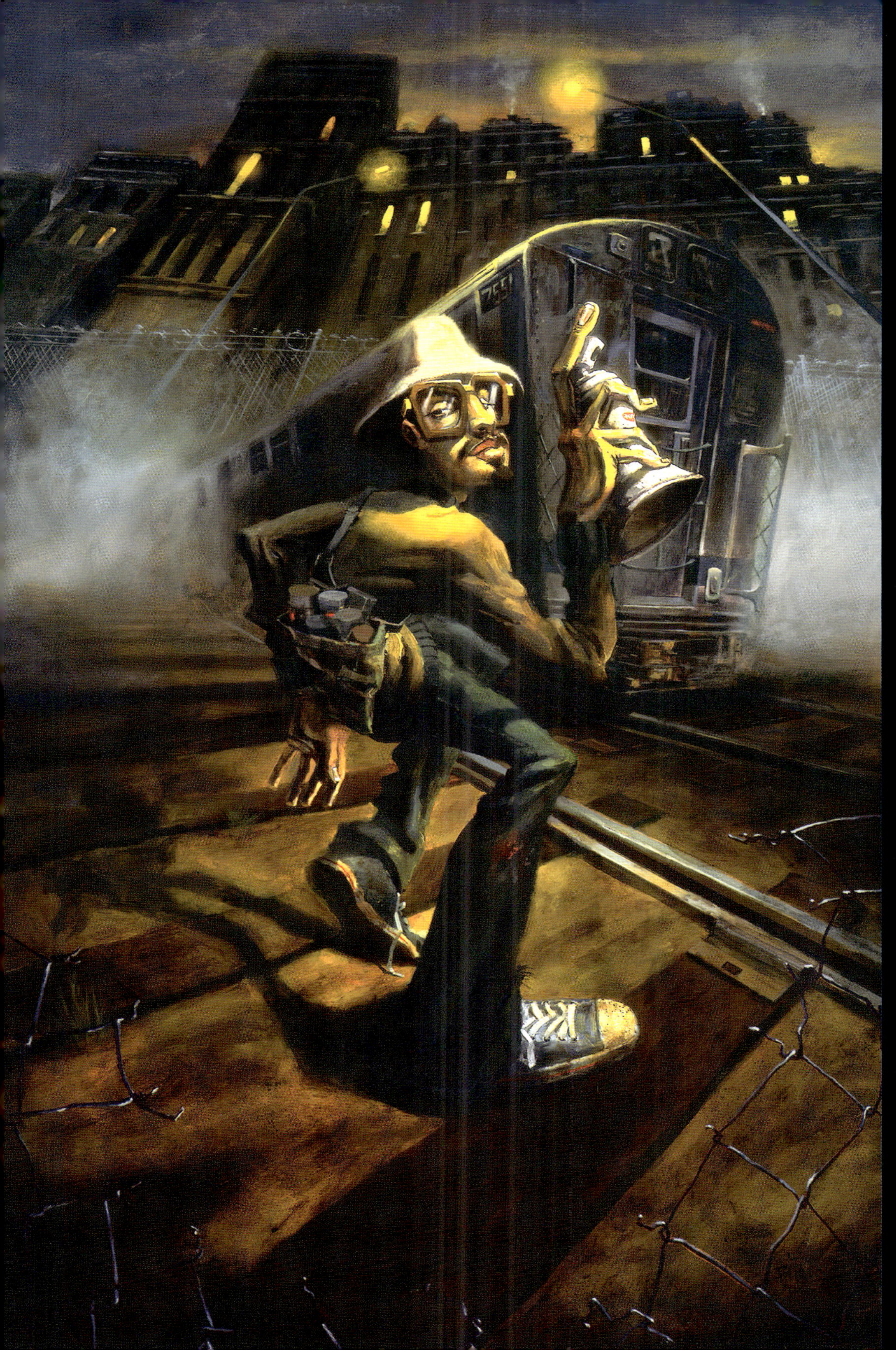

TRUMPET MAN

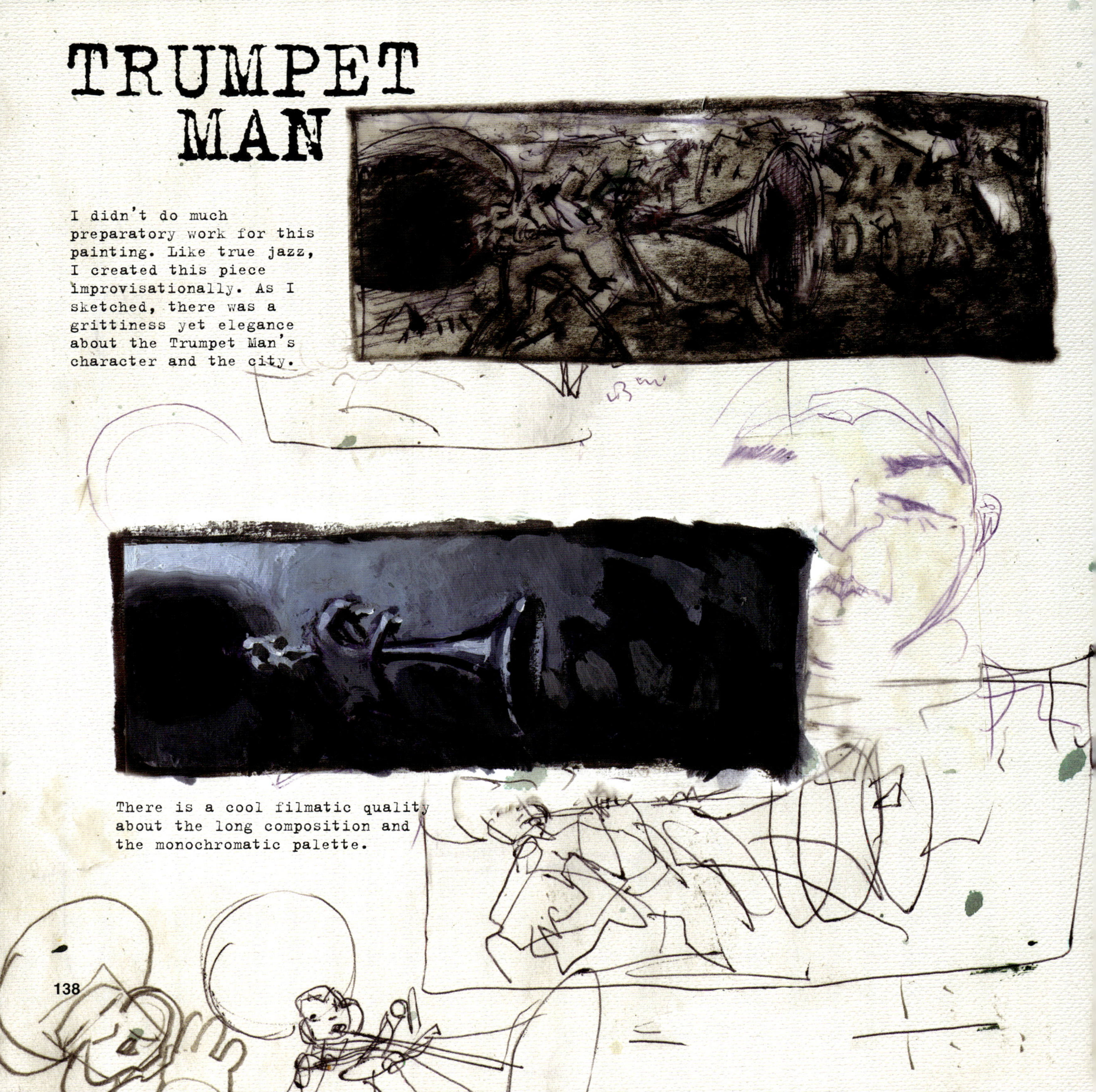

I didn't do much preparatory work for this painting. Like true jazz, I created this piece improvisationally. As I sketched, there was a grittiness yet elegance about the Trumpet Man's character and the city.

There is a cool filmatic quality about the long composition and the monochromatic palette.

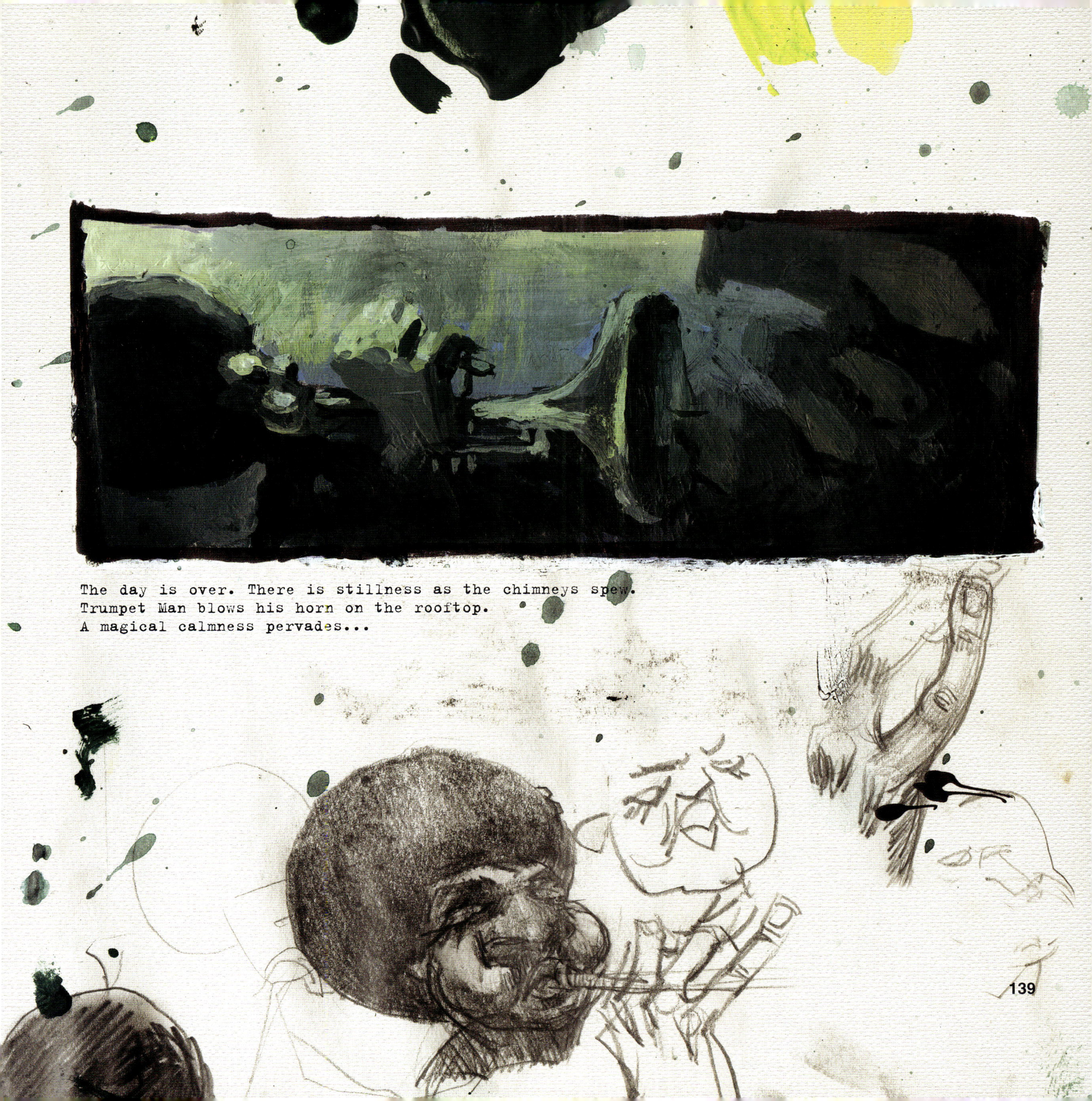
The day is over. There is stillness as the chimneys spew.
Trumpet Man blows his horn on the rooftop.
A magical calmness pervades...

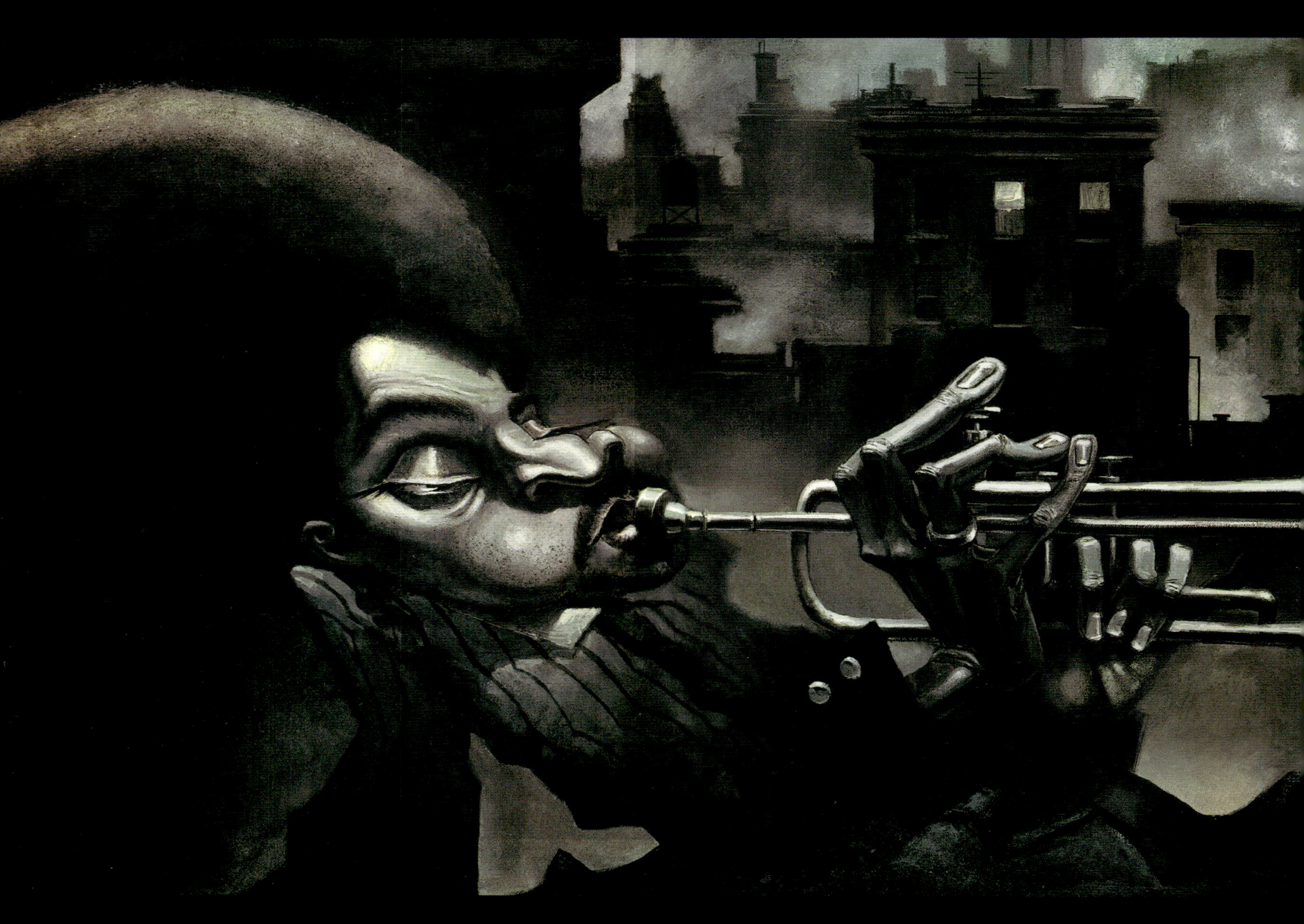

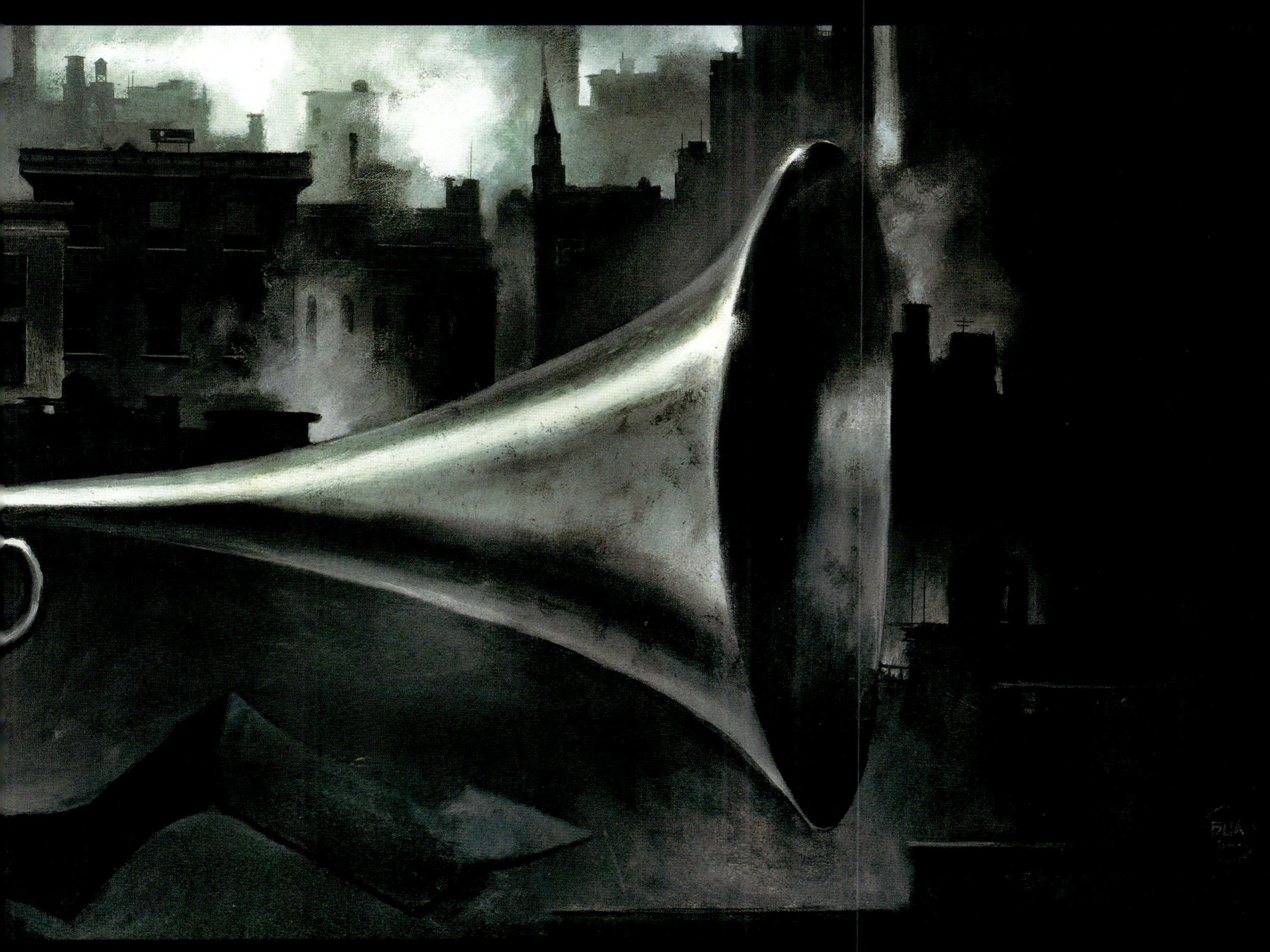

Trumpet Man 2004
Acrylic on Canvas
72 in. x 24 in.

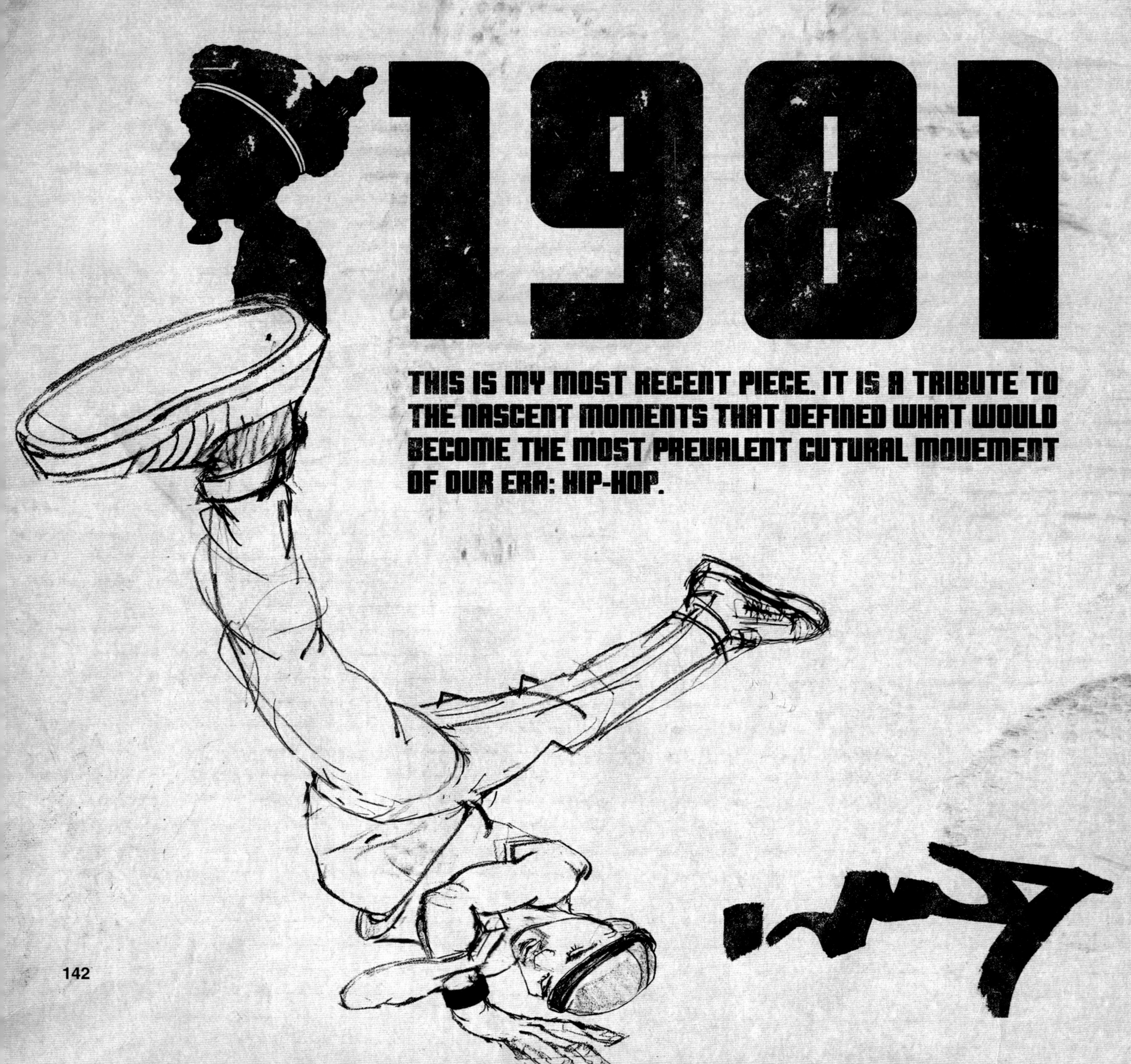

1981

THIS IS MY MOST RECENT PIECE. IT IS A TRIBUTE TO THE NASCENT MOMENTS THAT DEFINED WHAT WOULD BECOME THE MOST PREVALENT CUTURAL MOVEMENT OF OUR ERA: HIP-HOP.

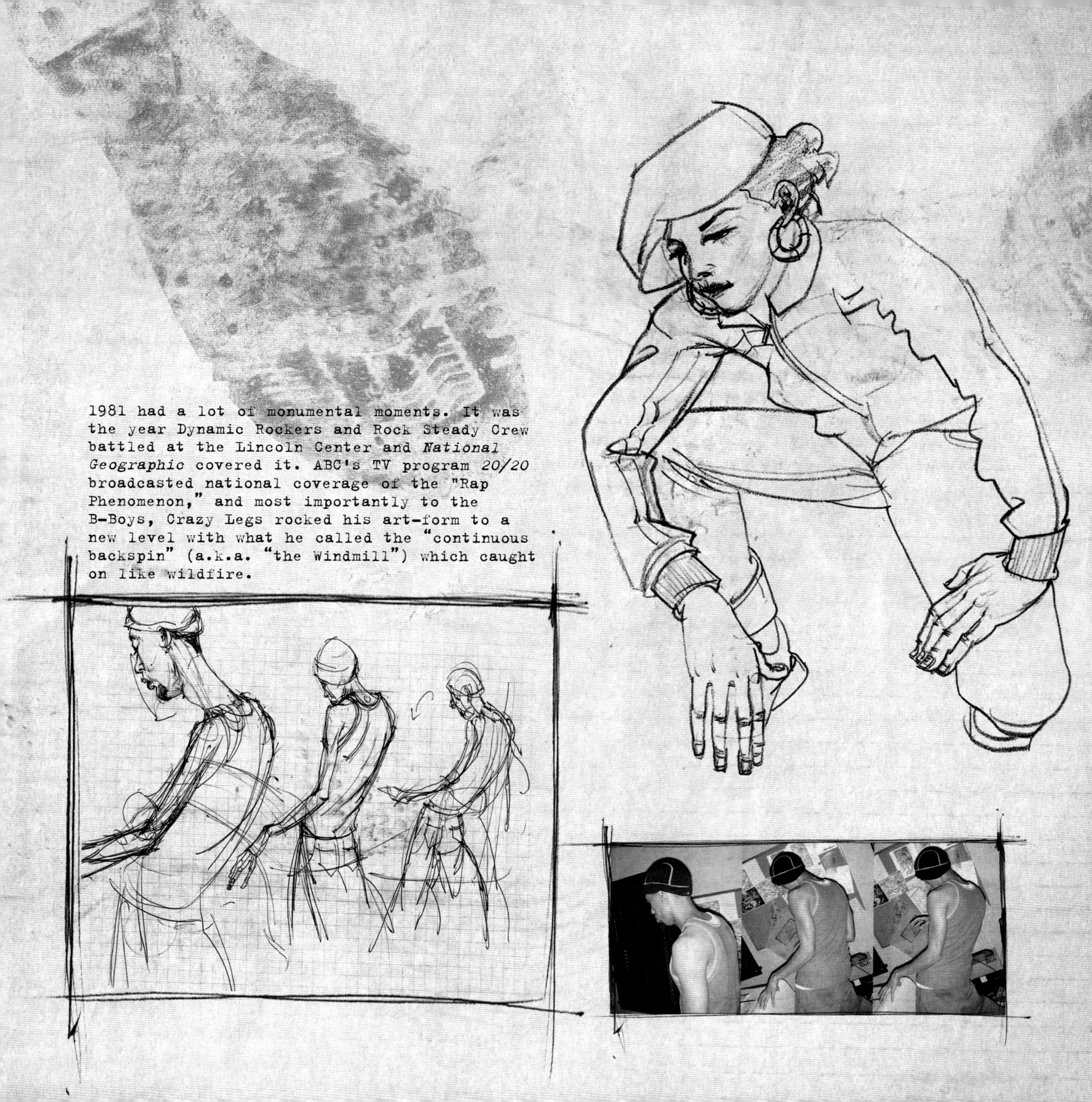

1981 had a lot of monumental moments. It was the year Dynamic Rockers and Rock Steady Crew battled at the Lincoln Center and *National Geographic* covered it. ABC's TV program *20/20* broadcasted national coverage of the "Rap Phenomenon," and most importantly to the B-Boys, Crazy Legs rocked his art-form to a new level with what he called the "continuous backspin" (a.k.a. "the Windmill") which caught on like wildfire.

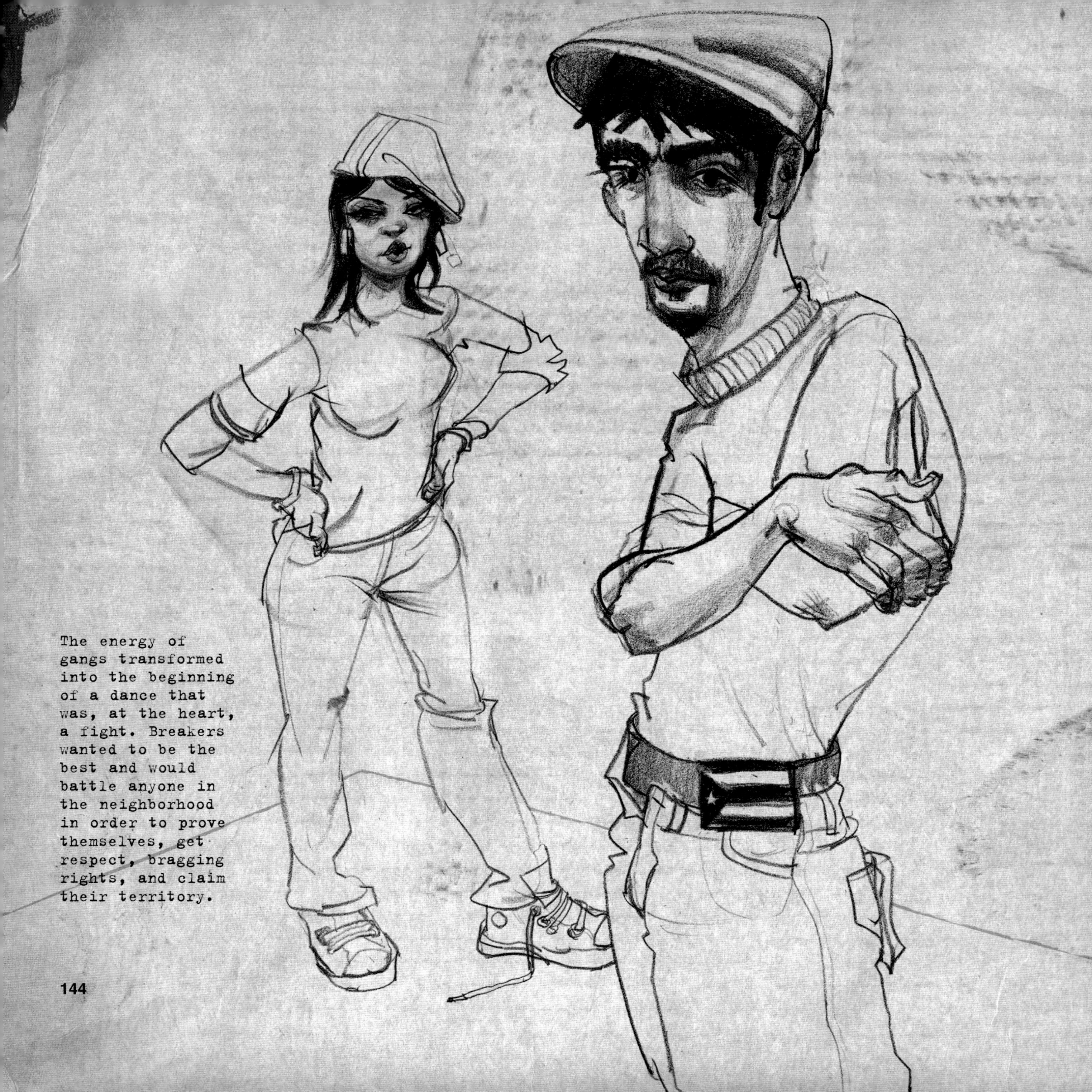

The energy of gangs transformed into the beginning of a dance that was, at the heart, a fight. Breakers wanted to be the best and would battle anyone in the neighborhood in order to prove themselves, get respect, bragging rights, and claim their territory.

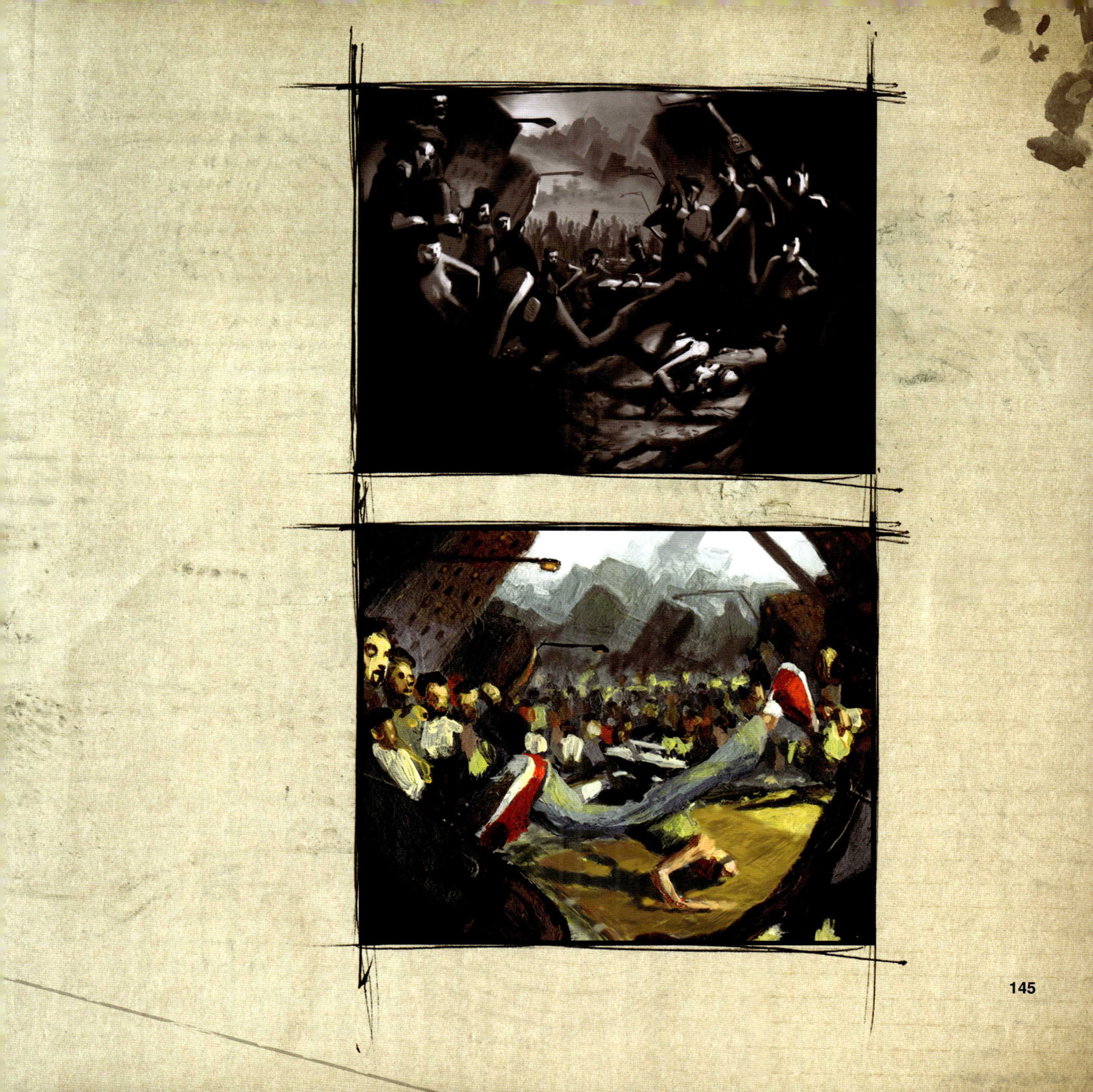

B-Boying was about style—aggressive, hard, and strong. That expression was best exemplified by the almighty Prince Ken Swift with the look that was called "the mugsy"—a look that was both hard and cool. The faces, the hard rock B-Boy stance and all the rugged poses were stylized renditions of fearlessness and aloofness amidst the ruckus backdrop of a tough city. The culture emanated the flavor and savoir faire of "cool" while it also created an avenue for self expression. It fostered positive creativity for a lot of people, myself included. I watched and danced while I soaked up rhythms that would come out later in my artwork. We all knew we were in the middle of something great.

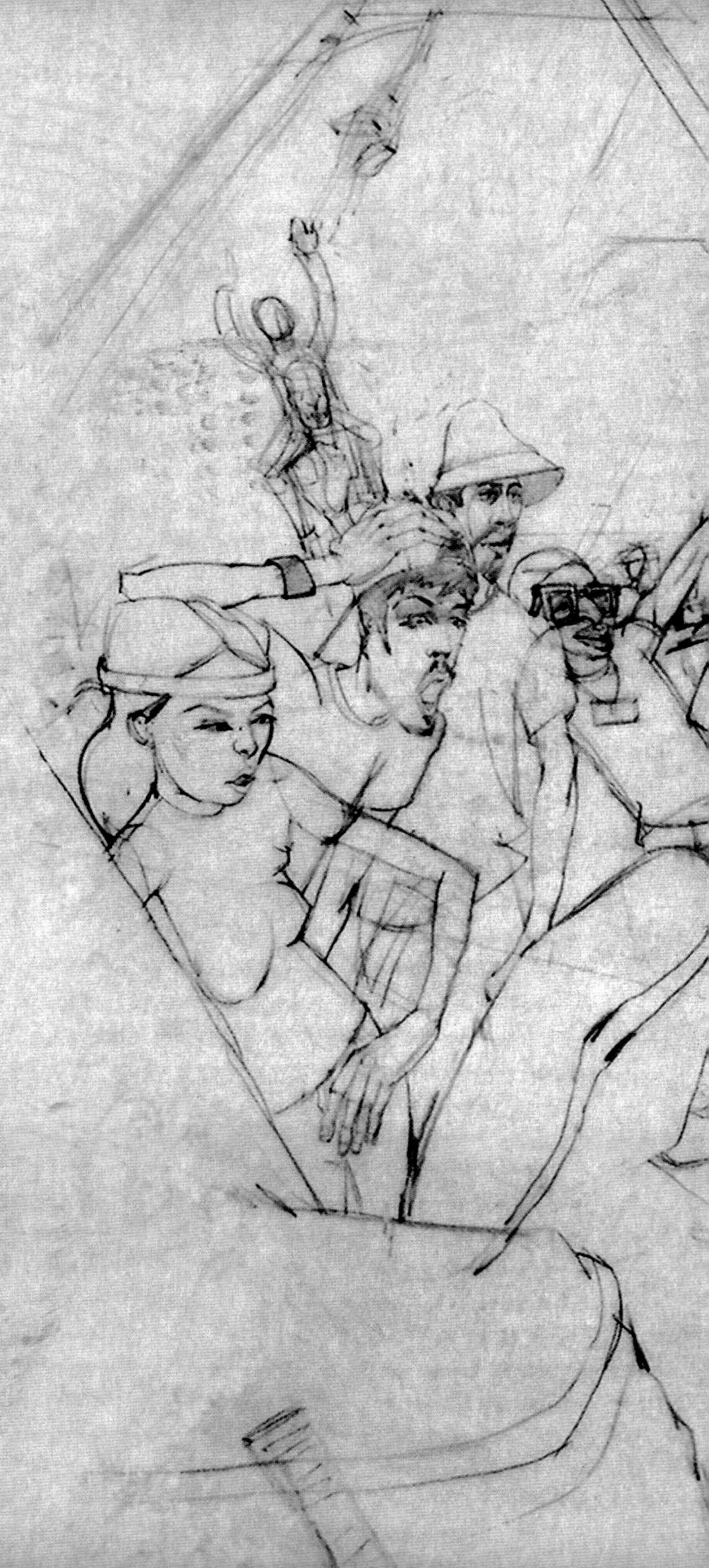

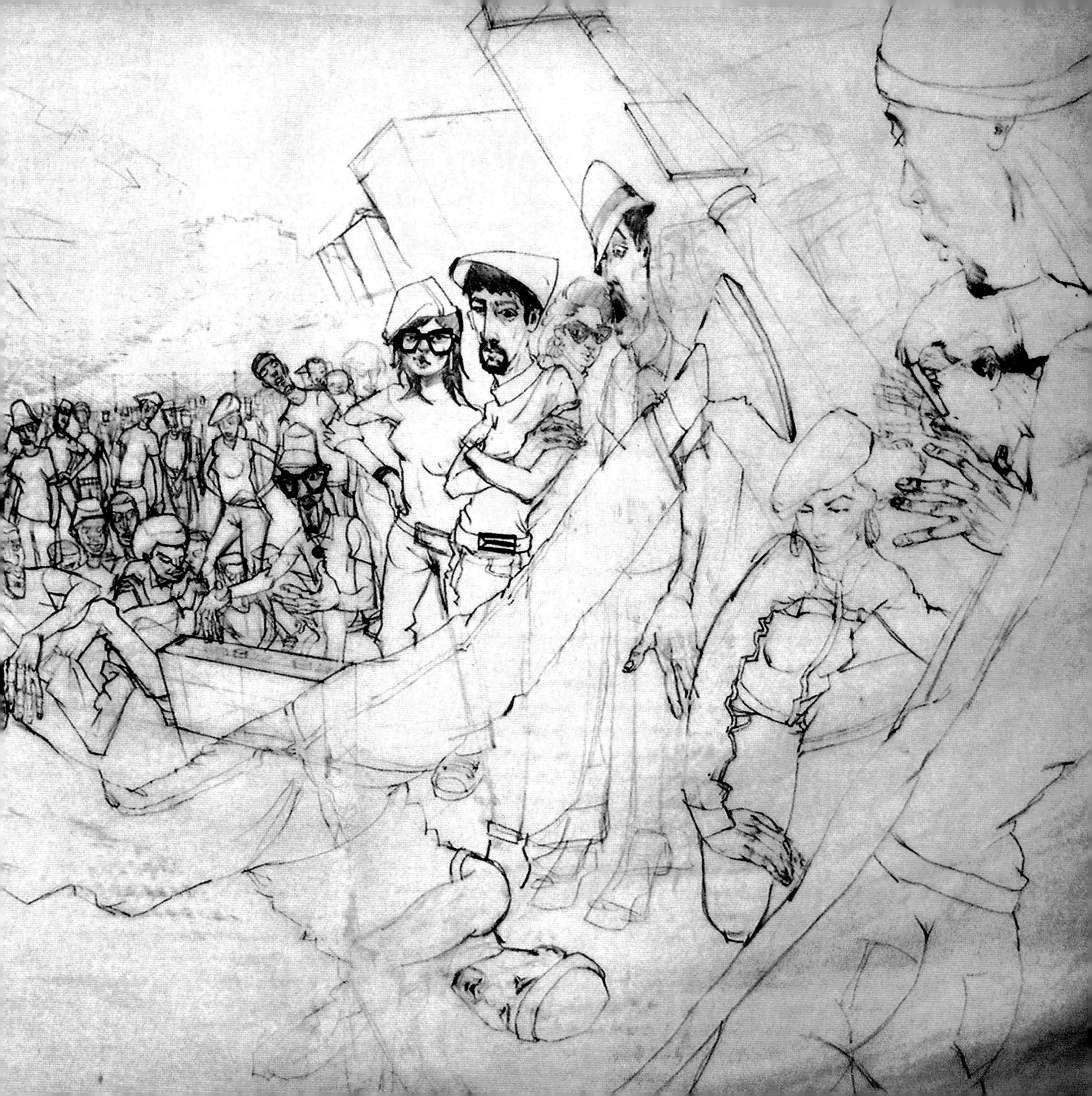

Great painters such as Rembrandt, Van Eyck, Rubens, and Velasquez painted popes, kings, and the aristocracy, people whom their societies deemed important. "1981" represents my larger-than-life community of heroes and Hip-Hop disciples, gathered together and dressed in the gear of their time. They feel greatness; they know they are seeing something new burgeoning, the rare attainment of originality. Jaws drop, hearts beat faster, inspiration, pride, and "this-is-it!" energy runs through the crowd.

These are the roots and the soul of everything that would later be classified into "elements." Absent from the textbooks, "1981" is an historical snapshot of time—a look back to a moment that held the future.

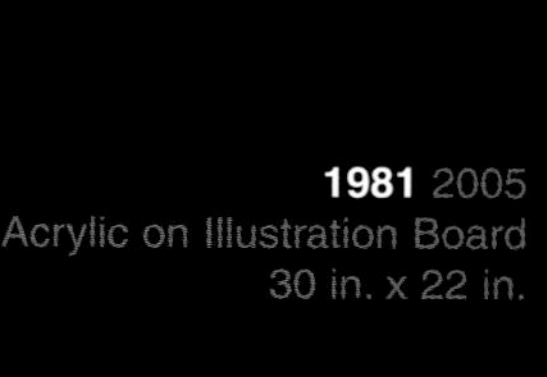

1981 2005
Acrylic on Illustration Board
30 in. x 22 in.

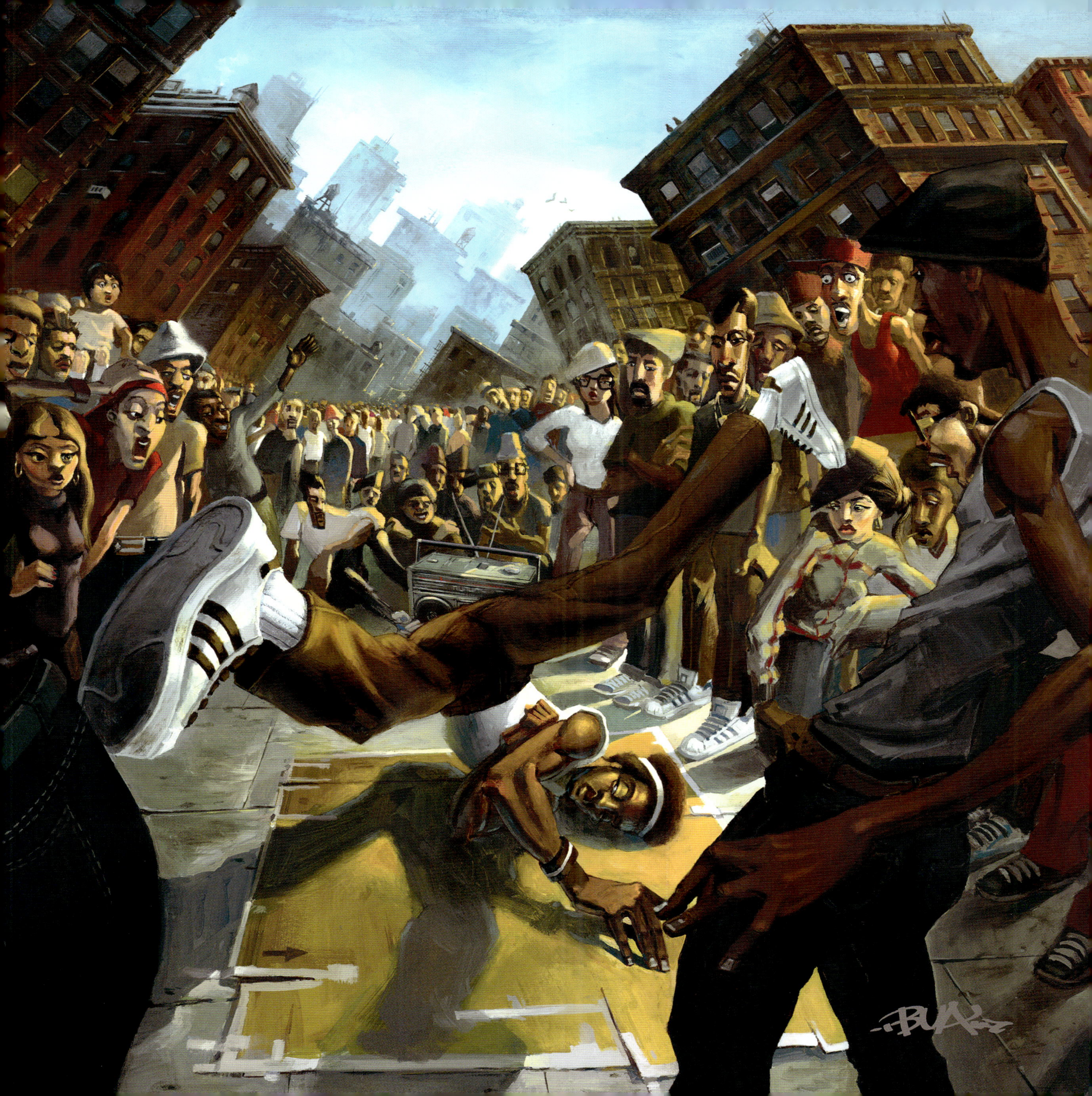
BUA

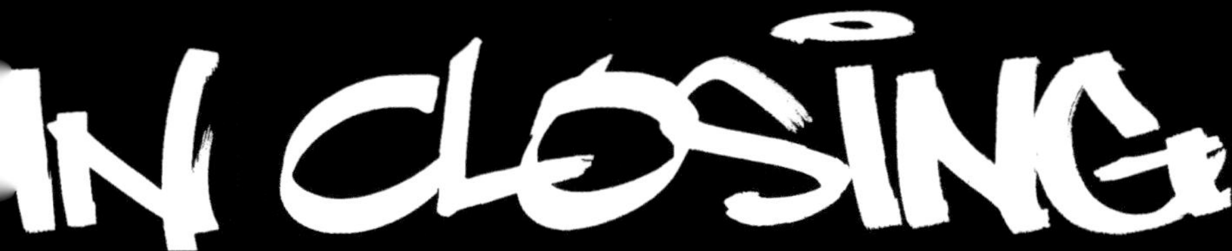

For over one hundred years, New York City has been called a melting pot. In my era, during the birth of Hip-Hop, it had already melted. I had the opportunity to mix with all these unique people who had grown from this metropolis. In my art I like to capture the true moments representing people in a state of just "being" in their element. My art is a way of paying tribute to the unsung heroes who I feel give the city its true flavor:

The fearless Artist who writes graffiti in the face of the law; taking back public space, claiming his right to have a voice in the city that is more his than the corporate giants who bombard the city with advertisements of lies.

The Breaker who wants to be the best and will battle anybody to prove it, to get respect and bragging rights in the neighborhood that is his.

The DJ who plays the drums, guitar, and bass. He's the beat conductor orchestrating the rhythms of the block party like an urban Mother Nature.

The Baller, who plays with his heart to find a better life. His environment defines his game. He plays cool, smooth, and at the same time hard.

The working class cats that play jazz for the love of it and not for the money of it.

The gamblers in the underworld who have fun, hangin', chillin', or just plain buggin' out.

These characters were cool because they were survivors— I respected them. They represent the deeper meaning of cool, which was about truth, excellence, pride, strength, freedom, and self-expression. Buddha said that if there are two roads, take the harder one. Well these cats didn't have a choice. They traveled the harder road and it made them jaded, but at the same time stronger. If you looked underneath their hardness, they were compassionate, understanding, and forgiving. In the face of adversity, you see the truth. You dig deeper. These characters in my paintings were in my life. Their experiences made them real, made them raw, made them important.

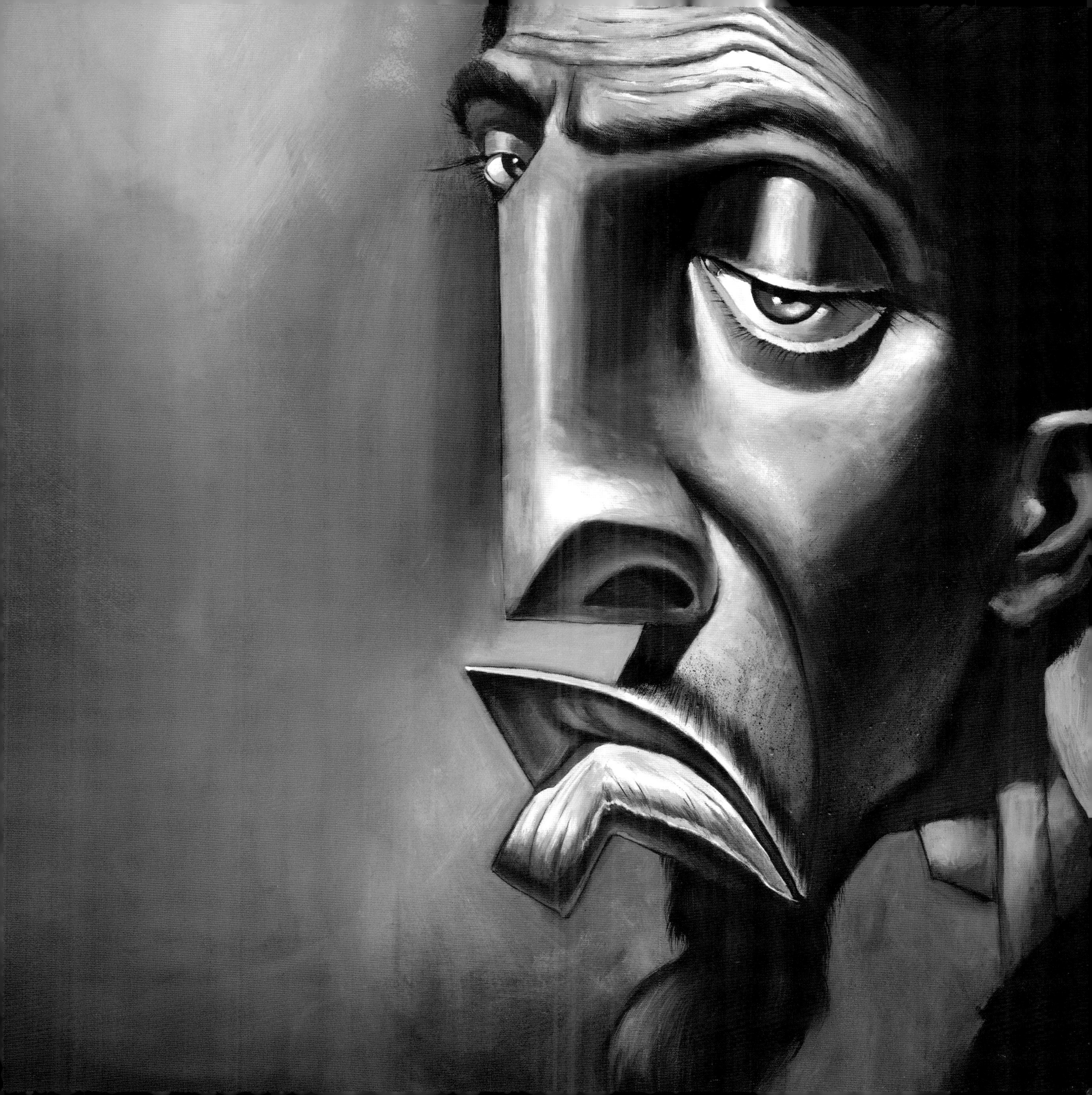

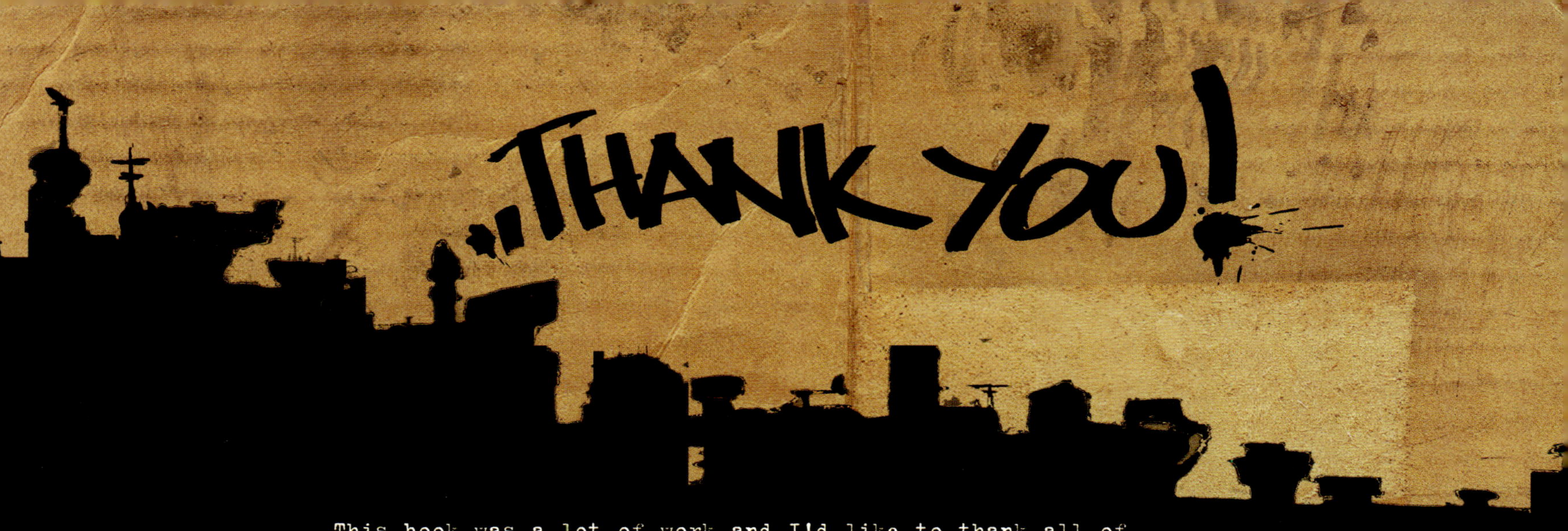

This book was a lot of work and I'd like to thank all of y'all without whom this would never have happened.

First and foremost Kara, who worked full-time but devoted all her off time to this book. Her sense of aesthetics and color is impeccable. With her sharp eye and her incredible ability to kern one word for 45 minutes until it's perfect, this book reached new levels of beauty. She was the greatest art director I could have ever had. Between the birth of our daughter and the positive energy she supports me with, she is truly superwoman—the most special person in the world.

Akira, my daughter, my light, who has made me look deep within to find patience and humility and in doing so has made me see what it really means to be a man. During the making of this book she always made the crew take dance breaks. A future B-Girl. She truly is ONE.

Sophie Bambuck, for managing BUA Studios (and my insanity). Her input was insightful, humorous, and at times annoying...but usually correct. There are not many people in the world as honest and dedicated as her. She's one in a billion.

Duane Cardinez who designed the beginnings of this book with us. We share similar aesthetics partly because he is from Bed-Stuy, Brooklyn. His ideas are fresh, raw and out of the box. Big ups to D-money.

Ruby Roth, a friend and great artist in her own right. She did so much for this book it's ridiculous. Not only did she contribute countless hours of research, editing, and composing, she also added her powerful artistic voice which

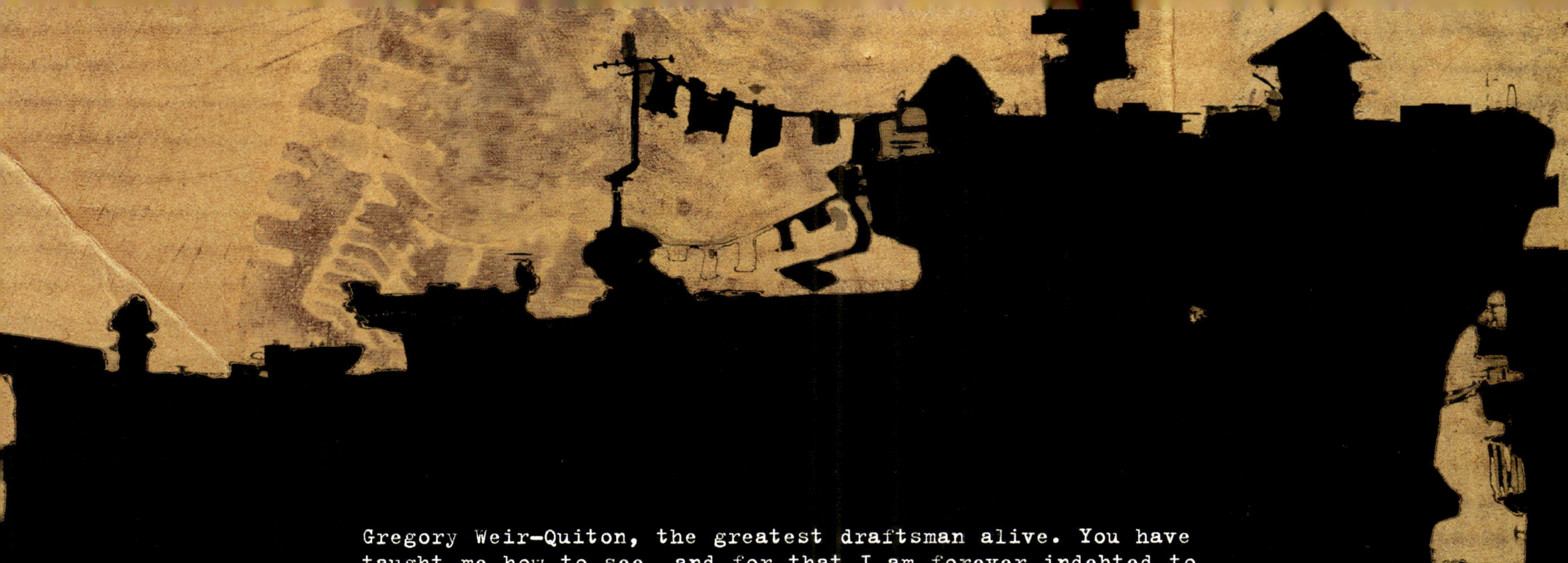

Gregory Weir-Quiton, the greatest draftsman alive. You have taught me how to see, and for that I am forever indebted to you.

Ruben Hickman, who is not only my best friend but an inspiration. I believe that Ruben is the best all around artist that I've ever been exposed to. He has been my greatest teacher.

Jason Andors, whose insightful humor has proved invaluable to keeping this book truly raw and funny. I couldn't have done it without him...Okay...Now that he just walked out of the office, let me be honest, of course I could have! Wait he just walked back in. He's amazing...

Seth Fleischman at HarperCollins, who called me as a fan and soon became a friend. When he found out that I had already invested years of sweat equity into a book that was just waiting to be published, he brought it straight to Judith Regan. The rest is history.

Judith Regan, who is a pioneer in her field. She believed in my vision and wasn't afraid to introduce it to the public, like so many before her were.

Doug Grad at HarperCollins, who I talked to every day that this book was in the works. He made sure my writing was up to par...and let me know when it wasn't. Thank you for giving me the freedom to write what I wanted, but the structure that allowed me to do it well.

Richard Ljoenes, who gave us great direction and redirection until the book was just right. Endless changes, endless thanks.

Suzanne Wickham, whose excitement, positivity, and support was an inspiration to all.

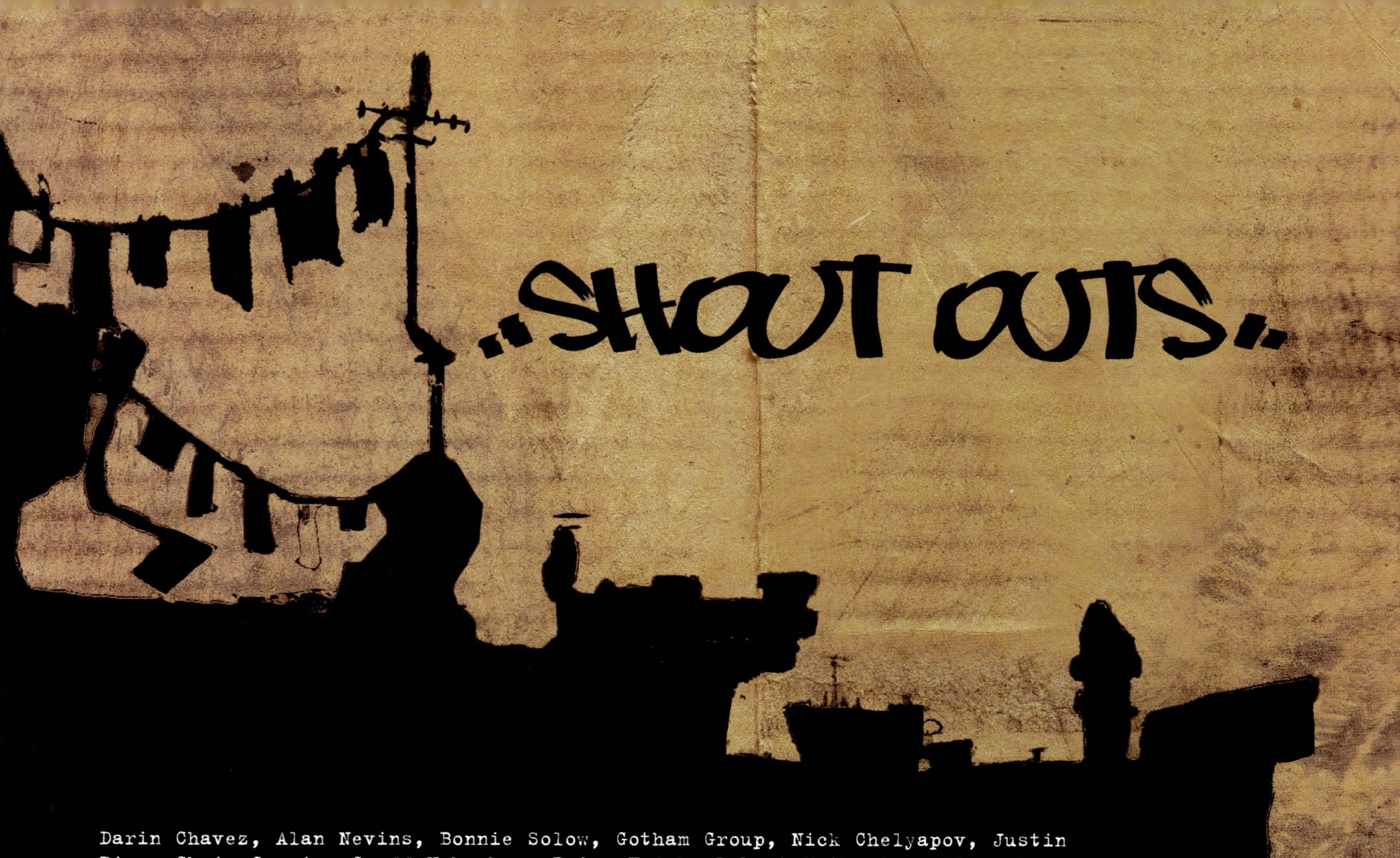

SHOUT OUTS

Darin Chavez, Alan Nevins, Bonnie Solow, Gotham Group, Nick Chelyapov, Justin Diaz, Chris Garcia, Geoff Nahashon, Brian Hajek, Robert Nathaniel, Mia Mitchell, Mike Gadow, Tom Turner, Katherine Koyanagi, Debbie Liebling, Bob Teitel, Rene Rigal, Joe Boucher, Mark McJimsey, Joel Kuwahara, Michael Brams, Michael Siegel, Kirk De Micco, Scott Greenberg and IDT, IDPR, John King (Dust Brothers), Bobby Mackston, Nathan Ratcliffe, Jared Sandrew, Steven Acuna, Lisa Northrup, Helen Robinson, Tom Goedde, Matt Frauman, Jerry Marshak and Shannon Van Dorn, Gary Meyer, Shakespeare, David Miller, Anita Arze, David Wolfe, Isaac "West" Rubenstein, Kahlil Zulu "Serge" Williams, Erik Lindenauer, Ale Smith, Trevor Clark, Tamara Rawitt, Steve Weiss, Uncle John, NYC Express and Julie Arenal, Wilpower (Air Force Crew), Steen and his brother Peter, Cisco, Kool Herc, Prince Whipper Whip (Fantastic 5 MCs), Mr. Wiggles, Crazy Legs, Rahzel, DJ QBert, Elmore Leonard, Aaron McGruder, Luis Rodriguez, Ali Shaheed Muhammad, Grandmaster Caz, Big Daddy Kane, Tony Parker, Eva Longoria, Saul Williams, Carl Jones, Martin Luther, Dan Brinkle, David Lipman, Fidel Rodriguez, Nate Geezy, Jointz Mag, Ryan, Cathy and Glen Yoshimoto, John McCaughey, Eliah Bornstien, Naomi and Howard (Off the Wall on Haight Street), Bruce Teleky, Franco, Yoko Sato, B-Boys, B-Girls, all my bugged out childhood friends, and all the fans who kept asking and pushing me to come out with a book.

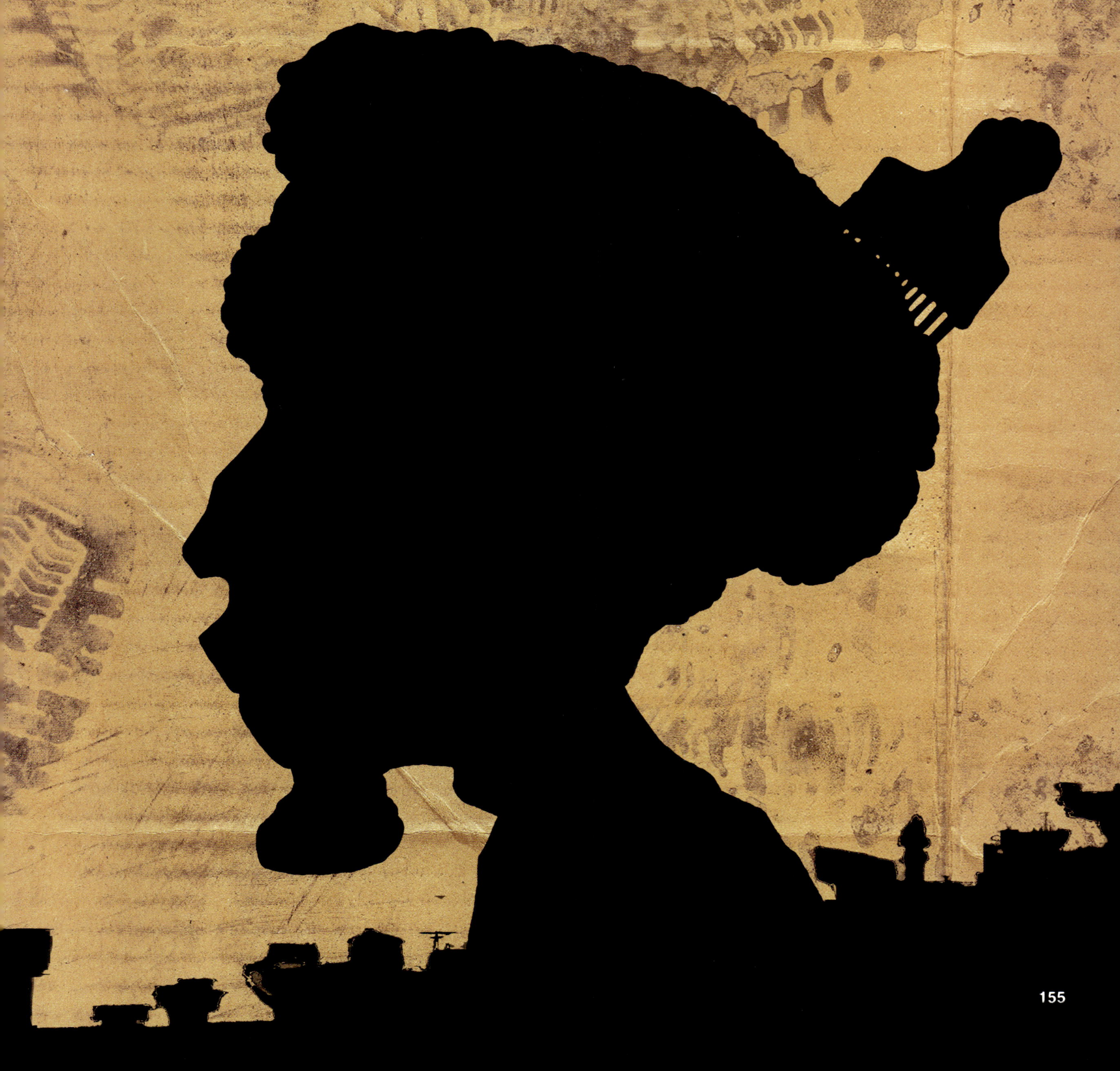

RESPECT...

Mom rockin' the old school fro.

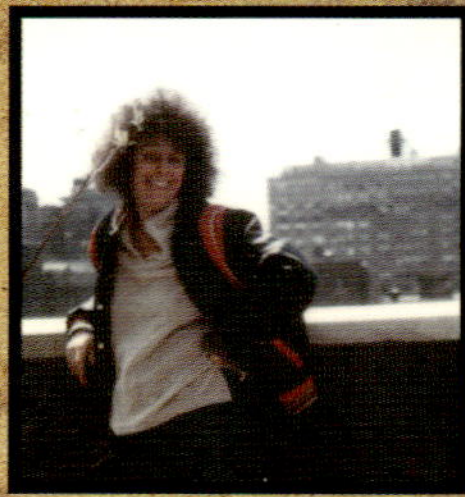

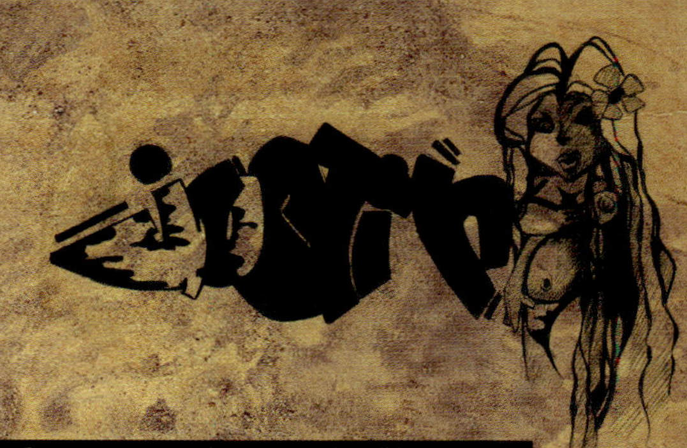

My mom coped with being a single parent from the day my dad went to get milk when I was two days old and never came back. She worked full-time to raise me and dealt with tough neighborhoods and my charming, delinquent friends. At the same time, she always found the energy to expose me to amazing art and culture. She was always a champion of my work. When my high school art teacher discouraged me from entering an art competition because my work was "unrefined, and too street," my mom said in typical New York fashion, "Fuck her, is she nuts? I'll give you the money. You enter it!" I did and I won a financial scholarship. She truly believed in me and that's why I am who I am today. I love you, Mom!

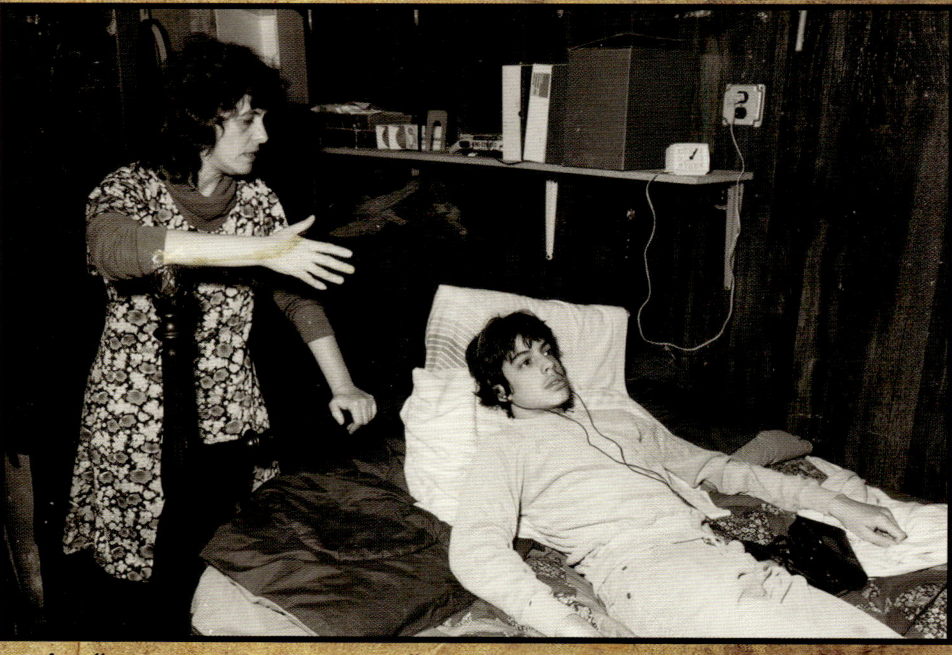

Mom's "Get up you lazy bum" pose.

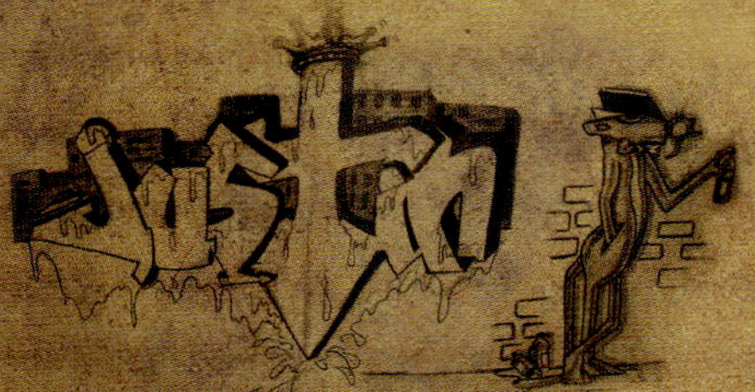

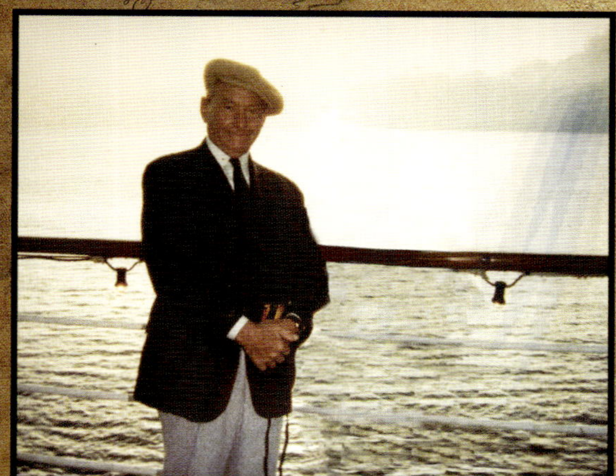

My grandfather always wore suits and a cap. He was from the old, old school generation.

My grandfather was an artist—a sculptor, painter, and an accomplished letterer. He lettered the original Felix the Cat, Prince Valiant, and had his own comic strip called "Frantic." Growing up during the Depression, he had an intense work ethic and was very sympathetic to the poor and working class, coming from a very poor family himself.

Thus, he was a big fan of artists who were socially and politically motivated like Kathe Kollwitz, Bruegal the elder, Rembrandt, Charles Bragg, and Hokusai. These artists were on his walls and I grew up exposed to these masters. My grandfather had strong philosophies about social injustices and was a voice, like these artists were, for the common man. His influence on me, artistically and socio-politically, affected how I saw the world and how I would later paint it. He was a great supporter of my work and one of my few and true heroes.

BACK IN THE DAYS

CONVENT AV

W 135 ST

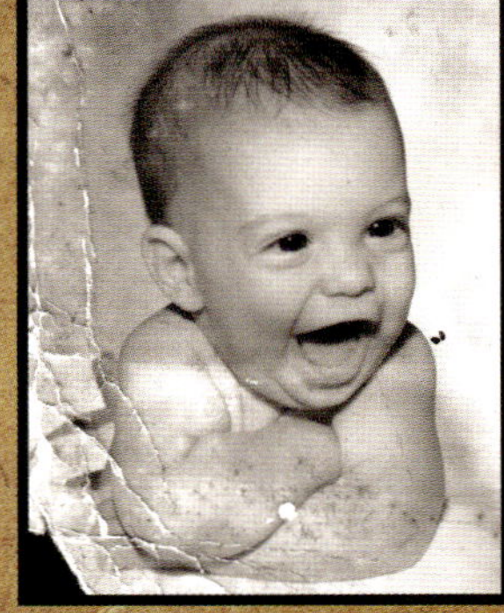

My first ever B-Boy pose.

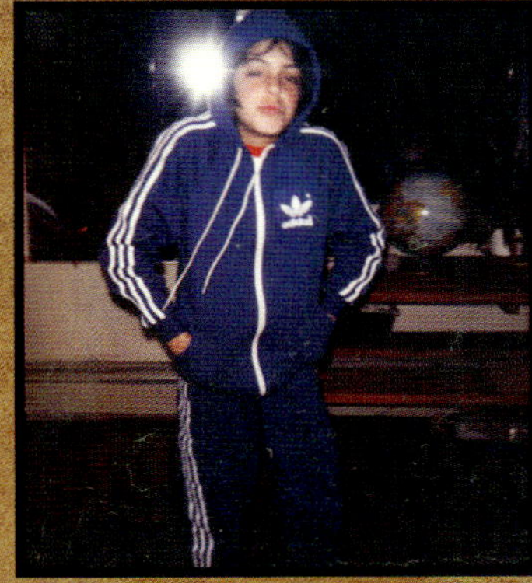

Chillin' 1977.

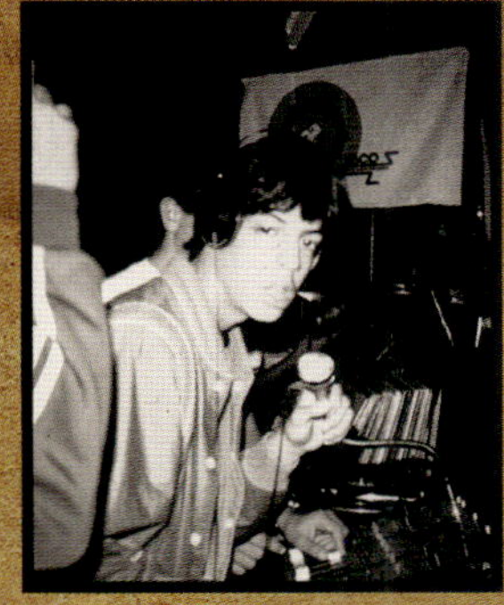

On the mic 1984.

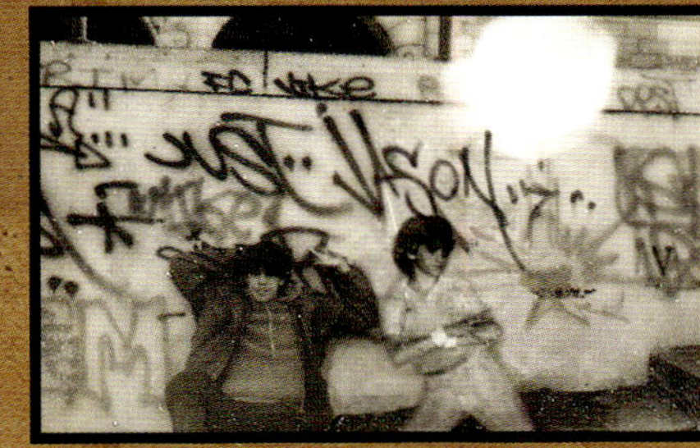

Me and my boy Jason gettin' up.

Streetdancers Breaking Into The Big Time

By BONNIE JERDAN
Post-Courier Reporter

The performances of the Spoleto Express Breakdancers will be "hot and fresh," the show's assistant choreographer says, and the vibrant energy and enthu-

Breakdancers replacing opera

GREENVILLE (AP) — The opera performance scheduled as part o… been … placed … and … dance… The… held a… sched… Furm… Audit…

The change was made late Tuesday, according to Elizabeth Mont-…

and dance troupe. The breakdancers perform routines choreographed for … to original music.

…kets to each performance were … Charleston. In Greenville, the … program will cost $10 per …

…ders of opera tickets may keep … for the new offering or return … for a refund, Mrs. Montgom-… …aid.

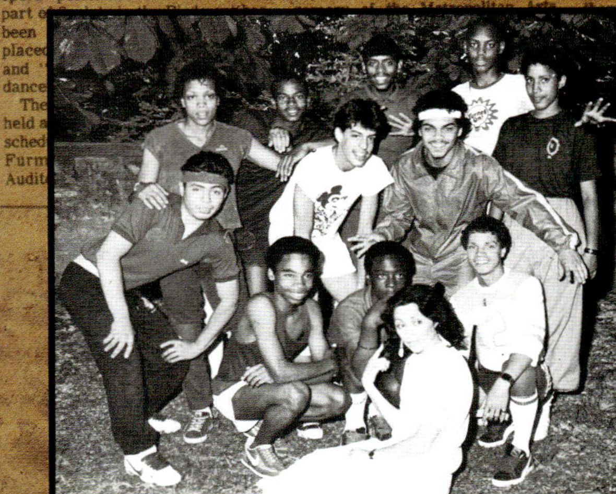

Me and my crew, New York Express, with choreographer Julie Arenal.

Double-stacked boomboxes.

Turning a craze into culture

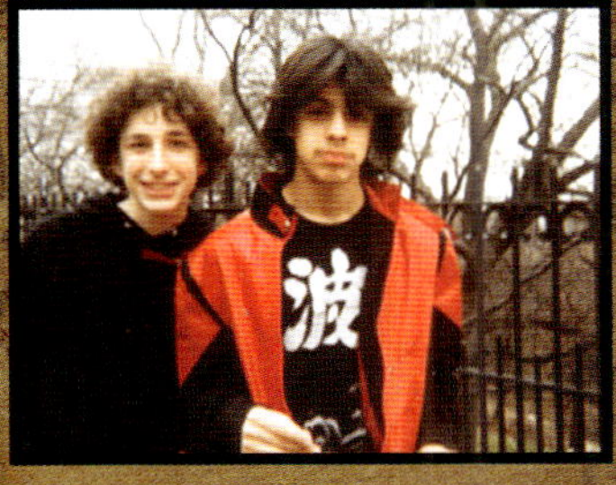

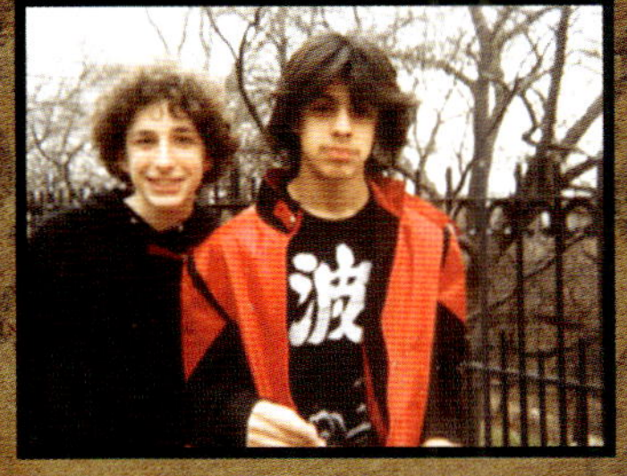

Cutting class with Eli on 135th Street.

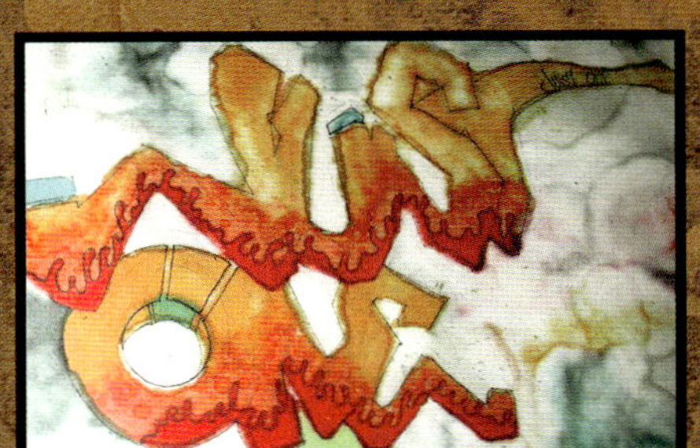

My first graf piece, age 12.

Breaking out of the ghetto

Andreas Panayi

HOW'S your moonwalk coming on? Been practising the wave recently? And if your breaking is generally a little

Breakdancers Drawing Sell-Out Crowds Daily

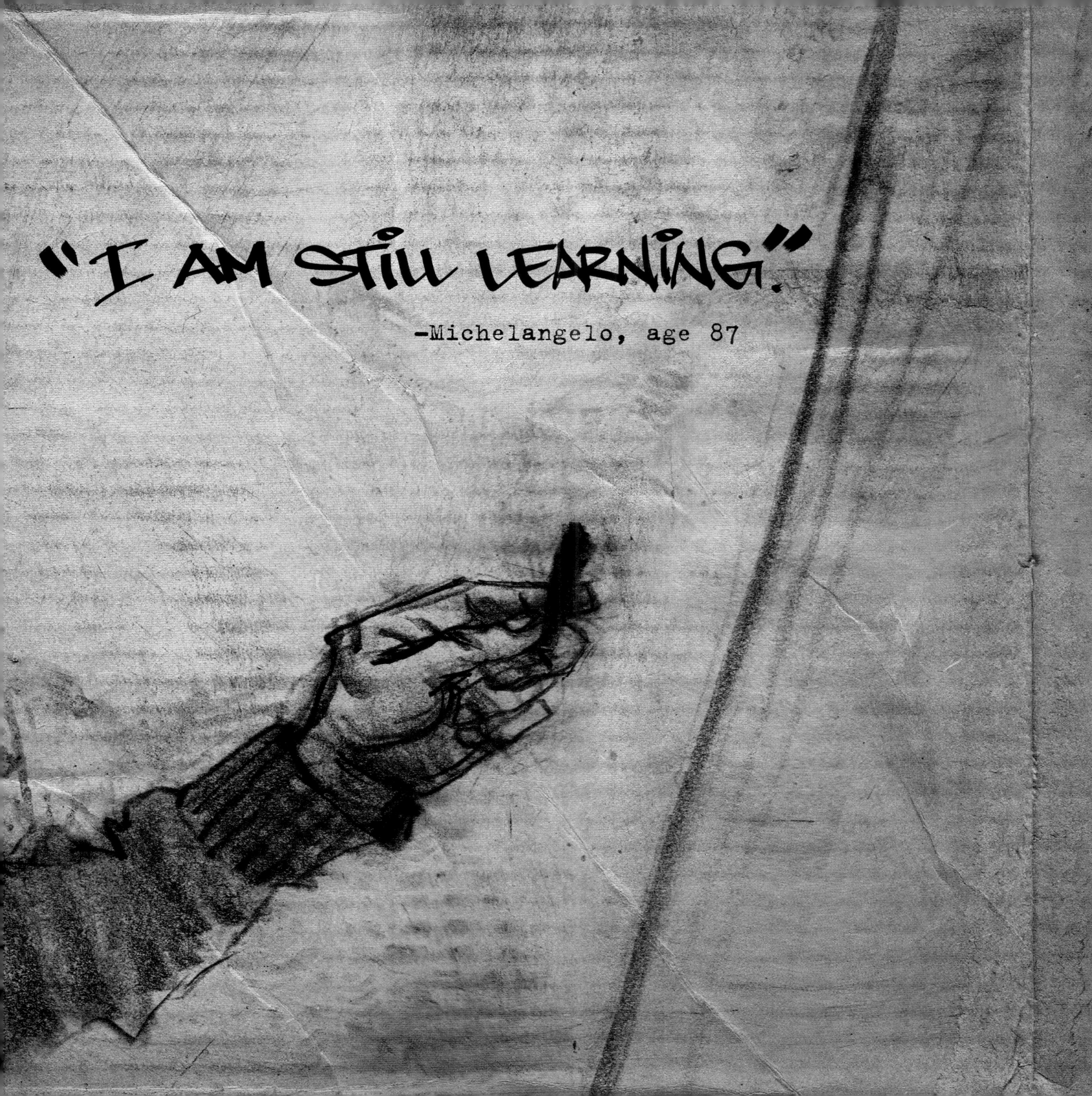
"I AM STILL LEARNING."
-Michelangelo, age 87

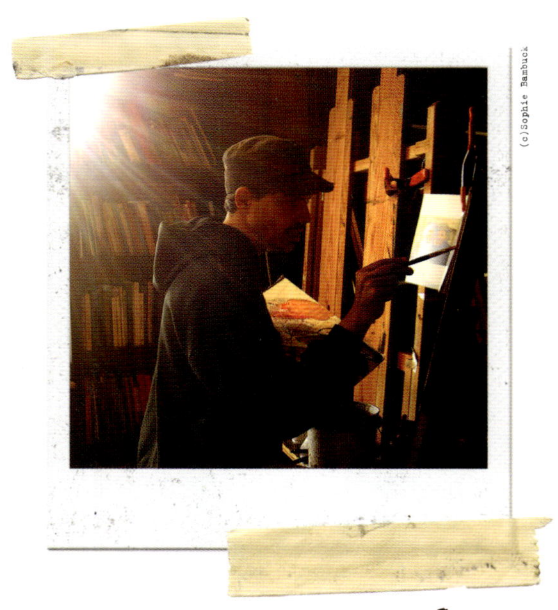

(c)Sophie Bambuck

BUA

Since the early 1990s, Justin BUA has been making a mark in the art world with the unique style he has named Distorted Urban Realism, spearheading a new genre of art. Born in 1968 in New York City's untamed Upper West Side and raised in Manhattan and East Flatbush, Brooklyn, BUA was fascinated by the raw visceral street life of the city. He attended the Fiorello H. LaGuardia High School of Music & Art and the Performing Arts and complemented his education by writing graffiti and performing worldwide with break-dancing crews. BUA went on to the Art Center College of Design in Pasadena, California, where he earned a B.F.A. in Illustration. He currently resides in Los Angeles and teaches at the University of Southern California.